PRONUNCIATION OF FRENCH

Articulation and Intonation

By

Jeanne VARNEY PLEASANTS
Associate Professor
Columbia University

Translated by Esther EGERTON
Head of Department of Romance Languages
High School, Plainfield, N. J.

Fourth Reprint

1960

Copyright 1933
Jeanne Vidon VARNEY

Lithoprinted in U.S.A.
EDWARDS BROTHERS, INC.
ANN ARBOR, MICHIGAN

To my son, Bernard.

INTRODUCTION

This book, written at the request of a great number of my American pupils at the Institute of Phonetics of the Sorbonne, is the transcription, in condensed form, of my teaching both there and elsewhere since 1920. In it I have incorporated the result of my experience not only with American students in France, but also as a student myself at an American University of which I am a graduate, as well as that of two additional years of residence in the United States, during which I made a practical study of the American theory and system of education. I believe, therefore, that the book will prove useful to American students of French.

Since making the first draft five years ago, I have in turn worked on it and laid it aside, making each time that I took it up some modification--more often than not of a negative character, that is to say, the omission of portions of the text to the end of greater simplicity. Whenever I found myself confronted by the necessity of treating a complex question such as that of intonation, I tried to reduce it to its simplest expression by casting aside everything that was too complicated and elaborate.

Inasmuch as there are several books which study the question of the pronunciation of French from a historical or scientific point of view, it seemed useless for me to add to their number. Limiting myself therefore to the description of sounds and to the explanation of rules which govern French articulation and intonation, I have omitted all historical and scientific discussion of the subject and have sought to give to this book the virtue and value of immediate utility. For the same reason, I have avoided as much as possible recourse to phonetic symbols and have omitted any reference to the phonetic triangle. Here, as in my oral teaching, I have intended to present a practical, reliable and simple guide to French pronunciation.

Phonograph records are often of great practical aid to a student of phonetics, especially if he has a good ear. There are now in preparation a series of records designed to accompany the exercises and reading lessons. By their use, a student will be able to compare and check his own pronunciation with that of a French person.

In order to facilitate the use of the book, I have avoided as much as possible both footnotes and reference to material on other pages than the one on which a given subject is discussed, and thus at times I have been obliged to repeat short paragraphs. Very infrequently I have repeated a rule or list, but only when it seemed important that the student should become thoroughly familiar with it.

I have nowhere compared French sounds to English sounds for the purpose of indicating any similarity between them. Inasmuch as the fundamental principles of articulation of the two languages are so very different, it seems unprofitable to attempt to establish even the slightest connection. The only apparent exception which I have permitted myself is in the discussion of the French closed e, which with the greatest caution and from one point of view only I mention with the English short i.

I wish here to express my thanks to the following persons: Dr. WILLIAM RALEIGH PRICE, State Supervisor of Modern Languages of the University of the State of New York, and Monsieur HUBERT PERNOT, Professor at the Sorbonne for their interest in my book; Mademoiselle N. PERNOT, who read a part of the manuscript; my friend, Madame BARA de TOVAR, of the Institute of Phonetics of the Sorbonne, for her tireless patience pitilessly put to the test during the pronunciation aloud of several thousand words; my sister, Mademoiselle LINE VIDON (now Madame Maxime Barret) who formerly gave courses in phonetics at the University of Grenoble (Patronage des Etrangers, and who kindly read part of my manuscript, filling several gaps in my treatment of liaison; Mademoiselle BERTHE des COMBES FAVARD, authority in the matter of teaching pronunciation of our language to Americans, and Monsieur LOUIS CHAPARD, Instructor of French in the University of Michigan, both of whom have shown great interest in the book; my husband, CHARLES E. VARNEY, who read the completed manuscript; and although last, by no means least, my pupil and friend, Miss ESTHER EGERTON, Head of the Department of Romance Languages, Plainfield High School, Plainfield, New Jersey, not only for her translation, but also for many useful suggestions made possible by her comprehension of the needs and difficulties of American students and her practical experience in teaching. Without her encouragement and assistance I should not have completed the book at this time.

                              JEANNE VIDON-VARNEY

   New York, June, 1932.

   The lines above were written in June, 1932. I should like today, more than a year later, to speak here of my debt to Monsieur PIERRE FOUCHÉ, Director of the Institute of Phonetics of the Sorbonne, under whose direction I have taught during the year just past. I wish especially to thank him not only for his invaluable advice with regard to my own studies but also for the privilege of attending his lectures. As a consequence I have felt the need of making some modifications in my two chapters on intonation, in order to follow more closely his method which respects the truth in all its details.

   Plainfield, September, 1933.

TABLE OF CONTENTS

Introduction..III

PART I.

Chapter I. PRELIMINARY NOTES........................... 1

    Phonetics. Use of the phonetic alphabet. Good pronunciation.

Chapter II. THE SPEECH ORGANS.......................... 4

    Movable organs: vocal chords, tongue, lips, soft palate. Immovable or rigid organs: teeth, teeth-ridges, hard palate, nasal cavity.

Chapter III. THE FRENCH SYLLABLE....................... 8

Chapter IV. "THE FRENCH ACCENT"........................ 8

Chapter V. THE FRENCH VOWEL............................ 14

    Each vowel a single sound. Each vowel pronounced on a single note. Flexibility of tongue. Groove formed lengthwise in tongue. Flexibility of lips. Movements of jaw.

Chapter VI. THE VOWELS................................. 18

    Figures. Exercises for practice. Reading exercises. Vocabulary. Mistakes to be avoided. Classification of the vowels: anterior a, posterior a, closed vowels, open vowels, nasal vowels, mute e. Duration. Anterior a, a; posterior a, $ɑ$; ou, u; closed o, o; closed e, e; closed eu, $ø$; i, i u, y; open o, $ɔ$; open e, $ɛ$; open eu, $œ$; mute e, $ə$. Supplementary reading exercises. Nasal vowels: spelling. Duration. Mistakes to be avoided. an, $ã$; on, $õ$; in, $ɛ̃$; un, $œ̃$. Supplementary reading exercises.

Chapter VII. THE SEMI-VOWELS (SEMI-CONSONANTS)........... 43

    Definition. Semi-vowel ou, w. Semi-vowel u, $ɥ$, yod, j. Supplementary reading exercises.

Chapter VIII. THE CONSONANTS........................... 49

Classification: voiced, voiceless; plosives, fricatives, sibilants, hushing consonants, nasals, laterals or liquids, bi-labials, labio-dentals, dentals, palatals, uvular. Law of anticipation. Release. p, b, d, t, k, g, f, v, s, z, ch, ʃ; ʒ, ʒ; m, n, gn, ɲ; l; front lingual rolled r; uvular r; Parisian r. Supplementary reading exercises.

PART II.

Chapter IX. SYLLABIFICATION............................. 85

Chapter X. INTONATION.................................. 87

Stress group. Breath-group. Normal stress. Intensity. Musical pitch. Stress for emphasis. Declarative sentences. The rising part. The falling part. Interrogative sentences. Exclamatory sentences.

Chapter XI. MUTE e, ə 117

Spellings. General considerations. When completely silent. When pronounced. In monosyllables. Special observations.

Chapter XII. LIAISON...................................127

General considerations. Obligatory. Prohibited. Optional. Change of sound in liaison.

Chapter XIII. LIAISON OF N OF NASAL VOWELS.............136

General rule. an, ɑ̃; on, ɔ̃; in, ɛ̃; un, œ̃.

Chapter XIV. LINKING...................................140

Chapter XV. ASSIMILATION...............................141

Definition. Regressive. Progressive.

Chapter XVI. VOWEL HARMONY.............................143

Chapter XVII. DOUBLE CONSONANT.........................144

Chapter XVIII. PRONUNCIATION OF H......................145

Chapter XIX. PRONUNCIATION OF X........................146

Chapter XX. PRONUNCIATION OF DONC, PLUS, SENS, TANDIS
QUE, TOUS..................................147

Chapter XXI. PRONUNCIATION OF THE NUMERALS..............149

    Pronunciation of ten first numerals, according to position. Pronunciation of numerals from onze to mille. Notes.

Chapter XXII. PRONUNCIATION OF OU+VOWEL, OF U+VOWEL,
OF I+VOWEL................................155

PART III.

LEXICON

Chapter XXIII. POSTERIOR a, ɑ............................158

Chapter XXIV. ANTERIOR a, a.............................160

Chapter XXV. CLOSED o..................................163

Chapter XXVI. OPEN o, ɔ................................166

Chapter XXVII. CLOSED e................................167

Chapter XXVIII. OPEN e, ɛ..............................169

Chapter XXIX. CLOSED eu, ø.............................170

Chapter XXX. OPEN eu, œ................................171

Chapter XXXI. ou, u....................................172

Chapter XXXII. i.......................................172

Chapter XXXIII. u, y...................................174

Chapter XXXIV. an, ɑ̃...................................174

Chapter XXXV. on, ɔ̃....................................177

Chapter XXXVI. in, ɛ̃...................................178

Chapter XXXVII. un, œ̃..................................180

Chapter XXXVIII. SEMI-VOWEL ou, w......................181

Chapter XXXIX. SEMI-VOWEL u, ɥ.........................183

Chapter XL. YOD j 184
Chapter XLI. THE SOUND AND LETTER p 185
Chapter XLII. THE SOUND AND LETTER b 186
Chapter XLIII. THE SOUND AND LETTER t 187
Chapter XLIV. THE SOUND AND LETTER d 190
Chapter XLV. THE SOUND AND LETTER k 191
Chapter XLVI. THE SOUND AND LETTER g 193
Chapter XLVII. THE SOUND AND LETTER f 194
Chapter XLVIII. THE SOUND AND LETTER v 195
Chapter XLIX. THE SOUND AND LETTER s 196
Chapter L. THE SOUND AND LETTER z 198
Chapter LI. THE SOUND AND SPELLING ch, $\int$ 200
Chapter LII. THE SOUND $ʒ$ 201
Chapter LIII. THE SOUND AND LETTER m 201
Chapter LIV. THE SOUND AND LETTER n 203
Chapter LV. THE SOUND AND SPELLING gn, $ɲ$ 204
Chapter LVI. THE SOUND AND LETTER l 205
Chapter LVII. THE SOUND AND LETTER r 206
Chapter LVIII. A FEW COMMON WORDS OFTEN MISPRONOUNCED ... 207

Index of Spellings 209
Index of words used as examples 215
Index of subjects treated 244

PART I

Chapter I.
PRELIMINARY NOTES

1. PHONETICS. The noun "phonetics," as well as the corresponding adjective "phonetic," will be frequently used in this book. It seems desirable, therefore, to include at the very beginning a short discussion of these words.

For many people the term "phonetics" has an unfortunate signification, since they associate it, though incorrectly, merely with the phonetic symbols--which to them seem dry, artificial, forbidding, dead. In reality, however, the phonetic symbols form only a small portion of this subject. Indeed, from one point of view it would not be incorrect to say that they are not essential to it at all, being merely a part of its nomenclature--convenient, it is true, but not indispensable to the study of the subject in its largest aspect. It will be seen that they play only a small role in the present book.

What then is phonetics? It is the study of the sounds of a language, of the proper way to produce them, to group them, and to stress them, in order to express all our sentiments, all our ideas, our sensations, joys, sorrows, hopes. The oral use of a language is its most important expression. By means of vowels whose timbre may be infinitely varied--sometimes full and rich, sometimes thin and shrill, sometimes deep and sonorous--in turn gay or sad, intense or restrained, by means of consonants at times clearly and rapidly articulated and at others purposely retarded, by means of the ceaseless rise and fall of the voice, we may express to others a thousand shades in the color of our thought.

Is it possible then to say that the subject of phonetics is dry, artificial, dead?...What study could be more living? What, more gracious?

II. USE OF THE PHONETIC ALPHABET. The adjective "phonetic" as applied to a spoken language indicates perfect regularity of agreement between its separate sounds and the alphabet which furnishes the elements of its written expression. That French is not a phonetic language is evident from the following facts:

1. Each separate letter of the alphabet does not always represent a sound, (in the word août, for example, four letters represent only one sound).

2. The same sound may be represented by several different letters (in the words ça, ce, se and nation, the letters ç, c, s, and t are pronounced in the same way).

3. The same letter may represent different sounds (in the words ce and car, the letter c represents the sounds

s and k).

One may easily understand, therefore, in dealing with such a language, the advantage of using an alphabet in which each sound is represented by a single letter or symbol and in which each letter or symbol represents a single sound.

I assume that every advanced student of French understands the significance of the phonetic symbols; but for those who dislike to use them, I have adopted (except for the Exercises for Practice) in the cases where the phonetic symbol and the letter of the ordinary alphabet are not the same for the representation of a given sound, the following arrangement:

For each vowel, I have used (except infrequently in lists of sounds) before the proper phonetic symbol, the letter or group of letters which usually represents that vowel sound in the ordinary alphabet, together with the word closed, open, mute, nasal, posterior or anterior when necessary:

open o, ɔ

For each consonant, I have used (except infrequently in lists of sounds) before the proper phonetic symbol, the letter or group of letters which usually represents that consonant sound in the ordinary alphabet:

ch, ʃ

For this purpose I have used the symbols of the International Phonetic Alphabet, with which most Americans who have taken advanced courses in French are familiar.

Name of sound	Symbol	Example
anterior a	a	patte
posterior a	ɑ	pâte
closed o	o	rose
open o	ɔ	robe
closed e	e	été
open e	ɛ	lait
closed eu	ø	deux
open eu	œ	neuve
ou	u	loup
u	y	du
i	i	lit
mute e	ə	le
on	ɔ̃, õ	mon
an	ã	dans
in	ɛ̃	fin
un	œ̃	chacun
semi-vowel ou	w	louis
semi-vowel u	ɥ	lui
yod	j	bien, soleil, vieille

Name of sound	Symbol	Example
p	p	papa
b	b	bébé
t	t	ta
d	d	dans
k	k	quatre
g	g	gai
f	f	folle
v	v	va
s	s	son
z	z	rose
ch	ʃ	chat
j	ʒ	juge
m	m	maman
n	n	nez
gn	ɲ	gagne
l	l	lit
r	r	rien

: indicates that the sound represented by the preceding symbol is long.
:: indicates that the sound represented by the preceding symbol is very long.
' indicates that the following syllable is stressed.
* indicates that the following sound receives the stress for emphasis.
‿ indicates liaison or linking; in a few cases, a nasal vowel.
⏋ indicates that liaison, linking or elision is impossible.
| indicates the end of a stress-group.
‖ indicates the end of a breath-group.

III. GOOD PRONUNCIATION. What is good pronunciation in French?

It would be false to assert that there is only one which is good. Carefully directed and supervised teaching in French schools tends more and more, it is true, to standardise pronunciation; but there still remain many variations, more or less marked, in the speech not only of different regions, but even of different individuals of the same region. That there are not two persons whose pronunciation is exactly the same is as true in France as in any other country.

However, speaking in general terms, one may say that cultivated persons native to a given region all show in their speech habits certain common characteristics. Usually the model recommended to foreigners is that of Paris. But it must be remembered that Paris is not all of France--(far from it!) and that there are several provincial pronunciations which are not only agreeable to the ear but from the historical point of view, are as good as that of the capital.

Nevertheless it has seemed to me proper for three reasons to base my discussion of French speech on the Parisian, or rather upon one of the Parisian pronunciations--first, because this it is that "sets the style in good pronunciation"; second, because it is beautiful, rich, and sonorous; and third, because the majority of foreigners who study in France pass the greater part of their time in Paris.

But even there one is faced with the necessity of choosing the pronunciation which he wishes to adopt. That of the uneducated classes is of course out of the question. Of the two others, one may be called the ultra-modern; one, the classic (but classic in the French sense, "capable, because of its perfection, of serving as a model"). The former, that of some members of the very young generation, tends by the law of least resistance to reduce all vowels to uncertain sounds (which might be called middle, being neither open nor closed) and to identify two nasals which are by nature as different as in and un, thus giving to the pronunciation of our language the effect of something lacking precision, dull, impoverished. The latter pronunciation is characterized by good taste, by sounds enunciated clearly but without exaggeration, by sonorous vowels, whose timbre is clearly open or closed; and it has preserved as a precious part of its heritage a sound nonchalantly suppressed by the younger generation--the posterior a, so rich, so deep, so vibrant, capable of suggesting by its beauty and nobility a whole world of sentiment, sensations, ideas.

I have chosen the latter.

Chapter II.
THE SPEECH-ORGANS

The speech-organs are divided into two groups:
    A. The movable organs
    B. The immovable organs
A. The movable organs are:
    1. The vocal chords
    2. The tongue
    3. The lips
    4. The soft palate, of which the tip is called the uvula
B. The immovable organs are:
    1. The teeth
    2. The teeth-ridges

3. The hard palate
4. The nasal cavity
MOVABLE ORGANS
1. VOCAL CHORDS, (fig.1, V.C.). The vocal chords are, in reality, not chords at all, but the edges of the windpipe. They are situated in the larynx. The space between

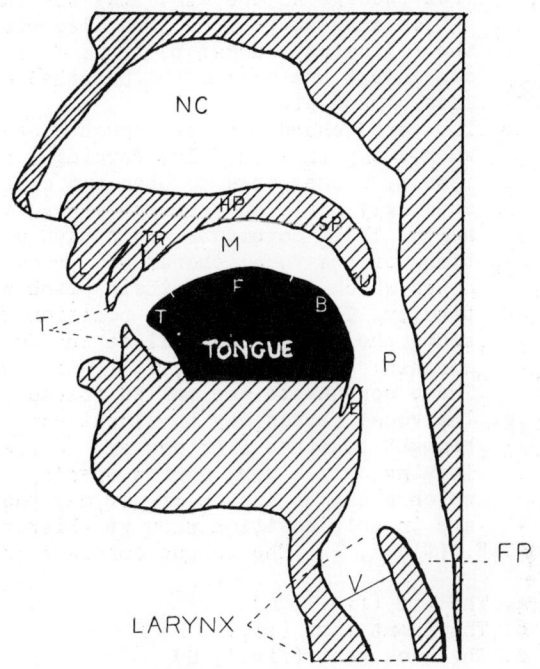

Fig.1-The Organs of Speech.
B Back of tongue. E Epiglottis. F Front of tongue. FP Food passage. HP Hard palate. L Lips. M Mouth. NC Nasal cavity. P Pharynx. SP Soft Palate. T Teeth. TR Teeth ridge. U Uvula. VC Vocal chords.

the vocal chords is called the glottis.
LARYNX, (fig.1, larynx). The larynx is the upper extremity of the passage which permits the release of the air from the lungs to the pharynx. Most people use indifferently, to indicate the same phenomenon, the terms "vibrations of the larynx" and "vibrations of the vocal chords".

PHARYNX, (fig.1, P). The pharynx is the space in the throat which is located immediately behind the mouth, and through which the air passes from the larynx to the mouth or the nose.

POSITION OF THE VOCAL CHORDS. The vocal chords may assume different positions:

    a. The vocal chords may be separated, leaving free passage to the air. They are in this position when we breathe, and also when we make the following sounds: p, t, k, f, s, ʃ. These consonants are called the breathed or voiceless consonants.

    b. The vocal chords may be brought together in such a way that the air, forcing a passage for itself, causes them to open and close with exceedingly rapid but perfectly regular movements. These movements are spoken of as vibrations of the vocal chords and produce musical notes which vary as to their pitch and intensity. They are in this position when we sound the vowels, as well as the following consonants: b, d, g, v, z, ʒ, m, n, l, ɲ, r. These consonants are called voiced consonants.

    c. The vocal chords may be almost completely brought together from one end to the other, leaving only a very narrow opening through which a slight amount of air may pass. They are in this position when we whisper.

2. TONGUE, (fig.1, C). The tongue consists of four parts:

    a. The tip (fig.1, T)
    b. The front part (fig.1, F)
    c. The back part (fig.1, B)
    d. The side-edges, parallel to the molars.

The different parts of the tongue may move with great rapidity and extreme flexibility, thus taking the most varied positions and producing an infinite number of modifications of the sound produced by the vocal chords.

3. LIPS, (fig.1, L). The lips include:

    a. The corners of the mouth
    b. The upper lip
    c. The lower lip

The corners of the mouth may be separated (as for e, i) or brought together (u, o), and the lips may take very different positions. For example, they may be opened vertically (ɑ), opened horizontally (a), completely closed (p, m), or thrust forward (ʃ, ʒ), etc. These different positions modify the sound produced by the vocal chords.

4. SOFT PALATE, (fig.1, S.P.). The soft palate includes:

a. The soft palate, as it is generally understood (fig.1, SP).
b. The uvula or tip (fig.1, U).

The soft palate may be lowered to a greater or less degree, thus leaving an opening which permits the air to pass partially or entirely through the nose ($\tilde{a}, \tilde{o}, \tilde{\varepsilon}, \tilde{\infty}$, m, n, $\textit{ɲ}$) or it may be raised, so that the entrance to the nasal cavity is completely closed, and the air is thus prevented from passing through the nose but is forced out through the mouth.

IMMOVABLE OR RIGID ORGANS

1. TEETH. The two rows of teeth (upper and lower) include each 4 incisors, 2 canines, 4 pre-molars, and 4 or 6 molars.

2. TEETH-RIDGES, (fig.1, TR). The teeth-ridges are that part of the upper and lower jaws in which are embedded the roots of the teeth.

3. HARD PALATE, (fig.1, HP). The hard palate, called also roof of the mouth, is the part of the palate which is located between the teeth-ridges and the soft palate.

The tip, the side-edges, the front and back parts of the tongue may be brought into contact, to a greater or less degree, either with the teeth, the teeth-ridges, or the hard palate, thus modifying the space in the interior of the mouth, and consequently the sound produced by the vocal chords.

4. NASAL CAVITY, (fig.1, NS). The nasal cavity is the double canal of the nose by which the sound formed by the vocal chords escapes. At the same time the soft palate is lowered sufficiently to permit the entrance of the air.

IMPORTANT REMARK. In speaking French, the soft palate, the lips, and the tongue are much more easily moved, more supple, more flexible than in speaking English. The lips may be thrust far forward or drawn far back. The tongue takes numerous positions which to Americans seem exaggerated; for example, it may be raised much higher either in the rear,(u,o) or in the front,(e, i, y). It changes position with a rapidity and a flexibility unknown in English.

But the great difference in the articulation of the two languages consists not only in the varied positions which the organs may take, but the extreme suppleness, flexibility and rapidity with which they move. In order to acquire a clear and precise pronunciation it is necessary to do gymnastic exercises for the purpose of giving practice to the muscles of these organs, in the same way in which a violinist trains the muscles of his fingers by exercises which he repeats regularly each day.

Chapter III.
THE FRENCH SYLLABLE

Although the subject of syllabification is to be treated at length in a later chapter, the student before going further, should here understand one of the fundamental principles of division into syllables in French, for this principle has a noticeable effect on pronunciation. Where a _single_ consonant separates two vowels, this consonant is sounded with the second vowel, thus forming what is called the regular French syllable: consonant plus vowel. The contrast between the English and French principle of syllable division may be seen by the comparison:

English   French
cap-able   ca-pable
am<u>us</u>-<u>ing</u>   am<u>u</u>-<u>sant</u>

A detailed discussion of the subject of Syllabification will be found in Chapter IX.

Chapter IV.
"THE FRENCH ACCENT"

It may at first thought seem strange that before beginning the study of isolated sounds I stop to consider the problem of intonation--or, as it is popularly known, "the French Accent." I do this because it is by his faults in intonation that a foreigner may be detected in France even more quickly than by his faults in pronunciation, and French people find the former far more shocking to the ear than the latter.

If the student pronounces the reading lessons which have been arranged for each sound, without having any idea of French intonation, he will run the risk of forming incorrect speech-habits from which he will later rid himself only with difficulty. For this reason I take up this subject here, although I do it in a very brief way and use for illustration only declarative sentences, reserving detailed discussion for a later chapter (X).

With the very first French word that the student speaks he may use correct intonation. In what then does it consist? It consists chiefly in two phenomena, which occur not separately but simultaneously--certain syllables are marked by special stress and at the same time by a change of the musical pitch of the voice.

The unit of French speech is not as in English, the grammatical word, but the _stress-group_ (groupe rythmique, mot phonétique). This group, it is true, may contain only one grammatical word, but usually it consists of a group

of several words closely related in thought--such as a
noun subject with its modifiers, a pronoun subject with
its verb:
>   Venez
>   La petite fille│court
>   Elle court
>   Jean│ouvre la fenêtre

It is the <u>last pronounced syllable of each stress-group</u>
which is the most important for correct intonation, for it
is there that occur the special stress and the change of
musical pitch mentioned above.
- a. <u>Special stress</u>.
  This stress is marked in two ways:
  1. always by a greater force (intensity)
     given to the whole syllable and more
     particularly to its <u>vowel</u>. This stress
     is called therefore a vowel-stress,
     (accent vocalique).
  2. often by a lengthening of the vowel, as
     will be explained later. (p.20).

  NOTE: Every pronounced syllable of a
  stress-group is clearly sounded with
  equal force and equal duration until
  the last is reached. Then, as has been
  said above, the last syllable receives
  greater force than the preceding one,
  and often is somewhat lengthened. It is
  sometimes said that this French stress
  on the last syllable has no counterpart
  in English. This is not quite true; for
  an approximation of it may be found in
  some English sentences or expressions
  consisting altogether of monosyllables
  or of monosyllables with the exception
  of the last word:
  >   Here and 'there, to ex'cess
- b. <u>Change of musical pitch</u>; that is, a rising of
  the musical pitch of the voice when the sentence is not finished or a falling at the end
  of the sentence:
  >   <u>La petite fille│ court</u>

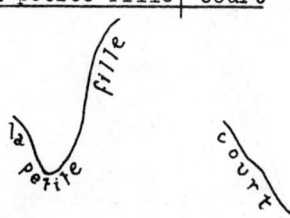

When the sentence is made up of only one
stress-group there is a rising and a falling
part without any pause whatsoever:
    Venez
    Elle court

When the sentence is made up of more than two
stress-groups, all those which correspond to a
question, to the expression of expectation, to
the arousing of curiosity and interest, form a
group whose final syllables progressively rise.
This group is spoken of as the rising part of
the sentence. On the other hand, all the
stress-groups which answer the questions proposed
in the rising part, thus satisfying expectation,
curiosity, and interest, form a
group whose final syllables progressively fall;
and this is known as the falling part. Thus,
in the sentence by A. Daudet,
    Monsieur le sous-préfet, grisé de parfums,
ivre de musique, essaye vainement de résister
au nouveau charme qui l'envahit, we have:
Question: Monsieur le sous-préfet grisé de
           parfums ivre de musique
Answer: essaye vainement de résister au
           nouveau charme qui l'envahit.

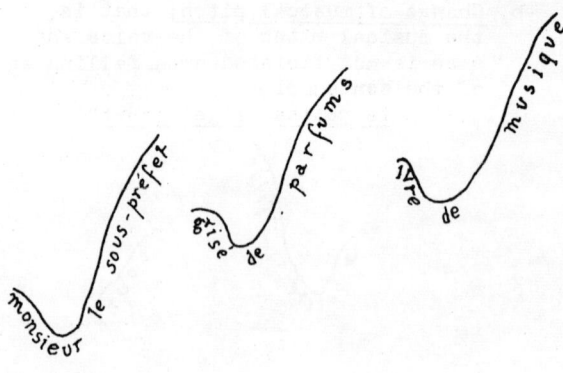

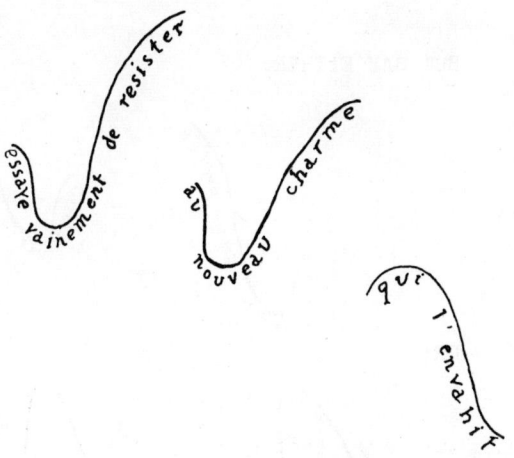

It is mainly in these two facts: <u>special stress</u> (marked by intensity and duration) and <u>change in the musical pitch</u> of the voice (marked by falling) that the secret of "the French Accent" lies.

To these two general laws should be added the four following observations:
    a. the note on which the first syllable of the whole sentence is pronounced is rather <u>low</u>.
    b. the rising of the pitch of the <u>voice</u> is not obtained in a monotonously regular ascent but by rich internal modulations:

DO NOT SAY:

OR:

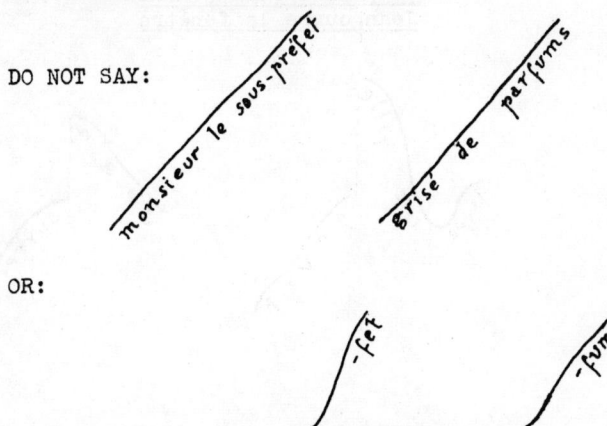

BUT SAY EITHER:

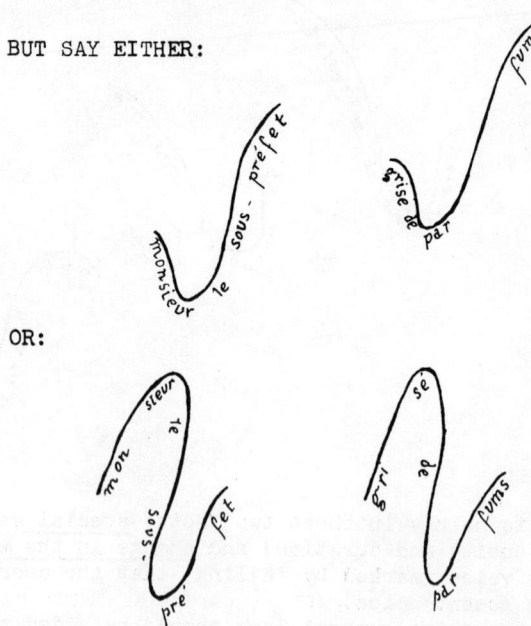

OR:

c. the note of the initial syllable of a stress-group is always very much lower than the note of the preceding stressed syllable. Remark in the following instances the drop of the musical pitch after <u>fille</u> and after <u>Jean</u>:
    La petite fille| court
    Jean| ouvre la fenêtre

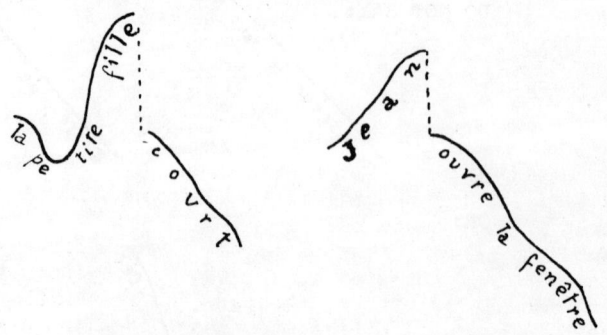

and also (in sentence already quoted) after -<u>fet</u>, -<u>fums</u>, -<u>sique</u>, -<u>ter</u>, <u>charme</u>:

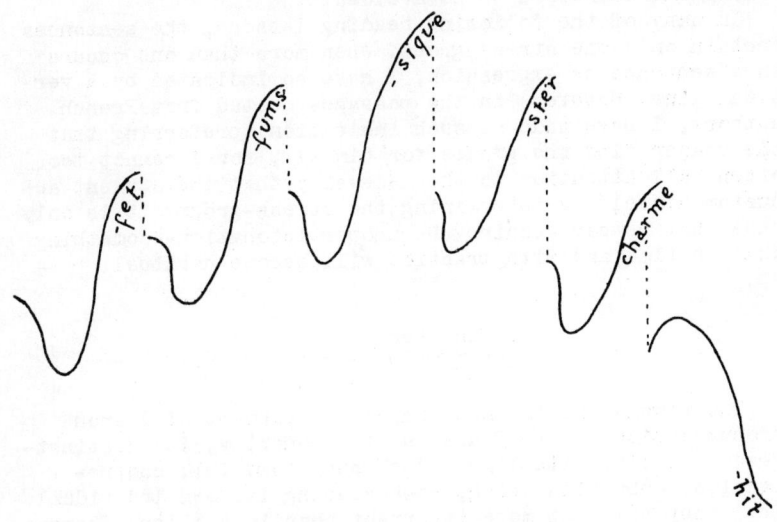

    d. the note on which the last syllable of the sentence is pronounced is very low:
        La petite fille|court
        Jean|ouvre la fenêtre

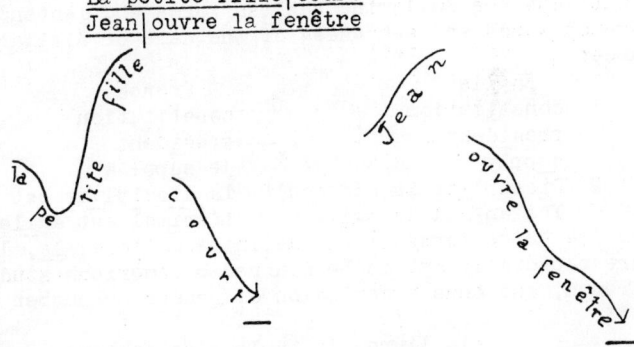

    Some teachers find that a useful method in connection with French intonation is that of counting. It is true that if one counts rapidly in English: "One, two, three; one, two, three, four; one, two, three, four, five;" he has used an approximation of the French intonation, but only an approximation, because even though the two elements of special stress and change of pitch are present, there are no internal modulations, these being replaced by a monotonous rising, and a staccato movement, unusual in

French and therefore to be avoided.

In many of the following reading lessons, the sentences contain only one stress-group. When more than one occurs in a sentence or expression, I have so indicated by a vertical line. However, in the passages quoted from French authors, I have made no such indication; preferring that the reader find the groups for himself, for I cannot too often call attention to the necessity that the student accustom himself to determining the stress-group. It is only thus that he can acquire the proper intonation--something that in time and with practice will become habitual.

Chapter V.
THE FRENCH VOWEL

The vowels are the most important element of French pronunciation. To them are due its sonority, its distinctness, its life, its light. Each one, powerful, comprehensive, unhurried, rich, each keeping its own individuality, they are much more important than in English. Whereas in English all unstressed vowels, and frequently stressed as well, (especially i, a, and u) are slurred and indistinct, in French they retain their own qualities and distinguishing characteristics. This fact is evident if one contrasts the following English words and sentences with French words and sentences of the same or similar appearance:

English	French
1. constitution	constitution
president	président
supply	je supplie
2. Discipline is difficult	La discipline est difficile
The animal is agile	L'animal est agile

The three forms of the definite article, le, la, les, are especially apt to be slurred by American students of French, and thus a confusion of gender or number is created:

le livre, la table, les cahiers

French vowels are pure; that is, each vowel represents a single sound, and each vowel is generally pronounced on a single note.

1. EACH VOWEL REPRESENTS A SINGLE SOUND.

It should be remembered that I use here the definition of the term diphthong from the point of view of the phonetician, that is the pronunciation in the same syllable, of two vowels of which one is stronger than the other; and this phenomenon is produced by the movement of one or more of the speech-organs, (tongue, lips, jaw) during the emis-

sion of the sound. In French there are no diphthongs.
    English   French
  a. blow   beau
  b. day   des

a. For the vowel sound of English "blow", the lips, at first open as for o are brought together as for ou, u: the tongue, at first slightly raised at the back as for o, is then lifted higher as for ou, u. These two movements take place <u>during the emission</u> of the sound, thus producing a diphthong.

For the vowel sound in French "beau", the lips even before the beginning of the sound, are pushed very far forward, the tongue is lifted a little at the back. The lips and tongue remain completely motionless during the emission of the vowel.

b. For the vowel sound of English "day", the tongue, at first slightly raised as for open e, ε, is raised somewhat more in the front part as for i. This movement takes place <u>during the emission</u> of the sound, thus producing a diphthong.

For the vowel sound in French "des", the tongue, lifted in the front part of the mouth, remains <u>motionless</u> during the emission of the vowel.

NOTE: In passing from one sound to another in these English diphthongs, the lips and tongue move <u>slowly</u> and <u>constantly</u>, thus producing intermediary sounds. This lingering transformation of sound, one of the greatest beauties of the English language, is unknown in modern French. When a French person pronounces two successive vowels they are never in the same syllable but always in two successive syllables, and the movements are extremely rapid.

In French the movements of the different organs are simultaneous and take place <u>before</u> the emission of the sound; they are not successive during the emission. It is only when the position has been taken that the vowel is pronounced, and it is only when the pronunciation has been finished that the speech-organs take either their normal position or the one preparatory to the following sound. The procedure is:
    1. preparation
    2. pronunciation
    3. relaxation or preparation for next sound.

Of course, in ordinary speech all this takes place rapidly, but it is a useful exercise for the student to retard the process in order to study its mechanics. There will be found in connection with the study of each sound an exercise for practice which should be done slowly at the beginning and <u>before a mirror</u> so that the student may compel his speech-organs to remain motionless during the pronunciation of each vowel.

2. EACH VOWEL IS PRONOUNCED ON A SINGLE NOTE.
(To this statement there are only exceedingly rare exceptions). Many American students of French, when speaking to a lady some distance away for the purpose of attracting her attention, say "Madame", singing the last syllable on several notes:

        ma da⌒me

In French, however long the vowel may be (and in this case it is never as long as in English), it is pronounced on a single note:

        ma — da — me

NOTE: The student should not confuse the terms "different note" (change in pitch) and "different sound" (change in articulation).

Several factors combine to give the French vowel all its characteristics. The chief ones to be studied are the following:
1. the flexibility of the tongue
2. the groove formed lengthwise in the tongue
3. the flexibility of the lips
4. the movements of the jaw
5. the separation of the teeth
6. the "attack" or beginning of the vowel.

1. THE FLEXIBILITY OF THE TONGUE. The tongue is supple, active, rapid in its movements. The tongue of most Americans is almost inactive, relaxed, incapable of elasticity, loath to assume extreme positions. It must be trained, and successful training can be accomplished only by regularly repeated exercises which by daily gymnastics will make the articulation smooth.

2. THE GROOVE FORMED LENGTHWISE IN THE TONGUE. The tongue is divided through the center by an axis. For the articulation of the vowels, the tongue is lifted or depressed on both sides of this axis, and forms a groove from back to front by which the air, already set in motion by the vocal chords, may escape freely. If this groove is obstructed at any point, the vowel is indistinct and dull.

3. THE FLEXIBILITY OF THE LIPS. The lips play a very important part in the articulation. Americans find great difficulty in separating the lips from the gums and are obliged to make a real effort in order to learn to push the lips forward, to move them with suppleness and rapidity. Exercises such as:

        i, u, i, y, i, u, i, y

will give to the lips this necessary flexibility. Furthermore, it is <u>both lips</u> which must be supple. Many Americans, while moving the lower lip sufficiently, keep the upper motionless.

4. THE MOVEMENTS OF THE JAW. Abrupt jerks of the jaw are to be avoided. The movements must be gentle. When the jaw is lowered for an open vowel, it should not be raised again immediately, as is often done by Americans, but only after the vowel has been pronounced with all the richness of timbre which characterizes it.

5. THE SEPARATION OF THE TEETH. Many students keep the jaws too close together and clench the teeth. In French the teeth are never clenched, even for the sounds during which they must be very close together, such as e, i. Otherwise the air could not pass freely.

6. THE "ATTACK" OR BEGINNING OF THE VOWEL. Contrary to the procedure in English, the "attack" or beginning of the French vowel is very gentle, --it begins by little vibrations which increase in size. One may represent in graphic form the English vowel as follows:

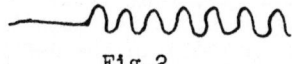

Fig.2

whereas the French vowel, so represented, is as follows:

Fig.3

In English, the vowel dies away; in French, it increases in vigor. (This increase takes place without movement of the speech-organs and without change in pitch).

If the student thoroughly understands and accepts the statements in the preceding pages and if he carefully studies the position of the speech-organs for each sound, he will discover that what is necessary is not an extraordinary effort of the muscles, but an extraordinary flexibility. If the organs are in their exact position, the muscles having been properly trained by means of the practice exercises, the effort will be scarcely noticeable. One should avoid the appearance of any effort or exaggeration and especially of any stiffness of the muscles. These, I cannot repeat too often, should be flexible and not strained.

When, in giving the position for the vowels, I use the word "tense", the student should remember that it means "not relaxed". It does not mean "strained".

It should never be forgotten that "a correct pronunciation is the result of the proper training of the muscles of the speech-organs." The American student must acquire a "new set of pronunciation-habits." (Knowles and Favard).

Chapter VI.
THE VOWELS

In this chapter, as well as in the two following, the purpose of which is to give to the pupil the clearest possible indication of the way to produce the separate sounds of French speech, I have made use not only of careful directions for the position of the speech organs, but also of various devices.

FIGURES. It has not been possible to include in this experimental edition the photographs and drawings of the original manuscript, about two hundred in number. They will, however, appear in the definitive edition. Within a few months, plates showing these figures may be obtained from the author. Similarly, many illustrative words and expressions, which have been omitted both in the text and in the lexicon, will be included in the definitive edition.

EXERCISES FOR PRACTICE. For each sound, I have arranged exercises intended to make the muscles of the tongue, lips, or the soft palate more flexible. It is only by daily repitition of these exercises that the pupil can acquire a good pronunciation. They may be compared to the finger training exercises of a student of the piano or violin; although often requiring not only an exaggeration but also a retardation of movement, they are intended to enable the student to move his speech-organs later with much greater flexibility and rapidity. They should be done before a mirror, for in no other way can the student have an accurate idea of the position of his speech-organs. No amount of theory by itself can compare in usefulness to theory reinforced by careful daily practice.

READING EXERCISES. For each sound I have composed also a reading exercise. Avoiding as much as possible long lists of isolated words, I have preferred to combine in short sentences or groups of words several examples of the sound under consideration, for thus of course it is most often found in speech. In addition, the student will find short paragraphs from our best French prose writers and poets, selections which are read in American High Schools and Colleges. In these paragraphs I have underlined the spelling of the sound studied.

VOCABULARY. By far the greater number of words employed in the reading exercises were selected from text-books for beginners; to these I have added others easy to understand because of the fact that they exist in the same or a similar form in English but with a different pronunciation, together with a considerable number of simple current expressions. It is only in rare instances that, in order to illustrate certain rules for which there are no well-known examples, I have used words which are scientific or somewhat unusual. In Part III, my lists of different spellings for each sound are complete.

MISTAKES TO BE AVOIDED. In order to combat incorrect tendencies which may have become habitual to Americans accustomed to speaking French, as well as to anticipate and make impossible the acquisition of such habits by beginners, I have inserted, at the foot of each page treating with a sound, a list of mistakes in articulation which Americans are especially prone to make. This list, arranged with the greatest care, is the result of observation through a long teaching experience.

Of course the technical explanations for the position of different organs are intended especially for students who have no "ear", or for those who, having a very delicate "ear", have never enjoyed the opportunity of studying oral French with a French person. It is hoped, too, that teachers may here find a model for their explanations of the speech phenomena, even though they may wish to simplify them in their own work.

CLASSIFICATION OF THE VOWELS

The vowels are classified as open, closed, and nasal; in addition to these three groups there are three other vowels of which one is said to be posterior and one anterior, and the mute e.

I have not followed the order generally adopted in treating the vowels. I have begun with the two a's, because when pronouncing these vowels the tongue may be said to be in a neutral position, which is very easy to take, and because they may be classed neither among the closed nor among the open. Next I have taken up the closed vowels, starting with the one for which the tongue is drawn back the farthest and proceeding to the one for which it is advanced the farthest. Then I have treated the open vowels, proceeding in the same way as for the closed, then the mute e; lastly, I have discussed the nasal vowels.

1. ANTERIOR A, a. Anterior a is so called because its point of articulation is in the <u>front</u> or <u>anterior</u> part of the mouth.

2. POSTERIOR A, ɑ. Posterior a is so called because its point of articulation is in the <u>back</u> or <u>posterior</u> part of the mouth.

3. CLOSED VOWELS. There are six closed vowels, so call-

ed because during their pronunciation the jaws are fairly close together and the contact between the tongue and the palate is very marked. These vowels, starting with the one whose point of articulation is farthest back in the mouth and proceeding to the one of which it is the farthest forward, are:

$$u, o, e, \emptyset, i, y$$

4. OPEN VOWELS. The open vowels are so called because for their pronunciation the lower jaw is dropped (the mouth is open); consequently, the contact of the tongue with the hard palate is less marked than in the case of the corresponding closed vowels. They are, starting with the one whose point of articulation is farthest back:

$$\mathit{ɔ, ɛ, œ}$$

5. NASAL VOWELS AND MUTE E. I shall treat nasal vowels and the mute e at a later point.

It must not be supposed that these vowels mentioned above are the only ones which exist in French, for there is really a far greater number. In the case of a French woman whose pronunciation is the most cultivated that I have ever had the privilege of hearing, I have noted no less than eight a's! And nearly as great a range is distinguishable in her other vowels. But I feel that it is sufficient to limit my teaching to two a's, two o's, two e's, two eu's, one ou, one u, one i, four nasals and the mute e. When the pupil can pronounce these vowels perfectly, according each one the timbre, the amplitude, the richness that combine to give it beauty, he may feel that he has accomplished a great deal.

DURATION

Stressed vowels are long when they are placed before the following sounds or groups of sounds: r, ʒ, z, v, vr.

Posterior a, ɑ, is long when it is placed before one or more sounded consonants.

In other positions, the vowels are short.

In order to facilitate the handling of the book I have adopted a somewhat unusual arrangement. The student will find on each even page the description of the position taken by the various speech-organs in the production of a given sound, together with a warning against certain mistakes which an American is especially prone to make. On the opposite page, the odd, he will find exercises for practice, and reading lessons. Additional exercises will be found at the end of the chapter. The student should of course make an effort to master one sound before attempting another.

ANTERIOR A, a

TONGUE
- TIP: touching and even protruding beyond lower teeth.
- BACK AND FRONT: fairly free, flat. Whole tongue placed higher in mouth than for posterior a, ɑ.
- MUSCLES: relaxed.

LIPS
- CORNERS OF MOUTH: in normal position.
- OPENING: horizontal.
- MUSCLES: not very tense.

TEETH Space between upper and lower teeth: 3/4 inch.

AVOID

1. Raising front part of tongue too high: (whence sound resembling open e, ɛ).
2. Separating jaws too widely.
3. Slurring of a in the article la, and in unstressed syllables.
4. Giving nasal quality, when placed before m, n, or gn, ɲ

POSTERIOR A, ɑ

TONGUE
- TIP: flattened, behind lower teeth, touching them.
- BACK: slightly raised.
- FRONT: flat.
- Whole tongue placed lower in mouth than for anterior a.
- MUSCLES: fairly tense.

LIPS
- CORNERS OF MOUTH: in same place as in normal position.
- OPENING: vertical.
- MUSCLES: relaxed.

TEETH Space between upper and lower teeth: 3/4 inch.

AVOID

1. Raising back of tongue too high.
2. Relaxing muscles of tongue too much.
3. Separating lips too little.
4. Pronouncing with nasal quality when before m, n, or gn, ɲ.

FOR PRACTICE. Before mirror.
TO TRAIN TONGUE, LIPS, AND JAW TO REMAIN MOTIONLESS:
Pronounce a as long as possible, taking care to have mouth
wide open. Repeat several times.
READING LESSON

SHORT. La, ma, sa, là, tabac, chat. J'ai mal à l'estomac. J'ai du tabac|dans ma tabatière. La femme|et le chat. Le Carnaval de Venise. A bon chat,| bon rat. Elle a du tact. La table|de la salle. Evidemment. Prudemment. Solennel.
LONG. La part|du barbare. Il est tard. C'est rare. J'achète|du lard. C'est dommage. Elle a mis du fard.
SHORT AND LONG. Papa|a à aller dans le Var. A la barre, l'avocat parle. Le tabac| lui fait mal à l'estomac. Il va à la gare.

Elle l<u>a</u>v<u>a</u> l<u>a</u> vaisselle, usant ses ongles roses sur les pot<u>e</u>ries gr<u>a</u>sses et le fond des c<u>a</u>ss<u>e</u>roles. Elle savonn<u>a</u> le linge s<u>a</u>le. les ch<u>e</u>mises et les torch<u>o</u>ns qu'elle faisait sécher sur une corde; elle desc<u>e</u>ndit à l<u>a</u> rue chaque matin, les ordures, et mont<u>a</u> l'eau, s'<u>a</u>rrêtant à chaque étage pour souffler. (Maup<u>a</u>ssant)

"Oui! mais s'il est s<u>a</u>ge, Sur son doux vis<u>a</u>ge L<u>a</u> Vierge se pencher<u>a</u>, Et longtemps lui parler<u>a</u>."
(Desbordes-V<u>a</u>lmore)

FOR PRACTICE. Before mirror.
TO TRAIN LIPS AND TONGUE: a, ɑ, a, ɑ, a, ɑ
Do not pronounce while moving tongue or lips. Pronounce
only when they are in position.
READING LESSON

SHORT. Bas, las, trois, ah! cas. En tous cas. Il est las. Ils sont trois. Le roi|donne la croix. Il croît.
LONG. Pâte, câble, vase, fable, phrase. Le gros câble. La flamme jaunâtre. Une belle âme. La fable de l'âne. Il se fâche. Elle est lâche.
SHORT AND LONG. Il a trois ânes. Le bas du cadre. Jacques| habite un château|à Blois. Le roi|est las et pâle.
POSTERIOR AND ANTERIOR A.
Mât, ma. Mâtin, matin. Châsse, chasse. Mâle, malle. Pâte, patte. Grâce, trace. Madame| est pâle. Jacques| passe par là.

Nous mangeons dans la première salle, au milieu de gens très r<u>â</u>pés, très affamés, qui r<u>a</u>clent leurs assiettes silencieusement.-Ce sont presque tous des hommes de lettres, me dit J<u>a</u>cques à voix b<u>a</u>sse. (Daudet).
Il faisait un fr<u>oi</u>d à fendre les dolmens, un de ces fr<u>oi</u>ds déchirants qui c<u>a</u>ssent la peau...(Maup<u>a</u>ssant)

Elle brame
Comme une âme
Qu'une flamme
Toujours suit.

(Victor-Hugo)

OU, *u*

TONGUE
- TIP: behind ridge of lower incisors.
- BACK: raised in direction of junction of hard and soft palate.
- MUSCLES: tense.

LIPS
- LIPS: very rounded, pushed forward.
- CORNERS OF MOUTH: brought forward, held tense.
- OPENING: horizontal rather than vertical.
- MUSCLES: tense.

TEETH   Space between upper and lower teeth: 1/10 inch.

AVOID

1. Raising tongue too much in front of mouth and not enough in back.
2. Relaxing muscles too much.
3. Moving lips or tongue while pronouncing vowel.
4. Throwing lips forward insufficiently.
5. Changing tone while pronouncing vowel.

CLOSED O, *o*

TONGUE
- TIP: brought back farther than for ou, *u*; consequently, not touching ridge of lower incisors.
- BACK: raised in rear of mouth, not as much as for ou, *u*, and touching hard palate on both sides in region of last molars.
- MUSCLES: tense.

LIPS
- LIPS: pushed very far forward.
- CORNERS OF MOUTH: brought forward, held very tense.
- OPENING: slight, horizontal.
- MUSCLES: tense.

TEETH   Space between upper and lower teeth: 1/4 inch.

AVOID

1. Moving tongue while pronouncing: (whence diphthong: o-*u*).
2. Relaxing muscles too much.
3. Moving lips and lower jaw.
4. Changing tone while pronouncing.

FOR PRACTICE. Before mirror.
TO TRAIN TONGUE, LIPS, AND JAW TO REMAIN MOTIONLESS.
Pronounce *u* as long as possible without stopping. Repeat
several times.

READING LESSON

SHORT. Sou, doux, loup, bout,
fou. J'ai un sou. Elle coud.
Tu joues. La roue de l'auto.
Le Doubs| est une rivière. Il
est jaloux. Tout d'un coup.
Le clown du cirque.
LONG. Bouge, rouge, Louvre,
douze. La robe| est rouge.
Elle est jalouse. Ils sont
douze. Je vais à Tours. Il
ferme| la porte du Louvre. Il
lit toujours. Elle bouge.
SHORT AND LONG. La nounou| la
trouve|sur la pelouse. Tout
d'un coup,| elle l'ouvre.

D'heure en heure on se disait: "Maintenant, ils sont
à Eyguières, maintenant, au
Parad<u>ou</u>". Puis, t<u>ou</u>t à c<u>ou</u>p,
vers le soir, un grand cri:
"Les voilà!" et là-bas, au
lointain nous voyons le
tr<u>ou</u>peau s'avancer dans une
gloire de p<u>ou</u>ssière. Toute
la r<u>ou</u>te semble marcher
avec lui. (Daudet)
Comme un bruit de f<u>ou</u>le,
Qui tonne et qui r<u>ou</u>le,
Et tantôt s'éc<u>ou</u>le
Et tantôt grandit.
(Victor Hugo)

FOR PRACTICE. Before mirror.
TO TRAIN TONGUE: *u, o, u, o, u, o*
Do not move lips. Do not pronounce while moving tongue.
Pronounce only when in position.

READING LESSON

SHORT. Eau, pot, p<u>ô</u>le, sauce,
trop. Il est tôt. Il est sot.
Il fait beau. Le chat| fait le
gros dos. Le pain chaud. Il
lui faut de l'eau. "Allô!..|
Allô!..."
LONG. Sauge, rose, pause,
mauve, chose. La sauge|est
une plante. J'ai quelque
chose. C'est une rose. Sa
veste est mauve. Elle pause.
Le pauvre.
SHORT AND LONG. L'eau chaude|
est dans le pot rose. Voici
un pauvre| Toto ôte son cha-
peau|et lui fait l'aumône.
CLOSED O AND OU, *u*. Dos,
doux, sot, sou, rôt, roux,
tôt, tout. L'eau bout.

...et quand il était là-
haut, assis <u>au</u> bon soleil,
sa mule près de lui, ses
cardin<u>aux</u> tout <u>au</u>tour, é-
tendus <u>aux</u> pieds des sou-
ches, il faisait déboucher
un flacon de vin de son cru,
--ce b<u>eau</u> vin, couleur de
rubis qui s'est appelé depuis le Chat<u>eau</u>-Neuf des
Papes, -et il le dégustait
par petits coups, en re-
gardant sa vigne d'un air
attendri. (D<u>au</u>det)
La voix plus h<u>au</u>te
Semble un grel<u>ot</u>,
D'un nain qui s<u>au</u>te
C'est le gal<u>op</u>;
(Victor-Hug<u>o</u>)

CLOSED E, e

TONGUE
- TIP: behind lower incisors, touching them.
- SIDE-EDGES: raised behind upper incisors and canines, touching pre-molars.
- MUSCLES: tense.

LIPS
- LIPS: showing front teeth.
- CORNERS OF MOUTH: in normal position.
- MUSCLES: tense.

TEETH Space between upper and lower teeth: 1/4 inch.

AVOID
1. Moving tongue while pronouncing.(whence diphthong: e-i).
2. Raising side-edges of tongue insufficiently.
3. Relaxing or stiffening muscles too much.
4. Uncovering front teeth too little.
5. Drawing corners of mouth too far apart.
6. Changing tone while pronouncing.
7. Exaggerating movements or tension.
8. Inserting the sound of yod, *j*, between a closed e and a following vowel in the same word, unless yod is written in the word;

créer	kreje	for	kree
océan	osejã	"	oseã
Européen	œropejẽ	"	œropeẽ

CLOSED EU, ø

TONGUE
- TIP: as for closed e: behind lower incisors, touching them.
- SIDE-EDGES: as for closed e: raised behind upper incisors and canines, touching pre-molars.
- MUSCLES: as for closed e: tense.

LIPS
- LIPS: as for ou, *u*: very rounded, pushed forward.
- CORNERS OF MOUTH: brought forward, held tense.
- OPENING: slight, horizontal.
- MUSCLES: tense.

TEETH Space between upper and lower teeth: 1/4 inch.

AVOID
1. Raising side-edges of tongue insufficiently.
2. Placing tip too far back, not touching lower incisors.
3. Relaxing muscles.
4. Separating lips too much without pushing them forward sufficiently.
5. Placing resonance in throat. Pronouncing on too low a note.

NOTE: In order to pronounce a clear closed eu, ø, try to pronounce a French closed e but with lips pushed forward and rounded.

FOR PRACTICE. Before mirror.

TO TRAIN LIPS AND TONGUE: e, o, e, o, e, o
Do not move jaw. Do not pronounce while moving lips and
tongue. Pronounce only when in position. (The position of
the speech-organs in French closed e and English short i,
as well as the sound, is approximately the same.)

READING LESSON

Tes, mes, les, ces, nez, bébé, thé. Les bébés|sont gais. J'ai du thé. Le nez|de la poupée. Nous avons deux pieds. Je vais les donner. J'irai chez l'épicier. L'hérédité. Vous aimez les poupées. Ces bébés|sont nés| l'été passé. L'hérésie|a été condamnée. La bonté et la beauté|sont deux qualités. J'ai des rosiers. Les cerisiers et les pommiers| sont des arbres fruitiers.

Et, vêtue comme une femme du peuple, elle alla chez le fruitier, chez l'épicier, chez le boucher, le panier au bras, marchandant, injuriée, défendant sou à sou son misérable argent. Il fallait chaque mois, payer des billets, en renouveler d'autres, obtenir du temps.

(Maupassant)

FOR PRACTICE. Before mirror.
I. TO TRAIN LIPS: e, ø, e, ø, e, ø
Do not move tongue or jaw. Do not pronounce while moving
lips. Pronounce only in position.
II. TO TRAIN TONGUE: ø, u, ø, u, ø, u
Do not move lips or jaw. Do not pronounce while moving
tongue. Pronounce only when in position.

READING LESSON

SHORT. Deux, peu, veut, jeu, ceux, oeufs. Je veux deux oeufs. Elle veut le cahier bleu. Eugène jeûne. Les malheureux|sont très nombreux. Il est veule. Il beugle.
LONG. Je suis malheureuse. Elle est affreuse. Tu es heureuse. Il va à Maubeuge.
SHORT AND LONG. Je veux qu'Eugénie|soit heureuse. Il a deux boeufs|dans la Meuse.
CLOSED E, e AND CLOSED EU, ø. Nez, noeud, des, deux, mes, meus, ces, ceux, fée, feu.

J'ai charge d'âmes, et je veux, je veux vous sauver de l'abîme ou vous êtes tous en train de rouler tête première...Demain lundi, je confesserai les vieux et les vieilles. Ce n'est rien...Jeudi, les hommes. Nous couperons court...Samedi, le meunier! ...Et si dimanche nous avons fini, nous serons bien heureux.

(Daudet)

I, i

TONGUE
- TIP: as for closed e: behind lower incisors, touching them.
- SIDE-EDGES: raised behind upper incisors a little more than for closed e and touching canines and part of incisors.
- MUSCLES: as for closed e: tense.

LIPS
- LIPS: as for closed e: showing front teeth.
- CORNERS OF MOUTH: as for closed e: drawn apart.
- MUSCLES: as for closed e: tense.

TEETH   Space between upper and lower teeth: 1/4 inch.

AVOID

1. Relaxing tongue too much.
2. Raising side-edges of tongue insufficiently.
3. Uncovering front teeth insufficiently.
4. Drawing corners of mouth too far apart.
5. Stiffening muscles.

U, y

TONGUE
- TIP: as for i: behind lower incisors, touching them.
- SIDE-EDGES: as for i: raised behind upper incisors, touching canines and part of incisors.
- MUSCLES: as for i: tense.

LIPS
- LIPS: very rounded, pushed forward.
- CORNERS OF MOUTH: brought forward; tense.
- OPENING: slight, horizontal.
- MUSCLES: tense.

TEETH   Space between upper and lower teeth: 1/4 inch.

AVOID

1. Moving tongue while pronouncing (whence two sounds: $j+y$)
2. Raising side-edges insufficiently.
3. Relaxing muscles.
4. Opening lips too wide; pushing them insufficiently forward.

NOTE: In order to pronounce a clear u, y, try to pronounce a French i, but with lips pushed forward and rounded.

FOR PRACTICE. Before mirror.
TO TRAIN TONGUE: e, i, e, i, e, i
Do not move lips. Do not pronounce while moving tongue.
Pronounce only when in position.

READING LESSON

SHORT. Dis, y, si, ni, ami, ceci, lit. Je dis merci | à Marie. Ni lui ni elle | n'a fini. Il lui dicte | une lettre. Il est triste. Prix unique. Six vitres. Dix pipes. La petite fille.
LONG. Il ouvre le livre. Il faut vivre. La lyre | qu'il a prise. Le rire | de l'homme ivre. Sur la rive. La frise grise.
SHORT AND LONG. La discipline | est difficile. La petite fille. Il tire le brise-bise. Il lit | dans le livre. Ils lui disent | de finir.

Tout le petit bois conspire pour l'empêcher de composer son discours...Monsieur le sous-préfet, grisé de parfums, ivre de musique, essaye vainement de résister au nouveau charme qui l'envahit. Il s'accoude sur l'herbe, dégrafe son bel habit, balbutie encore deux ou trois fois:
-Messieurs et chers administrés...Messieurs et chers admi...

(Daudet)

FOR PRACTICE. Before mirror.
I. TO TRAIN LIPS: i, y, i, y, i, y
Do not move tongue or jaw; for y push lips forward as rapidly as possible. Do not pronounce while moving lips. Pronounce only when in position.
II. TO TRAIN TONGUE: u, y, u, y, u, y
Do not move lips or jaw; for y raise front part of tongue very quickly forward. Do not pronounce while moving tongue.

READING LESSON

SHORT. Une, vue, du, rue, plus, tube. La tulipe | que j'ai vue. La musique russe. Tu sculptes une statue. Il a vendu | une plume. J'ai eu | une urne.
LONG. Juge, use, sur, pur, mur, cure. Le juge l'accuse. La robe s'use. La ruse du juge. Sur le mur. Tu es sûre.
SHORT AND LONG. Il accuse le rustre. La statue | est près du mur. Une rue du Vaucluse. Tu uses la plume.

Plus de dix fois, je ne mens pas, Gringoire, elle força le loup à reculer pour reprendre haleine. Pendant ces trèves d'une minute, la gourmande cueillait en hâte encore un brin de sa chère herbe; puis elle retournait au combat, la bouche pleine...-Oh! pourvu que je tienne jusqu'à l'aube...L'une après l'autre, les étoiles s'éteignirent. (Daudet)

OPEN O, ɔ

TONGUE
- TIP: flattened; touching lower teeth.
- BACK: raised less than for closed o; but slightly more raised than for posterior a, ɑ.
- FRONT: depressed.
- MUSCLES: tense.

LIPS
- CORNERS OF MOUTH: drawn slightly forward.
- OPENING: vertical.
- MUSCLES: relaxed.

TEETH   Space between upper and lower teeth: 5/8 inch.

AVOID

1. Raising front part of tongue too high (whence sound of open eu, œ).
2. Flattening back of tongue (whence sound of posterior a, ɑ).
3. Rounding lips insufficiently.
4. Giving nasal quality, when placed before m, n, or gn, ɲ.

OPEN E, ɛ

TONGUE
- TIP: behind lower incisors, touching them.
- SIDE-EDGES: raised behind pre-molars, touching them.
- MUSCLES: not very tense.

LIPS
- CORNERS OF MOUTH: drawn fairly far apart.
- OPENING: horizontal rather than vertical.
- MUSCLES: relaxed.

TEETH   Space between upper and lower teeth: 1/2 inch.

AVOID

1. Raising front part of tongue insufficiently.
2. Moving tongue forward (whence diphthong: e-i).
3. Separating jaws insufficiently.
4. Stiffening muscles.

FOR PRACTICE. Before mirror.
I. TO TRAIN JAW, LIPS, AND TONGUE: o, ɔ, o, ɔ, o, ɔ
For open o, ɔ, lower jaw and open lips as rapidly as possible. Do not pronounce while moving jaw, lips, and tongue. Pronounce only when in position.
II. TO TRAIN TONGUE AND LIPS: a, ɔ, a, ɔ, a, ɔ
Do not change position of lower jaw. Do not pronounce while moving tongue and lips. Pronounce only when in position.
III. TO TRAIN TONGUE: ɔ, ɑ, ɔ, ɑ, ɔ, ɑ
Do not move lips or jaw. Do not pronounce while moving tongue. Pronounce only when in position.

READING LESSON

SHORT. Robe, globe, ode, sol, code. La robe|est à la mode. La somme|est sur la note. L'homme|donne une pomme.
LONG. Il a tort. Il est mort. Tu dors. Laure sort. Le doge a une toge. La loge.
SHORT AND LONG. Paul|ouvre la porte de la loge. Paul| dort‖ et Laure|s'endort.

Il était une fois un homme qui avait une cervelle d'or; oui, madame, une cervelle toute en or. Lorsqu'il vint au monde, les médecins pensaient que cet enfant ne vivrait pas...Il vécut cependant et grandit au soleil comme un beau plant d'olivier. (Daudet)

FOR PRACTICE. Before mirror.
I. TO TRAIN TONGUE: a, ɛ, a, ɛ, a, ɛ
Do not move lips or jaw. Do not pronounce while moving tongue. Pronounce only when in position.
II. TO TRAIN JAW AND MUSCLES OF TONGUE: e, ɛ, e, ɛ, e, ɛ
For open e, ɛ, drop lower jaw as rapidly as possible and relax muscles of tongue. Do not pronounce while moving jaw. Pronounce only when in position.

READING LESSON

SHORT. Mais, c'est laid, fait, belle. Il se tait. Vous faites une lettre. Le geste| est ferme.
LONG. Terre, seize, neige. J'ai vu son père. C'est le seize. Il tombe de la neige. Son frère|est sur la chaise.
SHORT AND LONG. Pierre|passait près de la scène. Esther est avec Madeleine. Le père d'Esther|viendra le seize.
ANTERIOR A AND OPEN E. Mal, mêle. Balle, belle.

Madame Loisel semblait vieille maintenant. Elle était devenue la femme forte et dure et rude, des ménages pauvres. Mal peignée, avec les jupes de travers et les mains rouges elle parlait haut, lavait à grande eau les planchers. Mais, parfois...elle s'asseyait auprès de la fenêtre, et elle songeait à ce bal où elle avait été si belle et si fêtée. (Maupassant)

OPEN EU, œ

TONGUE
- TIP: behind lower teeth, touching them.
- SIDE-EDGES: as for open e, ε: raised behind upper pre-molars, touching them.
- MUSCLES: rather tense.

LIPS
- CORNERS OF MOUTH: drawn forward more than for open e, ε.
- OPENING: vertical, lower lip covering lower teeth.
- MUSCLES: relaxed.

TEETH   Space between upper and lower teeth: 5/8 inch.

AVOID
1. Flattening tongue (whence sound resembling mute e).
2. Rounding lips insufficiently.
3. Separating jaws insufficiently.
4. Pronouncing in a colorless manner, because of the fact that muscles are too relaxed.
5. Placing resonance in throat.

MUTE E, ə

TONGUE
- TONGUE: completely flat.
- TIP: rounded, behind lower teeth.
- MUSCLES: absolutely relaxed.

LIPS
- CORNERS OF MOUTH: in normal position.
- OPENING: slight.
- MUSCLES: absolutely relaxed.

TEETH   Space between upper and lower teeth: 1/3 inch.

AVOID
1. Placing tongue too high (whence sound resembling u in English word but).
2. Opening mouth too much or too little.
3. Placing resonance in throat.
4. Slurring of _e_ especially in _le_, article.

(The subject of retaining or omitting mute e, ə, under different circumstances, is fully discussed in Chapter XI).

FOR PRACTICE. Before mirror.
I. TO TRAIN LIPS: ɛ, œ, ɛ, œ, ɛ, œ
Do not move jaw or tongue. Do not pronounce while moving lips. Pronounce only when in position.
II. TO TRAIN LIPS AND LOWER JAW: ø, œ, ø, œ, ø, œ
Separate lips and drop jaw as rapidly as possible. Do not pronounce while moving lips and jaw. Pronounce only when in position.

READING LESSON

SHORT. Seul, neuf, jeune, boeuf, peuple. Il est seul. Le jeune peuple. La feuille de papier. La jeune fille. Le petit oeuf.
LONG. Coeur, heure, neuve, soeur, fleuve. Elle pleure. C'est le bonheur. Sa soeur a peur. Elle a des malheurs.
SHORT AND LONG. La jeune fille|cueille une fleur. Ma soeur|a grand'peur.

...L'éducation du co̱eur se fait par les mères et tu connais la mienne...Elle a fait de moi un piocheu̱r, un savant. La science a rempli ma vie. Tu en as été le se̱ul repos, le se̱ul sourire, la se̱ule je̱unesse (Pailleron). Un co̱eur ne̱uf, c'est comme une maison ne̱uve, ce ne sont pas les vrais locataires qui essuient les plâtres... (Pailleron)

─────────────────────────────

FOR PRACTICE. Before mirror.
TO TRAIN TONGUE AND LIPS: 1.   ø, ə, ø, ə, ø, ə
Do not pronounce while moving tongue or lips. Pronounce only when in position.
2.   œ, ə, œ, ə, œ, ə
Do not pronounce while moving tongue, lips, and jaw. Pronounce only when in position.

READING LESSON

STRESSED. Dis-le̱. Prends-le̱..
...et que̱, sur ce̱, et ce̱. Ces poèmes sont de...? Ne̱ viens pas. Redis-lui. Debout les morts. Le|est masculin. Ce,| adjectif démonstratif. De̲,| préposition. Me̱,| te̱,| se̱,| sont des pronoms.
UNSTRESSED, (but clearly pronounced). Il me̱ l'a dit. Il te̱ voit. Il me̱ parlø. Brusque̱ment. Libre̱ment. Juste̱ment. Propre̱ment. Semblable̱ment. Terrible̱ment. Parle̱ment. Humble̱ment. Noble̱ment. Vous aime̱riez. La chaisø de mon frère.

Jø te̱ dis encore toi parcø que̱ nous sommøs seuls, mais tout à l'heurø, devant lø monde, ce̱ sø ra: vous, tout lø temps: vous. La comtessø de Céran m'a fait l'honneur de m'inviter à lui présenter ma jeunø femmø et à passer quelques jours à son château dø Saint-Germain. Or, le̱ salon dø Madamø de̱ Céran est un des trois ou quatre salons les plus influents dø Paris...Tout dépend d'elle, de̱ nous, de̱ toi!

(Paille̱ron)

SUPPLEMENTARY READING EXERCISES

I. OU AND CLOSED O.
u, o

Dos, doux, sot, sou, rôt, roux, tôt, tout. L'eau bout. Le gros pot| est lourd. Les roues de l'auto| roulent sur la route. La nounou| ôte le chapeau| et la blouse de Toto. Au mois d'août| il fait chaud. Les douze apôtres. Le toutou et Toto| sautent sur la pelouse. La choucroute| est sur le fourneau. Le nouveau couteau. Les rouleaux de journaux| sont de l'autre côté.

II. CLOSED E AND I.
e, i

Fée, fit; des, dis; ces, si; nez, ni; les, lis; ré, ri; bée, bis, mes, mis. Félicité et Lili| y ont été. Disciplinez-les. J'ai fini |de répéter les poésies. Emilie| les a imités. Renée| a pris ses livres. Il y a dix cerisiers| chez Amélie. Emile| a été chez l'épicier. L'iniquité. Il a imité| le rire d'Andrée. Disciplinez-les. La petite fille| est intimidée. Il a pris| les poupées de Josée| et il les a cassées. Ridé, édile, plaisir, miné, érigé, intimer, je finirai, épicier, j'irai, frisé, livré, délivré.

III. CLOSED E AND CLOSED EU.
e, ø

Nez, noeud, des, deux, mes, meus, ces, ceux, fée, feu, bée, boeufs. Deux nez, des noeuds, les deux, ces oeufs, tes deux oeufs, ces jeux. J'ai deux dés. Les deux aînés| sont ces deux-là. Ces deux malheureux bébés| ont été trouvés| abandonnés. Eugénie| veut un peu de papier. Des yeux bleus,| des cheveux dorés,| et un nez retroussé.

IV. I AND U.
i, y

Dire, dure; dîne, dune; sire, sur; bise, buse; mise, muse; ride, rude. L'inutile sublimité. L'illustre ministre. L'usine| est minuscule. La cupidité du public. Une pilule.

V. OU AND U.
u, y

Moulu, pourvu, Mulhouse, moussu, couture, humour, fourrure, sous, su, mou, mû, bouche, bûche, rousse, russe, pouce, puce. La couturière| a voulu une fourfure de loutre. Jules| a couru tout le jour| sur la mousse. Pourvu que la nourriture de Jules| ne soit pas une nourriture trop lourde.

VI. OU, I AND U.
u, i, y

Doux, dis, du; sou, si, su; loup, lis, lu; joue, j'y, jus. Le tissu| d'une blouse russe. Le supplice du loup. Dis-tu doux? Sur six sous.

VII. CLOSED EU AND U.
ø, y

Jeu, jus; peu, pu; deux, du; noeud, nu; boeufs, bu; meus, mu. Le jeu du gueux. Ceux du duc. Jules et Hugues| jeûnent. Les deux oeufs de Luc. Scrupuleux, tuberculeux, tu veux, brumeux, nu, noeud. Tu as vu

le tuberculeux. Tu es peu
scrupuleux. Les deux oeufs|
sont sur le feu. Jules |veut
du feu.

VIII. CLOSED O AND OPEN O.
o,ɔ
Bône, bonne; hôte, hotte;
côte, cote; l'hôte, Loth;
saute, sotte; taupe, tope;
saule, sole; pôle, Paul;
môle, molle. Comme j'aurai
chaud. Laure et Paule| coupent
les roseaux. Auto| pour automobile, *oto| pur ɔtomɔbil*.
Photo | pour photographie,
foto|pur fɔtɔgrafi. Paul|
fait l'aumône au pauvre.

IX. ANTERIOR A AND OPEN O.
a,ɔ
Malle, molle. Bal, bol.
Salle, sol. Dague, dogue.
Cale, colle. Dard, dort.
Tard, tort. Mort, mare. Sort,
sarre. Baobab, catalogue, patronage, paradoxal, odorat,
apostolat, apostrophe, philosophe. Laure| part ,avec sa malle. Jeanne a tort |de parler
si fort. Jeanne raccommode| la
sacoche d'Adolphe. La catastrophe de Carcassonne.
Marc a tort| d'apostropher le
soldat.

X. ANTERIOR A AND OPEN E.
a,ɛ
Mal, mêle. Balle, belle. Sa,
c'est. Salle, celle. Germaine|
parlait à Isabelle. Elle apparaît avec sa mère. Esther
a fait la quête |avec Madame.
La fenêtre |est ouverte. Germaine partait| hier |quand Madeleine arrivait. La mallette
de Jeannette| est pleine de
lettres.

XI. CLOSED E AND OPEN E.
e,ɛ
Et, est; ces, c'est; mes,
mais; des, dais; ré, raie;
les, lait; nez, n'est; fée,
fais; tes, tait. L'été|
avait été très sec. Les
poupées d'Esther| étaient de
vraies beautés. Les prés et
les prairies| avaient été
plantés d'arbres fruitiers|
et d'herbes vertes.

XII. OPEN O AND OPEN EU.
ɔ,œ
Mort, meurs, port, peur,
sort, soeur; corps, coeur,
sole, seule; noble, meuble.
Le cor|sonne à neuf heures.
Ta soeur sort seule. Le
jeune veuf| porte un monocle.
Laure fait bon accueil| à sa
soeur. Elle raccommode| la
seule culotte de Paul.

XIII. ANTERIOR A, OPEN O
AND OPEN EU.
a,ɔ,œ
Sole, seule, sale; d'or,
d'heure, d'art; corps,
coeur, car; mords, meurs,
mare. A la bonne heure.
Malheur à la bonne. La robe
neuve de Madame. Ma soeur|
part à la Havane.

XIV. OPEN E AND OPEN EU.
ɛ,œ
Jeune, gêne; soeur, sert;
peur, père; meurs, mère;
seul, sel. Elle cueille| la
feuille de lierre. La jeune
Hélène |sert le beurre et
l'oeuf| à sa soeur. La jeune
veuve |allait au club. Elle
gêne sa soeur. Leur mère
meurt. Elle a peur |de son
père.

XV. CLOSED E, CLOSED EU, OPEN E AND OPEN EU.
$e, ø, ɛ, œ$

Mes, mais, meus, meurt. Epée paix, peu, peur. Ces, sait, ceux, soeur. Nez, n'est, noeud, neuf. Sa mère se meurt. Elle plaît à sa soeur. Jeannette| cueille de belles fleurs. Seule,|elle est demeurée au prieuré. Heureusement pour ceux-ci,| elle n'est demeurée que deux heures;| après | elle s'est échappée.

XVI. CLOSED EU, OPEN E AND MUTE E.
$ø, ɛ, ə$

De, deux, d'heure; ne, noeud, bonheur; ce, ceux, soeur; me, meus, meurt; que, queue, coeur. Je veux que ta soeur| me cueille deux fleurs. L'heureuse Renée |veut revenir à Montreuil. La malheureuse |est en deuil.

XVII. CLOSED E, CLOSED EU, OPEN EU AND MUTE E.
$e, ø, œ, ə$

Me, mes, meus, meurt; de, des, deux, d'heure; que, quai, queue, coeur; ce, ces, ceux, soeur. Les deux dés de ma soeur. Le bleu| est la couleur de Renée. Vous danseriez de bon coeur. Le feu|est dans la cheminée. La soeur d'Eugénie| part demain. Je veux deux fleurs. Les deux soeurs pleurent.

(The following passage contains examples of every vowel studied so far, eleven in number).

M. Seguin n'avait jamais eu de bonheur avec ses chèvres.
Il les perdait toutes de la même façon: un beau matin, elles cassaient leur corde, s'en allaient dans la montagne, et là-haut le loup les mangeait. Ni les caresses de leur maître, ni la peur du loup, rien ne les retenait. C'était, paraît-il, des chèvres indépendantes, voulant à tout prix le grand air et la liberté.
Le brave M. Seguin, que ne comprenait rien au caractère de ses bêtes, était consterné. Il disait:
--C'est fini; les chèvres s'ennuient chez moi, je n'en garderai pas une.
Cependant il ne se découragea pas, et, après avoir perdu six chèvres de la même manière, il en acheta une septième; seulement, cette fois, il eut soin de la prendre toute jeune, pour qu'elle s'habituât mieux à demeurer chez lui.
Ah! Gringoire, qu'elle était jolie la petite chèvre de M. Seguin! qu'elle était jolie avec ses yeux doux, sa barbiche de sous-officier, ses sabots noirs et luisants, ses cornes zébrées et ses longs poils blancs qui lui faisaient une houppelande! C'était presque aussi charmant que le cabri d'Esmeralda, tu te rappelles, Gringoire?--et puis, docile, caressante, se laissant traire sans bouger, sans mettre son pied dans l'écuelle. (Daudet)

THE NASAL VOWELS

SPELLING: in general, any vowel followed by a single n or m in the <u>same</u> syllable. (Double n or m, with few exceptions, denasalizes a preceding vowel):

    in-tro-duc-tion   but   i-nu-tile
    a-ban-don   "   do-nner
    fen-te   "   fe-nêtre

There are four nasal vowels, each one corresponding to an ordinary vowel. In the articulation of the ordinary vowels, the soft palate is raised so as to touch the back of the pharynx (fig. 1,P, p.5) thus preventing exhalation of air through the nose. In the articulation of the nasal vowels, the soft palate is lowered (fig.1,SP, p.5) thus allowing exhalation of air through the nose as well as through the mouth.

There is no sound completely nasal in French, that is to say, there is no sound for which all the air passes through the nose; part of it, a considerable part, always passes through the mouth; hence, the nasal vowels are only <u>partly</u> nasal. Students should bear this fact in mind and, when practicing, they should always take care that part of the air passes through the mouth.

Since the written n or m found in the spelling of a nasal vowel is only the mark of nasalization, it has no pronunciation of its own; it is completely silent. Many students have a strong tendency to pronounce these letters and only with difficulty rid themselves of this habit. It is especially for the benefit of such students, that the last exercise of the practice drill for each nasal vowel has been arranged.

DURATION

Stressed nasal vowels are long when they are placed before one or more sounded consonants.

In other positions, nasal vowels are short.

MISTAKES TO BE AVOIDED

The following mistakes, frequently made by foreigners in the articulation of the four nasal vowels, should be avoided:
1. Jerking jaw at beginning.
2. Lowering soft palate insufficiently (whence vowel insufficiently nasal) or on contrary, lowering it too much (whence indeterminate sound).
3. Moving back of tongue toward palate, during pronunciation of vowels (whence sound of **ng** in English word sing).
4. Closing lips during pronunciation of vowel (whence n or m).

ON, ɔ̃ or õ

TONGUE as for o
- TIP: flattened, touching lower teeth.
- BACK: raised less than for closed o, but slightly more than for posterior a, ɑ.
- MUSCLES: tense.

LIPS as for o
- LIPS: pushed very far forward.
- CORNERS OF MOUTH: brought forward, held tense.
- OPENING: horizontal.
- MUSCLES: fairly tense.

TEETH Space between upper and lower teeth: 1/4 inch.

MECHANISM
- As larynx begins to vibrate, tongue, lips and jaw are being brought into position and soft palate is lowered to allow part of breath to pass through nose.

AVOID
1. Closing lips during pronunciation (whence sound of m).
2. Rounding lips insufficiently.
3. Nasalizing open o, ɔ, when placed before nn, mm, or gn, ɲ.
4. Confusing on, ɔ̃, with an, ã.

AN, ã
CORRESPONDS TO POSTERIOR A, ɑ

TONGUE
- TIP: flattened, behind ridge of lower incisors, touching it.
- BACK: slightly raised.
- MUSCLES: fairly tense.

LIPS
- CORNERS OF MOUTH: in normal position.
- OPENING: vertical rather than horizontal.
- MUSCLES: relaxed.

TEETH Space between upper and lower teeth: 3/4 inch.

MECHANISM
- As larynx begins to vibrate, tongue, lips and jaw are being brought into position, and soft palate is lowered to allow part of air to pass out through nose.

AVOID
1. Raising front part of tongue too high.
2. Opening lips insufficiently.
3. Nasalizing anterior a, a, rather than posterior a, ɑ, when placed before nn, mm, or gn, ɲ.
4. Confusing an, ã, with on, ɔ̃.

FOR PRACTICE. Before mirror.
Do not pronounce while moving tongue, lips, or jaw. Pronounce only when in position.
I. TO TRAIN SOFT PALATE: $a, \tilde{a}, a, \tilde{a}, a, \tilde{a}$
Do not move lips, tongue, or jaw during whole drill.
II. TO TRAIN TONGUE, LIPS, AND JAW TO REMAIN MOTIONLESS:
Pronounce an, $\tilde{a}$, for half a minute uninterruptedly.

READING LESSON

SHORT. Banc, sans, lent, maman. Le banc du marchand. Tous les ans. Quel temps fait-il? Il fait du vent.
LONG. Chante, lente, range. Elle est lente. Elle est blanche. Blanche danse. Les marchandes| vendent de la viande. Le chantre|va au temple.
SHORT AND LONG. En entendant le chant,| l'enfant danse. La marchande|vend le banc à Jean.

Elle franchissait d'un saut de grands torrents qui l'éclaboussaient au passage de poussière humide et d'écume. Alors, toute ruisselante, elle allait s'étendre sur quelque roche plate et se faisait sécher par le soleil. (Daudet)

Il fuit, s'élance,
Puis en cadence
Sur un pied danse
Au bout d'un flot.
(Victor-Hugo)

FOR PRACTICE. Before mirror.
Do not pronounce while moving tongue, lips, or jaw. Pronounce only when in position.
I. TO TRAIN SOFT PALATE AND LIPS: $o, \tilde{o}, o, \tilde{o}, o, \tilde{o}$
Do not move tongue or jaw during whole drill.
II. TO TRAIN TONGUE, LIPS, AND JAW TO REMAIN MOTIONLESS:
Pronounce on, $\tilde{o}$, for half a minute uninterruptedly.
III. TO TRAIN EAR, AS WELL AS LIPS, TONGUE, AND JAW:
$\tilde{a}, \tilde{o}, \tilde{a}, \tilde{o}, \tilde{a}, \tilde{o}$

READING LESSON

SHORT. Bon, on, son, long. Ils sont longs. Nous partons. Ils vont sur le pont. L'a-t-on fait promptement?
LONG. Monde, longue, oncle, ongle. Tout le monde. Il la gronde. Il a honte. Elle est longue. Il y en a onze. Elle est prompte.
SHORT AND LONG. Les bonbons de l'oncle. On lui fait honte. Le lion,| on le dompte. Léon le gronde.

Non, non, va! c'est bien ici que se font, défont et surfont les réputations, les situations et les élections, où, sous couleur de littérature et beaux-arts, les malins font leur affaire...(Pailleron)

Leur essaim gronde:
Ainsi, profonde,
Murmure une onde
Qu'on ne voit pas.
(Victor-Hugo)

IN, $\tilde{\varepsilon}$

TONGUE
- TIP: behind lower incisors, touching them.
- SIDE-EDGES: raised behind pre-molars, touching them; not, however, as for open e, ε.
- MUSCLES: not very tense.

LIPS
- CORNERS OF MOUTH: fairly far apart.
- OPENING: horizontal.
- MUSCLES: relaxed.

TEETH Space between upper and lower teeth: 1/2 inch.

MECHANISM As larynx begins to vibrate, tongue, lips, and jaw are being brought into position, and soft palate is lowered to allow part of air to pass out through nose.

AVOID

1. Permitting side-edges of tongue to occupy too much room in mouth, thus preventing air from passing out freely.
2. Separating corners of mouth too much.
3. Nasalization of i when placed before one n vowel:
   Inutile $\tilde{\varepsilon}nytil$ for $inytil$
   Inepte $\tilde{\varepsilon}n\varepsilon pt$ " $in\varepsilon pt$

UN, $\tilde{œ}$

TONGUE
- TIP: behind lower teeth, touching them.
- SIDE-EDGES: raised behind upper pre-molars, touching them.
- MUSCLES: rather tense.

LIPS
- CORNERS OF MOUTH: drawn forward a little more than for in, $\tilde{\varepsilon}$.
- OPENING: horizontal.
- MUSCLES: relaxed.

TEETH Space between upper and lower teeth: 5/8 inch.

MECHANISM As larynx begins to vibrate, tongue, lips, and jaw are being brought into position, and soft palate is lowered to allow part of air to pass out through nose.

AVOID

1. Raising front part of tongue insufficiently behind upper teeth.
2. Rounding lips insufficiently (whence the sound of $\tilde{\varepsilon}$).
3. Slurring un, article.
4. Placing resonance in the throat.

FOR PRACTICE. Before mirror.
Do not pronounce while moving tongue, lips or jaw. Pronounce only when in position.
I. TO TRAIN TONGUE AND SOFT PALATE: ε, ε̃, ε, ε̃, ε, ε̃
Do not move lips, or jaw during whole drill.
II. TO TRAIN TONGUE, LIPS, AND JAW TO REMAIN MOTIONLESS:
Pronounce in, ε̃, for half a minute uninterruptedly.
III. TO TRAIN EAR, AS WELL AS TONGUE, LIPS, AND JAW:
ã, ε̃, ã, ε̃, ã, ε̃
READING LESSON

SHORT. Pain, vin, mien, faim. J'ai du pain et du vin. Il peint la salle de bains. Il craint le chien. Le chien Rintintin.
LONG. Prince, dinde, sainte, sphinx. La sainte. Elle est peinte. Les belles teintes. Elle porte le linge.
SHORT AND LONG. J'ai quatre-vingts timbres. Elle a peint| le sphinx.
AN, ã, and IN, ε̃. Mente, mainte. Fente, feinte.

Au même moment une trompe sonna bien loin dans la vallée. C'était ce bon monsieur Seguin qui tentait un dernier effort.
-Hou! hou!...faisait le loup. -Reviens! reviens... criait la trompe. (Daudet)

C'est la plainte
Presque éteinte
D'une sainte
Pour un mort.
(Victor-Hugo)

FOR PRACTICE. Before mirror.
Do not pronounce while moving tongue, lips or jaw. Pronounce only when in position.
I. TO TRAIN SOFT PALATE: œ, œ̃, œ, œ̃, œ, œ̃
II. TO TRAIN TONGUE, LIPS, AND JAW TO REMAIN MOTIONLESS:
Pronounce un, œ̃, for half a minute uninterruptedly.
III. TO TRAIN MUSCLES OF TONGUE, AND LIPS, AS WELL AS EAR:
ε̃, œ̃, ε̃, œ̃, ε̃, œ̃
READING LESSON

SHORT. Un, quelqu'un, chacun, l'un, aucun. Il a vu quelqu'un. Les uns vont à Verdun, les autres à Melun. Le parfum. Il est à jeun. Il est importun.
LONG. Humble, défunte, emprunte. Il emprunte. La défunte était une humble personne.
SHORT AND LONG. L'importun| emprunte à chacun. La défunte de Melun. Un humble.
IN, ε̃, AND UN, œ̃. Daim, d'un. In, un. Quint, qu'un.

NOTE: In the following passage the sounds ε̃ and œ̃ are underlined:
"-Moi, Je n'entre pas. Je suis un ami de Dieu.
"-Tu es un ami de Dieu...
Eh! b...de teigneux! Que viens-tu faire ici?..."-Je viens...Ah! ne m'en parlez pas, que je ne puis plus me tenir sur mes jambes...Je viens, je viens de loin... humblement vous demander...
(Daudet)

SUPPLEMENTARY READING EXERCISES

I. AN AND ON.

Banc, bon; pan, pont; dans, dont; ambre, ombre; pente, ponte; bande, bonde. Mentant, montons, menton, montant; pensant, ponçons, pensons, ponçant; lançant, long son, lançons, l'on sent. Nous pensons au bon temps. On entend | l'oncle de la marchande. Blanche a honte | devant tant de monde. Le ballon de l'enfant | est rond. Sans son enfant | la maman est dolente. Les enfants | sont dans le fond de la chambre. Mon oncle | vient en chantant. Ils vont au temple | le dimanche.

II. AN AND IN.

Lent, lin; vent, vin; dans, daim; pense, pince; rance, rince. Du pain, de la viande et du vin. Le marchand | vend vingt timbres | à l'enfant. Le temps est incertain | ce matin. Prends garde au vent. Le prince | pense à la sainte. Le temple | est peint en blanc. Jean | boit de l'absinthe. Jean | joue avec le singe.

III. AN, ON, IN AND UN.

Ment, Moeung; lent, l'un; quand, qu'un; dans, d'un; dont, daim: quand, Quint, qu'on, qu'un. On en a vu un | en endosser un. Un bon pain blanc. L'enfant | a un fin parfum. Chacun | prend son pain et son vin. Le pinson | chante un refrain charmant. En entendant et en grondant l'enfant, | l'oncle songe | à un mensonge de son enfance | et cette pensée | le rend indulgent. Jean prend du pain. Son enfant est brun. Ils ont envahis | la Saintonge. Les pins et les sapins | sentent bon.

(The following passage contains examples of the four nasal vowels, all of which are underlined).

Pour aller au village, <u>en</u> desc<u>en</u>dant de m<u>on</u> moul<u>in</u>, <u>on</u> passe dev<u>ant</u> <u>un</u> mas bâti près de la route au f<u>on</u>d d'une gr<u>an</u>de cour pl<u>an</u>tée de micocouliers. C'est la vraie mais<u>on</u> du ménager de Prov<u>en</u>ce, avec ses tuiles rouges, sa large façade brune irrégulièrem<u>ent</u> percée, puis tout <u>en</u> haut la girouette du grenier, la poulie pour hisser les meules, et quelques touffes de fo<u>in</u> br<u>un</u> qui dépassent...
Pourquoi cette mais<u>on</u> m'avait-elle frappé? Pourquoi ce portail fermé me serrait-il le coeur? Je n'aurais pas pu le dire, et pourt<u>ant</u> ce logis me faisait froid. Il y avait trop de sil<u>en</u>ce autour...Qu<u>an</u>d <u>on</u> passait, les chi<u>ens</u> n'aboyaient pas, les p<u>in</u>tades s'<u>en</u>fuyaient s<u>ans</u> crier...A l'<u>in</u>térieur, pas une voix! Ri<u>en</u>, pas même un grelot de mule...S<u>ans</u> les rideaux bl<u>ancs</u> des fenêtres et la fumée

qui m̲ontait des toits, o̲n̲ aurait cru l'e̲n̲droît inhabité.
   Hier, sur le coup de midi, je revenais du village, et, pour éviter le soleil, je lo̲n̲geais les murs de la ferme, da̲n̲s̲ l'o̲m̲bre des micocouliers...Sur la route, deva̲n̲t̲ le mas, des valets sile̲n̲cieux achevaient.de charger une charrette de foi̲n̲...Le portail était resté ouvert. Je jetai u̲n̲ regard e̲n̲ passa̲n̲t, et je vis, au fo̲n̲d̲ de la cour, accoudé, --la tête da̲n̲s̲ ses mai̲n̲s,--sur une large table de pierre, un gra̲n̲d̲ vieux tout bla̲n̲c̲, avec une veste trop courte et des culottes en la̲m̲beaux...(Daudet)

Chapter VII.
THE SEMI-VOWELS OR SEMI-CONSONANTS

   There are three semi-vowels or semi-consonants in French. They are called by either of these two names, because in their articulation they are just half way between the vowels and the consonants.
   The main difference between a vowel and a consonant is that for the vowel there is always a free passage, a "groove" in the mouth from the back to the front, which allows the air to pass out easily without obstacle; whereas for the consonant, there is either a complete obstacle (p, b, t, d, k, g, m, n, ɲ), or a narrowing of the passage (f, v, s, z, ʃ, ʒ, l, r).
   For the pronunciation of the semi-vowels, the passage is neither as large as for the vowels nor as closed and narrow as for the consonants. The three semi-vowels correspond to three ordinary vowels but with a narrower space for the passage of the air.
   Moreover, while French vowels are very sonorous and very clear, the semi-vowels are less sonorous and less clear and all very short as compared with vowels, even the very short ones.
   In the articulation of semi-vowels, the student should take care to give to the speech-organs the same position as when forming the corresponding vowels (with a narrower passage for the air). As soon as the position is taken, instead of pronouncing that vowel he should immediately displace the speech-organs (lips and tongue) for the next sound; it is the displacement of the speech-organs which produces the semi-vowel.
   Furthermore, although the "attack" or beginning of the vowels in French is very smooth and soft, increasing in volume afterward, the "attack" of the semi-vowels is rather abrupt.

SEMI-VOWEL OU, *w*
CORRESPONDING TO THE VOWEL OU, *u*

TONGUE
- TIP: behind ridge of lower incisors.
- BACK: raised as high as possible in direction of hard palate, so that space between tongue and hard palate is very narrow.
- MUSCLES: very tense.

LIPS
- CORNERS OF MOUTH: Brought forward, held very tense.
- OPENING: horizontal.
- MUSCLES: very tense.

TEETH Space between upper and lower teeth: 1/10 inch.

MECHANISM

Cause larynx to vibrate from very beginning and start sound with much more force than for corresponding vowel. As soon as tongue, lips, jaw, and larynx are in position, instead of pronouncing the vowel ou, *w*, immediately displace speech-organs and pronounce next sound: it is the <u>displacement</u> of speech-organs which produces the semi-vowel.

AVOID
1. Raising tongue too much in front.
2. Permitting tongue to occupy too much room in mouth.
3. Pushing lips forward insufficiently.

SEMI-VOWEL U, *ɥ*
CORRESPONDING TO THE VOWEL U, *y*

TONGUE
- TIP: behind lower incisors, touching them.
- SIDE-EDGES: raised behind upper incisors, touching canines and part of incisors.
- BACK: lowered.
- MUSCLES: fairly tense.

LIPS
- LIPS: very rounded, pushed forward.
- CORNERS OF MOUTH: brought forward, held tense.
- OPENING: small, horizontal.
- MUSCLES: fairly tense.

TEETH Space between upper and lower teeth: 1/4 inch.

MECHANISM

Cause larynx to vibrate from beginning and start sound with much more force than for corresponding vowel. As soon as tongue, lips, jaw, and larynx are in position, instead of pronouncing the vowel u, *y*, immediately displace speech-organs and pronounce next sound: it is this <u>displacement</u> which produces the semi-vowel.

AVOID
1. Raising front part of tongue insufficiently.
2. Relaxing muscles.
3. Pushing lips forward insufficiently.

FOR PRACTICE. Before mirror.

TO TRAIN TONGUE, LIPS: u, i, u, i, u, i, wi
Pronounce each vowel distinctly and separately. Then,
after placing lips, jaw and tongue in position for u, instead of pronouncing u, pronounce i: it is this displacement of speech-organs which produces the semi-vowel

READING LESSON

Je dis oui. Il est couard. La loyauté du citoyen. L'Equateur. C'est quadrangulaire. Elle voit au loin, le casque qui pointe. Louis a moins de points que toi. Louise a joué avec la girouette. Je vis dans le lointain une alouette. Edouard est loyal envers ses concitoyens. Il faut avoir soin d'entretenir le foyer.

Je n'avais plus le coeur à jouer, vous pensez...oh! non... J'allais m'asseoir dans tous les coins et, regardant les objets autour de moi, je leur parlais comme à des personnes; je disais aux platanes:"Adieu, mes chers amis!" et aux bassins:"C'est fini, nous ne nous verrons plus!" Il y avait dans le fond du jardin un grand grenadier dont les belles fleurs rouges s'épanouissaient au soleil. (Daudet)

FOR PRACTICE. Before mirror.
I. TO TRAIN LIPS: y, i, y, i, y, i, ɥi
Pronounce each vowel distinctly and separately. Then,
after placing lips, jaw, and tongue in position for y, instead of pronouncing y, pronounce i: it is this displacement of speech-organs which produces the semi-vowel.
II. TO TRAIN TONGUE AND LIPS:
  1. wi, ɥi, wi, ɥi, wi, ɥi
  2. lwi, lɥi, lwi, lɥi, lwi, lɥi

READING LESSON

Je suis ruiné. Aujourd'hui c'est le huit juin. Lui, il la fuit. L'écuyer a essuyé le tuyau. La questure. C'est équilatéral. Le bruit de la pluie, sur la tuile. C'est lui qui l'a tué. Puis, j'enfile une aiguille. La cuisinière a fait cuire aujourd'hui huit plats à l'huile sur la cuisinière de la cuisine.

...Je ne suis pas un élève du tout, je viens ici comme maître d'étude; conduisez-moi chez le principal.
...Bamban s'était assis par terre à cause de ses jambes qui lui faisaient mal. Je m'assis près de lui. Je lui parlai...Je lui achetai une orange...J'aurais voulu lui laver les pieds. (Daudet)

SEMI-VOWEL YOD, j
CORRESPONDING TO THE VOWEL I, i

TONGUE
{ TIP: behind lower incisors, touching them.
SIDE-EDGES: raised behind upper incisors more than for 1.
BACK: somewhat raised toward hard palate, leaving only narrow canal for passage of air.
MUSCLES: more tense than for 1. }

LIPS { Inactive for yod, j, but in position of accompanying vowel. }

MECHANISM

Cause larynx to vibrate at beginning and start sound with much more force than for corresponding vowel. At beginning of word or between vowels, as soon as tongue is in position, instead of pronouncing i , i, immediately displace speech-organs and place them in position for next sound: it is this <u>displacement</u> of speech-organs which produces the semi-vowel. At end of word, keep larynx, lower jaw, and lips in position required for preceding vowel, place tongue in proper position for yod, j, and articulate it very clearly.

AVOID

1. Raising tongue insufficiently toward front.
2. Raising tongue insufficiently toward rear.
3. Relaxing muscles.
4. Making yod, j, partly or completely voiceless, that is to say, without vibrations of larynx.
5. Except under certain circumstances (p.   ), pronouncing yod, j, when placed before vowel, separately instead of together with vowel (bi-$\tilde{\varepsilon}$, instead of bj$\tilde{\varepsilon}$).
6. Articulating insufficiently when at end of word. (At first, students should add a mute e, θ, to pronunciation of final yod, j).
7. Inserting the sound of yod, j, between a closed e and the following vowel in the same word unless it is written in the word:

créer	kreje	for	kree
océan	osej$\tilde{a}$	"	ose$\tilde{a}$
européen	œropej$\tilde{\varepsilon}$	"	œrope$\tilde{\varepsilon}$
néant	nej$\tilde{a}$	"	ne$\tilde{a}$
et on	ej$\tilde{o}$	"	e$\tilde{o}$
nazaréen	nazarej$\tilde{\varepsilon}$	"	nazare$\tilde{\varepsilon}$

FOR PRACTICE. Before mirror.

I. TO TRAIN TONGUE: bi-ɛ̃, bi-ɛ̃, bi-ɛ̃, bjɛ̃
Pronounce each vowel distinctly and separately three times; then, in last word, after placing tongue in position for yod, *j*, immediately pronounce anterior a: it is the displacement of tongue which produces the semi-vowel yod.

II. TO TRAIN LIPS AND TONGUE:
1. ja, jo, ja, jo, ja, jo
2. aja, ojo, aja, ojo, aja, ojo
3. aj, oj, aj, oj, aj, oj

READING LESSON

Souiller, soulier; vouliez, voudriez; rien. Hier, elle ne voyait rien, mais ses yeux vont mieux. Dès son réveil, elle commence à travailler. Le soleil brille dans le ciel. L'ouvrier est fier. La vieille a un beau tablier. Le soulier de la petite fille. Soyez sérieux. Une vieille fille. Un vieillard. La veille de la fête. Elles voyagent sur un yacht. Vous ne voudriez pas. Ayant voyagé hier dans l'Ohio. La grenouille. Couleur de rouille. Les brouillards de Lyon.

On partit enfin. Je vois cela comme si c'était d'h*i*er: le vapeur chauffait contre le quai de Granville; mon père effaré, surve*i*llant l'embarquement de nos trois colis; ma mère inqu*i*ète ayant pris le bras de ma soeur non mar*i*ée, qui semblait perdue depuis le départ de l'autre, comme un poulet resté seul de sa couvée; et derr*i*ère nous, les nouveaux époux qui restaient toujours en arr*i*ère, ce qui me faisait souvent tourner la tête....Nous regard*i*ons les côtes s'enfuir, heureux et f*i*ers comme tous ceux qui vo*y*agent peu. (Maupassant)

          Dormeuse.
    Si l'enfant somme*ille*,
    Il verra l'abe*ille*,
Quand elle aura fait son m*i*el,
Danser entre terre et c*i*el.
              (Desbordes-Valmore)

SUPPLEMENTARY READING EXERCISES

(The following passages contain examples of the three semi-vowels, all of which are underlined).

A minuit, le gardien se levait, jetait un dernier coup d'oeil à ses mèches, et nous descendions. Dans l'escalier on rencontrait le camarade du second quart qui montait en se frottant les yeux; on lui passait la gourde, le Plutarque...Puis, avant de gagner nos lits, nous entrions un moment dans la chambre du fond, tout encombrée de chaînes, de gros poids, de réservoirs d'étain, de cordages, et là, à la lueur de sa petite lampe, le gardien écrivait sur le grand livre du phare, toujours ouvert:
Minuit. Grosse mer. Tempête. Navire au large.

Je courais la mer de Sardaigne en compagnie de sept ou huit matelots douaniers. Rude voyage pour un novice! De tout le mois de mars, nous n'eûmes pas un jour de bon. Le vent d'est s'était acharné après nous, et la mer ne décolérait pas.

Un soir que nous fuyions devant la tempête, notre bateau vint se réfugier à l'entrée du détroit de Bonifacio, au milieu d'un massif de petites îles...Leur aspect n'avait rien d'engageant: grands rocs pelés, couverts d'oiseaux, quelques touffes d'absinthe, des maquis de lentisques, et, çà et là, dans la vase, des pièces de bois en train de pourrir; mais, ma foi, pour passer la nuit, ces roches sinistres valaient encore mieux que le rouf d'une vieille barque à demi pontée, où la lame entrait comme chez elle, et nous nous en contentâmes.

Personne! Le bruit s'est tu...Du milieu des lambrusques mouillées, deux ou trois courlis s'envolent en secouant leurs ailes...Un peu de brise chante dans les arbres... Vers l'orient, sur la crête fine des Alpilles, s'entasse une poussière d'or d'où le soleil sort lentement...Un premier rayon frise déjà le toit du moulin. Au même moment, le tambour, invisible, se met à battre aux champs sous le couvert...Ran...plan...plan, plan, plan!

Le diable soit de la peau d'âne! Je l'avais oubliée. Mais enfin, quel est donc le sauvage qui vient saluer l'aurore au fond des bois avec un tambour?...J'ai beau regarder, je ne vois rien...rien que les touffes de lavande, et les pins qui dégringolent jusqu'en bas sur la route... Il y a peut-être par là, dans le fourré, quelque lutin caché en train de se moquer de moi...C'est Ariel, sans doute, ou maître Puck.

(Daudet)

Chapter VIII.
THE CONSONANTS

A consonant is a sound, whether or not accompanied by vibrations of the larynx, in the production of which the air, as it passes through the mouth, meets a complete or nearly complete obstruction. This obstruction may be caused by the lips or by the tongue.

A **voiced** consonant (Fr. **sonore**) is a consonant accompanied by vibrations of the larynx. The voiced consonant is **gentle** (Fr. douce): the air, having already been stopped a first time by the vocal chords or larynx, has less force when it reaches the obstacle formed by the lips or tongue.

A **voiceless** consonant (Fr. **sourde**) is a consonant not accompanied by vibrations of the larynx. The voiceless consonant is **strong** (Fr. forte): the air, not having been stopped by the vocal chords, since these are open and offer a free passage, has more force when it meets the obstacle formed by the speech-organs. It will later be seen that every voiceless consonant has its corresponding voiced consonant.

There are seventeen consonants in French.

I prefer to teach the formation and pronunciation of the consonants with very little reference to technical terms. However, as the student may find these terms in other books and wish to associate them with the material from two different points of view: **manner** in which they are articulated, and **place** where they are articulated.

A. According to the **manner** in which they are articulated, the consonants are classified as:
    1. plosive
    2. fricative
    3. sibilant
    4. hushing
    5. nasal
    6. lateral or liquid.

B. According to the **place** in which they are articulated, the consonants are classified as:
    1. bi-labial
    2. labio-dental
    3. dental
    4. palatal
    5. uvular.

A. CLASSIFICATION ACCORDING TO THE MANNER IN WHICH THE CONSONANTS ARE ARTICULATED.
                    I. PLOSIVES

VOICELESS	VOICED
p, t, k.	b, d, g.

These consonants are called plosive because they are the result of an <u>explosion</u>; the air forces the obstacle formed by the speech-organs to give way in order that it may pass out.

The plosives are also called <u>instantaneous</u> or <u>momentary</u> (Fr. <u>momentanées</u>) because, being the result of an explosion, their sound cannot be prolonged. We shall later see, however, that their silent part may be prolonged.

Contrary to what happens in pronouncing English plosives, the volume of air used in the pronunciation of the French plosives is very limited.

The articulation of such consonants includes three phases:
1. IMPLOSION: that phase when speech-organs are placed in position to close mouth at some point.
2. OCCLUSION: that phase when speech-organs remain in position.
3. EXPLOSION: (Fr. détente) that phase when speech-organs separate.

In French, the occlusion is always complete. It is during this phase that the muscles are most tense. (It is this part of the plosive consonant which, in case emphasis is desired, may be lengthened, continued. The speech-organs completely close the air passage and offer a resistance to the air, which is thus stopped in its rush. Then suddenly and rapidly, these organs separate and permit the air to escape, thus producing a <u>clear-cut</u> sound. (In English, the separation of the speech-organs is rather lax and slow, and the air is very abundant).

2. FRICATIVES

VOICELESS	VOICED
f.	v.

These consonants are called fricative (Lat. fricatus, rubbed), because they are produced by a light <u>rubbing</u> of the air against the upper and lower lip.

3. SIBILANTS

VOICELESS	VOICED
s	z

These consonants are called sibilant (Lat. sibilo:hiss), because they are <u>hissing</u> sounds.

4. HUSHING CONSONANTS

VOICELESS	VOICED
ch, ʃ	j, ʒ

These consonants are so called because they are the sounds which one uses in suggesting silence (<u>Hush!</u> sh<u>shsh</u>).

5. NASALS

VOICED

m, n, gn, ɲ

These consonants are called nasal because part of the air necessary for their pronunciation escapes through the nose. (The student should bear in mind, however, that they are not completely nasal and that part of the air escapes through the mouth).

These three consonants are usually voiced. They may, however, become voiceless through the process of a phenomenon called assimilation of which I shall speak later.

Gn, ɲ, is also called "mouillée" (English literal translation: wet), because the contact of a large part of the moistened tongue against the hard palate gives an impression of something wet.

6. LATERALS OR LIQUIDS
VOICED
l, r. (rolled).

These consonants are called lateral (Lat. latus, -eris, side) because they are produced by the escape of the air between an obstacle in the middle of the mouth and the sides. They are also called liquid (Lat. liquidus, fluid), because they are pronounced with a smoothly flowing sound and may easily be linked to other consonants. (Do not confuse, then, a "consonne mouillée" with a "consonne liquide").

These two consonants are usually voiced. They may, however become voiceless through the process of a phenomenon called assimilation of which I shall speak later.

Fricative, sibilant, hushing, nasal, and lateral or liquid consonants are also called continuant because they may be continued, prolonged.

The articulation of all these continuants includes three phases, as for the articulation of the plosive or instantaneous (momentary):

1. PREPARATION: that phase when speech-organs are placed in position.
2. PAUSE: (Fr. tenue) that phase when speech-organs remain momentarily motionless but do not relax.
3. RELEASE: (Fr. détente), that phase when speech-organs separate.

When the consonant is placed at the end of the word the student should take great care not to overlook the third phase which is essential in order to make the word clear to a listener.

There are three r's in French:
1. Rolled (Fr. r roulé).
2. Uvular (Fr. r uvulaire).
3. Parisian (Fr. r parisien ou grasseyé).

The r preferred by most cultured French people is the Parisian, but if a student is unable to acquire this r, either of the two others is acceptable.

B. CLASSIFICATION ACCORDING TO THE PLACE IN WHICH THE CONSONANTS ARE ARTICULATED.

1. BI-LABIALS

p, b, and m are called bi-labial because they are articulated by the two lips, one against the other (Lat. labia, lip:).

2. LABIO-DENTALS

f and v are called labio-dental because they are articulated by the lower lip against the upper teeth (Lat. dens, -tis: tooth).

3. DENTALS

d, t, l, n, s, z, rolled r, are called dental because they are articulated against the teeth or teeth-ridge.

4. PALATALS

k, g, ʃ, ʒ, Parisian r, are called palatal because they are articulated against hard palate.

5. UVULAR

Uvular r is so called because it is articulated by the tip of the soft palate or uvula.

NOTE: I have treated each consonant separately even in the case of those that correspond (as p and b), because usually not enough consideration is given to the fact that although similar, they are not exactly alike. It is the failure sometimes to observe this distinction that betrays the foreigner.

LAW OF ANTICIPATION
(LOI DE PRÉVOYANCE)

Before the articulation of a consonant, the lips must be, as nearly as possible, in the position required for the accompanying vowel. The term "accompanying vowel" indicates that vowel which either directly precedes or directly follows the consonant in the same syllable.

In French, it is the vowel which is all-powerful and which regulates the position of the organs for the articulation of the consonant, at every time it has the opportunity to do so.

ot: The lips must be pushed very far forward for closed o even before t is pronounced. It is in this position that t should be pronounced.

tɛ: The corners of the mouth must be drawn far apart for open e, ɛ, even before t is pronounced. It is only in this position that t should be pronounced.

ot: The lips must remain pushed very far forward until t is pronounced. It is only in this position that t should be pronounced.

ɛt: The corners of the mouth must remain drawn far apart until t is pronounced. It is only

in this position that t should be pronounced.
I repeat that this law of anticipation operates with
all consonants.

RELEASE (Fr. DETENTE)

The release is the phase in the articulation of a consonant which is the opposite of the preparation--the speech-organs suddenly leave the position which they have assumed and their muscles become relaxed. This it is that produces the <u>clear-cut</u> articulation of the last consonant or consonants of a stress-group. Consequently, if a speaker has not kept his muscles extremely tense during the pause, sufficiently complete and rapid relaxation is impossible, with the result that to a French person the last consonant or consonants are audible only very slightly if at all. This frequently causes him to misunderstand the speaker, or (when an adjective or variable noun is involved) to think that the masculine gender has been used when the feminine is required.

From the very beginning therefore, the student should make especial effort to articulate final consonants with the greatest distinctness. It may even be useful to him to pretend that a mute e, ə, exists after the final consonant. In this way he will probably be more successful in attaining sufficient articulation of the consonant or consonants.

Compare the following endings:

{ Il est Francais.
{ La prononciation français<u>se</u>.

{ Dans le tas.
{ La grande ta<u>ble</u>.

{ Le petit le fil.
{ La petite fi<u>lle</u>.

{ Dans le port.
{ J'ouvre la po<u>rte</u>.

{ Un poisson frit.
{ Une pomme fri<u>te</u>.

{ Le ruban vert.
{ La robe ve<u>rte</u>.

{ Le bon lait.
{ Le beau sole<u>il</u>.

{ Le beau genêt.
{ J'ouvre la fenê<u>tre</u>.

{ En tout cas.
{ Je vais à la ca<u>ve</u>.

{ Un sermon.
{ Une semon<u>ce</u>.
{ C'est un mon<u>stre</u>.

{ Il va à la mairie.
{ Il va en Amérique.

{ Dans la rue.
{ Il est Ru<u>sse</u>.
{ C'est un ru<u>stre</u>.

P, p

TONGUE Inactive.

LIPS
- LIPS: pressed against each other just inside the visible part.
- CORNERS OF MOUTH: more or less far apart or close together, depending on accompanying vowel.
- MUSCLES: tense.

MECHANISM

P is a strong consonant. Larynx does not vibrate. At very beginning, lips are pressed tightly together; the pressure gradually diminishes until separation of lips. Volume of air very small.

AVOID

1. Bringing exterior part of lips together.
2. Separating lips too slowly.
3. Relaxing muscles from beginning.
4. Releasing too much air (whence sound of English h after p).
5. Making p insufficiently audible at end of word.

B, p

TONGUE Inactive.

LIPS
- LIPS: pressed against each other just inside visible part.
- CORNERS OF MOUTH: more or less far apart or close together, depending on accompanying vowel.
- MUSCLES: relaxed.

MECHANISM

B. is a gentle consonant.
At very beginning, as larynx is caused to vibrate, lips are pressed tightly together; the pressure gradually diminishes until separation of lips. Volume of air very small.

AVOID

1. Bringing exterior part of lips together.
2. Separating lips too slowly.
3. Releasing too much air (whence sound of English h after b).
4. Stopping vibrations of larynx partly or incompletely at end of word or when b is followed by l or r at end of word (whence sound of p).

FOR PRACTICE. Before mirror.
Do not pronounce while moving tongue, lips, or jaw. Pronounce only when in position.
I. TO REDUCE BREATH AND TO SUPPRESS POSSIBLE SOUND OF H:
Pronounce: *pa, pa, pa,* before a sheet of thin paper. During the pronunciation of correct French p, the paper barely moves, whereas with an English p, it shows a pronounced movement.
II. TO TRAIN LIPS: 1. *pa, po, pa, po, pa, po*
                     2. *ap, op, ap, op, ap, op*
READING LESSON

"Paix"| dit-il. "Père,| viens avec moi." "Pan,| pan,| pan!| Ouvrez-moi." Papa|n'y va pas. Paris|est une belle ville. Paul vient. Parlons-lui. Partons. Donne-lui une tape. C'est un type. Il fait la lippe. Je veux|qu'il le rompe. Il allume la lampe. Il l'attrape. Il s'en occupe. Hep!

Il avait trente ans; sa taille était assez élevée pour que Paul auprès de lui, parut transformé en pygmée; son expression était intelligente, hautaine, et telle que personne, à première et même à seconde vue, ne lui eût octroyé l'auréole de la sainteté. (Labiche)

FOR PRACTICE. Before mirror.
Do not pronounce while moving tongue, lips, or jaw. Pronounce only when in position.
I. TO REDUCE BREATH, TO SUPPRESS SOUND OF H, AND TO FORCE VIBRATIONS OF LARYNX: 1. *ba, be, bi, bo, bu*
Have larynx vibrate as soon as lips close.
                     2. *ab, ɛb, ib, ob, ub*
Do not stop vibrations between vowel and consonant.
II. TO TRAIN LIPS: 1. *ba, bo, ba, bo, ba, bo*
                     2. *ab, ob, ab, ob, ab, ob*
READING LESSON

Bien faire. Blanche|est venue me voir. Bonjour,| boulanger,| donne-moi du pain. Blond| comme un chérubin. Bouche d'or. Ce mot a deux syllabes. Un gros tube. Elle méprise la plèbe. La femme de l'Arabe. Le bel habit. L'abbé Constantin. Le jambon. Elle embellit. Il abolit. Il aborde. Buvez| le bon vin de la bonbonne.

Elle se rappelait bien l'histoire de la construction de cet étage; c'était à la suite d'une trouvaille de bateau abandonné faite en Manche par le père Gaos et son cousin le pilote; la nuit du bal, Yann lui avait raconté cela....Par un escalier de bois blanc tout neuf, on la fit monter dans la chambre d'en haut qui était la gloire du logis.
(Loti)

T, t

TONGUE
- TIP: behind and against upper incisors, touching them very firmly.
- SIDE-EDGES: against upper teeth and ridge.
- MUSCLES: tense.

LIPS Inactive for t itself, but in position of accompanying vowel.

MECHANISM

T is a strong consonant. Larynx does not vibrate.
At very beginning, tip of tongue is strongly pressed against upper incisors; the pressure gradually diminishes until separation of tongue from teeth; tip then drops very rapidly, giving a clear-cut sound. Volume of air very small.

AVOID

1. Placing tip of tongue too far back in mouth.
2. Pressing tip of tongue insufficiently against teeth.
3. Relaxing muscles at very beginning.
4. Separating tip of tongue too slowly from teeth.
5. Releasing too much air (whence sound of English h after t).
6. Making t insufficiently audible at end of word.

D, t

TONGUE
- TIP: behind and against upper incisors.
- SIDE-EDGES: against upper teeth and ridge.
- MUSCLES: tense.

LIPS Inactive for d itself, but in position of accompanying vowel.

MECHANISM

D is a gentle consonant.
At very beginning, as larynx is caused to vibrate, tip of tongue is strongly pressed against upper incisors; the pressure gradually diminishes until separation of tongue from teeth. Tip then drops very rapidly, giving a clear-cut sound. Volume of air very small.

AVOID

1. Placing tip of tongue too far back in mouth.
2. Pressing tip of tongue insufficiently against teeth.
3. Relaxing muscles at very beginning.
4. Separating tip of tongue too slowly from teeth.
5. Releasing too much air (whence sound of English h after d).
6. Stopping vibrations of larynx partly or completely at end of word (whence sound of t).

FOR PRACTICE. Before mirror.
Do not pronounce while moving tongue, lips, or jaw. Pronounce only when in position.
I. TO REDUCE BREATH, TO SUPPRESS SOUND OF H, AND TO TRAIN TIP OF TONGUE:
Pronounce: *ta, ta, ta,* before a sheet of thin paper. During the pronunciation of correct French t, the paper barely moves, whereas with an English t, it shows a pronounced movement.
II. TO TRAIN JAW TO REMAIN MOTIONLESS AND TONGUE TO MOVE RAPIDLY: *ta, ta, ta*
Do not move jaw.
III. TO TRAIN LIPS: 1. *ta, to, ta, to, ta, to*
2. *at, ot, at, ot, at, ot*
READING LESSON

Tiens! Tel fils, tel père. Tôt ou tard. Tandis qu'il vient. Tapez fort. Il a hâte. Il parle à l'hôte. Vous êtes honnête. Le beau site. Sur la natte. La patte de la chatte. Il tape dans le tas.

Blanque<u>tte</u> eu<u>t</u> envie de revenir; mais en se rappelant le pieu, la corde, la haie du clos. elle pensa que main<u>te</u>nant elle ne pouvait plus se faire à ce<u>tte</u> vie et qu'il valait mieux res<u>ter</u>. (Daudet).

FOR PRACTICE. Before mirror.
Do not pronounce while moving tongue, lips, or jaw. Pronounce only when in position.
I. TO REDUCE BREATH, TO SUPPRESS SOUND OF H, AND TO FORCE VIBRATIONS OF LARYNX: 1. *da, de, di, do, du*
Cause larynx to vibrate at very beginning of consonant.
2. *ad, ɛd, id, od, ud*
Do not stop vibrations between vowel and consonant.
II. TO TRAIN JAW TO REMAIN MOTIONLESS AND TONGUE TO MOVE RAPIDLY: *da, da, da*
Do not move jaw.
III. TO TRAIN LIPS: 1. *dɛ, do, dɛ, do, dɛ, do*
2. *ɛd, od, ɛd, od, ɛd, od*
READING LESSON

Dis-le. Dix enfants. Donne-le. Dame fourmi. Dicte-lui la fable. Donnant, donnant. D'ailleurs, dire n'est pas faire. Il est timide. Il est malade. J'aime la salade. Je fais une promenade. L'onde est profonde. Il doit. Il dit. Tu diras à la grande amie. La distance est grande.

"Monsieur le préfet, je crois <u>d</u>evoir prévenir l'autorité que <u>d</u>eux insensés ont l'intention de croiser le fer <u>d</u>emain, à mi<u>d</u>i moins un quart"...il suffit quelquefois <u>d</u>'un quart d'heure! ..."A mi<u>d</u>i moins un quart... .Le ren<u>d</u>ezvous est à la porte <u>d</u>u gar<u>de</u>..."(Labiche)

K, k

TONGUE
- TIP: behind and against lower incisors.
- BACK: raised against hard palate.
- POINT OF ARTICULATION: not always same: depending upon accompanying vowel:
  a. If accompanying vowel is posterior, point of articulation is against soft palate.
  b. If accompanying vowel is anterior, point of articulation is against back part of hard palate.
- MUSCLES: tense.

LIPS Inactive for k itself, but in position of accompanying vowel.

MECHANISM

K is a strong consonant. Larynx does not vibrate. At very beginning, tip of tongue is placed behind and against lower incisors, and back of tongue is firmly pressed against hard palate; the pressure gradually diminishes until separation of tongue from palate. Then, back of tongue drops very rapidly, giving a clear-cut sound. Volume of air very small.

AVOID

1. Placing point of articulation too far back in mouth.
2. Pressing back of tongue insufficiently against hard palate.
3. Relaxing muscles from very beginning.
4. Separating back of tongue too slowly from hard palate.
5. Releasing too much air (whence sound of English h after k).
6. Making k insufficiently audible at end of word.

FOR PRACTICE. Before mirror.

Do not pronounce while moving tongue, lips, or jaw. Pronounce only when in position.

I. TO REDUCE BREATH, TO SUPPRESS SOUND OF H, AND TO TRAIN BACK OF TONGUE:
Pronounce: *ke, ke, ke,* before a sheet of thin paper. During the pronunciation of correct French k, the paper barely moves, whereas with an English k, it shows a pronounced movement.

II. TO TRAIN JAW TO REMAIN MOTIONLESS AND BACK OF TONGUE TO MOVE RAPIDLY: *ke, ke, ke*
Do not move jaw. After complete contact between back of tongue and hard palate, drop tongue as rapidly as possible.

III. TO TRAIN LIPS: 1. *ke, ko, ke, ko, ke, ko*
2. *ɛk, ok, ɛk, ok, ɛk, ok*

READING LESSON

Quiconque peut le casser. Coupable, il l'est. Quarante hommes. Qui vient? Que dit-il? Elle est dans le hamac. J'ai un sac. Sur le lac. J'apprends la physique. Il critique. L'oiseau ouvre le bec. Le trafic. Au Danemark. Le képi du soldat. Je vais à l'Académie. Un kilo de concombres. Le choléra. Un chrétien. L'expression est exquise. Quelques caricaturistes nous prêteront leur concours. Que crie donc Christian, là, à côté? A Carcassonne l'eau est calcaire. A New-York, le trafic est considérable. Isaac. J'ai un sac. Du tac au tac. Je vais à Québec. Le long bec. Il est sec. Le pic. Le diagnostic. Le Maroc. Jeanne d'Arc. Un viaduc.

De tous les jolis di̱ctons, proverbes ou adages, dont nos paysans passementent leurs dis̱cours, je n'en sais pas un plus pittoresqu̱e ni plus singulier qu̱e celui-ci. A quinze lieues autour de mon moulin, qu̱and on parle d'un homme rancunier, vindi̱catif, on dit: "Cet homme-là! méfiez-vous!...il est c̱omme la mule du pape qui garde sept ans son c̱oup de pied!" (Daudet)

        La rumeur approche
        L'ecẖo la redit;
        C'est c̱omme la c̱loche
        D'un c̱ouvent maudit.
                (Victor-Hugo)

G, g

TONGUE
- TIP: behind and against lower incisors.
- BACK: raised against hard palate.
- POINT OF ARTICULATION: not always same, depending on accompanying vowel:
  a. If accompanying vowel is posterior, point of articulation is against soft palate.
  b. If accompanying vowel is anterior, point of articulation is against back part of hard palate.
- MUSCLES: tense.

LIPS Inactive for g itself, but in position of accompanying vowel.

MECHANISM

G is a gentle consonant.
At very beginning, as larynx is caused to vibrate, tip of tongue is placed behind and against lower incisors, and back of tongue is firmly pressed against hard palate; the pressure gradually diminishes until separation of tongue from palate. Then, back of tongue drops very rapidly, giving a clear-cut sound. Volume of air very small.

AVOID

1. Placing points of articulation too far back in mouth.
2. Pressing back of tongue insufficiently against hard palate.
3. Relaxing muscles from very beginning.
4. Separating back of tongue too slowly from hard palate.
5. Releasing too much air (whence sound of English h after g).
6. Stopping vibrations of larynx, partly or at end of word or when it is followed by l or r at end of word (whence sound of k).

FOR PRACTICE. Before mirror.

Do not pronounce while moving tongue, lips, or jaw. Pronounce only when in position.

I. TO REDUCE BREATH, TO SUPPRESS SOUND OF H, AND TO FORCE VIBRATIONS OF LARYNX: 1. ga, ge, gi, go, gu
Cause larynx to vibrate as soon as back of tongue comes in contact with hard palate. Test by placing fingers on larynx.   2. $ag, \varepsilon g, ig, og, ug$
Do not stop vibrations between vowel and consonant; at first, one may even add a mute e, ə, to consonant to force vibrations of larynx.

II. TO TRAIN JAW TO REMAIN STILL AND BACK OF TONGUE TO MOVE RAPIDLY: ga, ga, ga
Do not move jaw. After complete contact between back of tongue and hard palate, drop tongue as rapidly as possible.
1. ga, go, ga, go, ga, go
2. ag, og, ag, og, ag, og

READING LESSON

Garde-la. Guide-le. Guy|est un petit garçon. Guiguite| est une petite fille. Gardons-nous| d'être goguenards. Garçon,| un café. Il donne la bague. Il est bègue. Il lègue. L'eau| a dépassé les digues. C'est un dogue. Il est rogue. Second. L'agrégé|a réussi à son agrégation. La guerre|a gagné la plus grande partie de la Gascogne. Gustave|se gargarise la gorge. Il est inexorable. En zigzag. Je vais à Dantzig. Je veux un grog. J'ai une bague. Mon collègue. Il se fatigue. Il parle plusieurs langues. Elle est longue. Un bouledogue. En Camargue. Les langues modernes. Je vais à Copenhague. Il est à Prague. C'est très vague. Il danse la gigue. Il est bilingue. Des meringues. Sur le catalogue.

Sa gaieté communicative, son esprit conciliant, le génie de l'organisation et des inventions drôlatiques qu'il possédait au plus haut degré en faisaient un compagnon charmant, égayaient notre vie et développaient mon amour.
                               (de la Brète)

   Ce bruit vague
   Qui s'endort
   C'est la vague
   Sur le bord;
    (Victor-Hugo)

F, ʃ

TONGUE Inactive.

LIPS
- LOWER LIP: internal part comes in contact with upper incisors, thus completely covering lower incisors.
- UPPER LIP: does not touch lower lip.
- CORNERS OF MOUTH: in position for accompanying vowel.
- MUSCLES: tense.

MECHANISM

F is a strong consonant. Larynx does not vibrate.
Internal part of lower lip comes in contact with upper incisors, completely covering lower teeth and leaving enough space for air to pass out continuously; then, separation of lip and teeth is very rapid, articulation extremely precise. Volume of air small.

AVOID

1. Pressing upper incisors against external part of lower lip.
2. Relaxing muscles.
3. Releasing too much air.
4. When lip and teeth separate, dropping lower jaw too much
5. Making f insufficiently audible at end of word.

V, ʋ

TONGUE Inactive.

LIPS
- LOWER LIP: internal part comes in contact with upper incisors, thus completely covering lower incisors.
- UPPER LIP: does not touch lower lip.
- CORNERS OF MOUTH: in position for accompanying vowel.
- MUSCLES: tense.

MECHANISM

V is a gentle consonant.
As larynx is caused to vibrate, internal part of lower lip comes in contact with upper incisors, completely covering lower teeth and leaving enough space for air to pass out continuously; then separation of lip and teeth is very rapid, articulation extremely precise. Volume of air small.

AVOID

1. Pressing upper incisors against external part of lower lip.
2. Releasing too much air.
3. When lip and teeth separate, dropping lower jaw too much.
4. Stopping vibrations of larynx partly or completely, at end of word (whence sound of f).

FOR PRACTICE. Before mirror.
Do not pronounce while moving tongue, lips, or jaw. Pronounce only when in position.
I. TO REDUCE BREATH AND TO ACQUIRE CORRECT POSITION OF LOWER LIP AND UPPER TEETH: Pronounce: ʃa, ʃa, ʃa, before a sheet of thin paper. During the pronunciation of correct French f, the paper barely moves, whereas with an English f, it shows a pronounced movement.
II. TO TRAIN LIPS: 1. ʃa, ʃo, ʃa, ʃo, ʃa, ʃo
                2. aʃ, oʃ, aʃ, oʃ, aʃ, oʃ

READING LESSON

Fais-le venir. Faites-la entrer. Faisons du bon travail. Faire une chose difficile. L'épitaphe. J'ai un phonographe. Le cinématographe. Un bon chef. L'affluence. C'est affreux. L'influence est bonne. Il a fait une affaire. Le fin fond de la France. Le fanfaron fanfaronne.

Naïvement, Yann racontait sa vie de pêcheur, ses fatigues, ses salaires, les difficultés d'autrefois chez ses parents, quand il avait fallu élever les quatorze petits Gaos dont il était le frère aîné...
...Ainsi, cette année, notre père m'a fait faire ces habits neufs que je porte.
(Loti)

FOR PRACTICE. Before mirror.
Do not pronounce while moving tongue, lips, or jaw. Pronounce only when in position.
I. TO ACQUIRE CORRECT POSITION OF LOWER LIP AND UPPER TEETH AND TO FORCE VIBRATIONS OF LARYNX:
                1. va, ve, vi, vo, vu
Cause larynx to vibrate at very beginning of consonant.
                2. aːv, ɛːv, iːv, oːv, uːv
Do not stop vibrations between vowel and consonant.
II. TO TRAIN LOWER JAW TO MOVE GENTLY: va, ve, vi, vo, vu
Drop jaw very little and very gently.
III. TO TRAIN LIPS: 1. va, vo, va, vo, va, vo
                2. aːv, oːv, aːv oːv, aːv, oːv

READING LESSON

Vas-y. Vont-elles à la gare? Vers elle. Vive l'Amérique. Viendra-t-il? Vaincre ou mourir. Je vais à la cave. Elle est brève. La veuve pleure. Elle est neuve. Qu'il vive. Un vilain voleur. Il casse la vitre. La vivacité d'Yvonne. Véra voyage avec ses voisins à travers les vallées.

On dansait à la vielle, au violon, les mêmes couples presque toujours ensemble. Quand lui venait la reprendre, après avoir par convenance dansé avec quelque autre, ils échangeaient un sourire d'amis qui se retrouvent et continuaient leur conversation d'avant...
(Loti)

S, s

TONGUE
- TIP: behind ridge of lower incisors, touching it.
- FRONT PART: raised behind lower and upper incisors, leaving very narrow space between them and teeth.
- SIDE-EDGES: touching upper incisors, canines, premolars and molars as well as their ridge.
- MUSCLES: very tense.

LIPS Inactive for s itself, but in position of accompanying vowel.

LOWER JAW Slightly pushed forward so that lower teeth are as far forward as upper.

MECHANISM

S is a strong consonant. Larynx does not vibrate.
As tip of tongue is placed behind ridge of lower incisors so that it touches it, front part of tongue is raised behind lower and upper incisors, leaving very narrow passage between it and teeth; at same time, side-edges of tongue are raised and placed against incisors, canines, premolars and molars, and against their ridge as well, while lower jaw is pushed slightly forward. Articulation very precise. Muscles tense.

AVOID

1. Lowering tip of tongue insufficiently.
2. Leaving too large space between front part of tongue and upper incisors.
3. Leaving canal, from molars to molars, too narrow.
4. Relaxing muscles.
5. Pronouncing on too low a note.
6. Making s insufficiently audible at end of word.
7. Uncovering upper incisors insufficiently.
8. Pronouncing s when sign of plural:

les livres	$lelivrs$	for	$leli:vr$
les tables	$letabls$	"	$letabl$
les filles	$lefijs$	"	$lefij$
les murs	$lemyrs$	"	$lemy:r$
les fauteuils	$lefotœjs$	"	$lefotœj$

FOR PRACTICE. Before mirror.

Do not pronounce while moving tongue, lips, or jaw. Pronounce only when in position.

I. TO TRAIN TIP AND FRONT PART OF TONGUE:
   sa, se, si, so, su
Keep tip of tongue behind ridge of lower incisors so that it touches them. Raise front part behind lower and upper incisors, leaving very small space between tongue and teeth. Muscles must be very tense.

II. TO TRAIN LIPS: 1. *sa, so, sa, so, sa, so*
                   2. *as, os, as, os, as, os*

READING LESSON

Ça et là. Servez-vous. Si grand. Ciel et terre. Sautez. Celle-là. Scandez ces vers. Je vais en classe. Je suis lasse. Je vais en Suisse. J'aime la sauce. Il faut qu'il finisse. Nous espérons. C'est assez. Une grosse émotion. Il est prétentieux. Je vais à Bruxelles. Sa soeur s'asseoit sur le siège. Six chasseurs sachant chasser sans chien. Pour qui sont ces serpents qui sifflent sur nos têtes? Combien, ces saucissons-ci? Ces saucissons-ci, six sous les six. Je demeure rue d'Assas. La rue Cujas et la rue Stanislas. Je vais à Arras. C'est un délice. Le train express. Une lettre expresse. Un edelweiss. Un omnibus. L'oremus. Vénus. Elle est basse. Qu'il le fasse. Une déesse. La Suisse. Une brosse. Elle est fausse.

Quand ils ont aperçu Monsieur le sous-préfet avec sa belle culotte et sa serviette en chagrin gaufré, les oiseaux ont eu peur et se sont arrêtés de chanter, les sources n'ont plus osé faire de bruit, et les violettes se sont cachées dans le gazon...Tout ce petit monde-là n'a jamais vu de sous-préfet, et se demande à voix basse quel est ce beau seigneur qui se promène en culotte d'argent. (Daudet)

   Il fuit, s'élance,
   Puis en cadence
   Sur un pied danse
   Au bout d'un flot. (Victor-Hugo)

Z, z

TONGUE
- TIP: behind ridge of lower incisors, touching it.
- FRONT PART: raised behind lower and upper incisors, leaving very narrow space between them and teeth.
- SIDE-EDGES: touching upper canines, pre-molars and molars as well as their ridge.
- MUSCLES: very tense.

LIPS Inactive for z itself, but in position of accompanying vowel.

LOWER JAW Pushed slightly forward so that lower teeth are as far forward as the upper.

MECHANISM

Z is a gentle consonant.
As larynx is caused to vibrate, tip of tongue is placed behind ridge of lower incisors so that it touches it, and front part of tongue is raised behind lower and upper incisors, leaving very narrow passage between it and teeth; at same time, side-edges of tongue are raised and placed against upper canines, pre-molars, and molars, and against their ridge as well. while lower jaw is pushed slightly forward. Articulation, very precise. Muscles, tense.

AVOID

1. Lowering tip of tongue insufficiently.
2. Leaving too large space between front part of tongue and upper incisors.
3. Leaving canal, from molars to molars, too narrow.
4. Relaxing muscles.
5. Pronouncing on too low note.
6. Uncovering upper incisors insufficiently.
7. Stopping vibrations of larynx partly or completely at end of word (whence sound of s).

FOR PRACTICE. Before mirror.

Do not pronounce while moving tongue, lips, or jaw. Pronounce only when in position.

I. TO TRAIN JAW, LIPS, AND FRONT PART OF TONGUE, AND TO FORCE VIBRATIONS OF LARYNX:
$$za, ze, zi, zo, zu$$
Push jaw forward so that it is as far forward as upper teeth. Keep tip of tongue behind ridge of lower incisors. Raise front part of tongue behind lower and upper incisors, leaving very small space between tongue and teeth; muscles very tense. Cause larynx to vibrate as soon as front part of tongue is raised. To test vibrations, place fingers on larynx.

II. TO TRAIN LIPS: 1. *za, zo, za, zo, za, zo*
　　　　　　　　　　2. *a:z, o:z, a:z, o:z, a:z, o:z*

READING LESSON

Zéro| est un chiffre. "Zouaves,| zouaves,| tenez ferme!" Zigzaguer| n'est pas marcher droit. Zézayer| est parler comme les petits enfants. J'aime les roses. Elle pause. Quelque chose. Une bonne cause. Les fleurs| sont dans le vase. Je l'ai mise. Elle use sa robe. Le cousin de Suzanne. Les enfants et les hommes. J'examine l'horizon. Zoé est inexorable. Le deuxième étage. Les hommes et les enfants| s'amusent. Le zézaiement de Suzanne| est chose désagréable. Suzanne| sème la zizanie| parmi les autres enfants. Le gaz. Berlioz. Trapèze. Ils sont treize. Il y en a quinze. Il est en bronze. J'en ai quatorze. La phrase. Le diocèse. Elle est Irlandaise.

Monsieur le sous-préfet, grisé de parfums, ivre de musique essaye vainement de résister au nouveau charme qui l'envahit. Il s'accoude sur l'herbe, balbutie encore deux ou trois fois:- messieurs et chers administrés...Messieurs et et chers admini...Messieurs et chers...(Daudet)

　　　　　Tandis qu'il se repose,
　　　　　Sa paupière rose,
　　　　　Pour la terre close,
　　　　　S'ouvre pour le ciel.
　　　　　　　　　　(Victor-Hugo)

CH, ʃ

TONGUE
- TIP: wide, raised toward front palate far forward.
- SIDE-EDGES: touching ridge of pre-molars and molars.
- MUSCLES: tense (pressure of tongue very strong).

LIPS
- Play important part in articulation of ch, ʃ: pushed far forward, forming a small megaphone.

RESONANCE

There are three different places where sound is amplified:
1. Between tip of tongue and back of mouth.
2. Between tip of tongue and upper incisors.
3. Between lips and teeth.

MECHANISM

Ch, ʃ, is a strong consonant. Larynx does not vibrate. At the same time that tip of tongue is raised toward front part of hard palate, side-edges come in contact with ridge of pre-molars and molars, while lips are pushed very far forward and form small megaphone; the different parts of this composite position must be taken simultaneously and before sound is uttered. Volume of air small. Muscles, tense.

AVOID

1. Pressing side-edges of tongue insufficiently against pre-molars and molars.
2. Lowering tip of tongue instead of raising it.
3. Bringing tip of tongue too far back.
4. Keeping lips inactive.
5. Pronouncing ch, ʃ, on too low a note.
6. Making ch, ʃ, insufficiently audible or even silent at end of word.

FOR PRACTICE. Before mirror.

Do not pronounce while moving tongue, lips, or jaw. Pronounce only when in position.

I. TO TRAIN TONGUE AND LIPS:
ʃa, ʃa, ʃa

Keep tip of tongue raised toward front part of hard palate. Side-edges of tongue must be brought into very firm contact with part of hard palate just above pre-molars and molars. Throw lips forward as much as possible.

II. TO TRAIN LIPS: 1. ʃa, ʃo, ʃa, ʃo, ʃa, ʃo
2. aʃ, oʃ, aʃ, oʃ, aʃ, oʃ

READING LESSON

Cher enfant. Chose vue. Chiffons. "Chauds, chauds," les marrons chauds". Chef de bande. Il triche. La jolie chatte. Elle est sèche. Cherchons. Le Général Hoche. Elle prend la hache. Elle apporte des bûches. Elle cherche. Il chérit son chat. Une hachette| est une petite hache. Elle cherche la chéchia. Le cheval de Charlotte. La vie est chère. Chacune a son cheval. La chevauchée des chevaliers. Six chasseurs| sachant chasser sans chien. Le chien|et le cheval de Chonchette. Dans la poche. Elle se cache. Elle est fraîche. En Autriche. C'est dimanche. Il marche. Il ouvre la bouche. Le maréchal Foch.

Tu penses, Gringoire, si notre ch**è**vre était heureuse. Plus de corde, plus de pieu...rien qui l'empê**ch**ât de gambader, de brouter à sa guise... C'est là qu'il y en avait de l'herbe! jusque par-dessus les cornes, mon **ch**er!...et quelle herbe! Savoureuse, fine, dentelée, faite de mille plantes...C'était bien autre **ch**ose que le gazon du clos!...La **ch**èvre blan**ch**e, à moitié soûle, se vautrait là-dedans, les jambes en l'air et roulait le long des talus, pêle-mêle avec les feuilles tombées et les **ch**âtaignes.

(Daudet)

La rumeur appro**ch**e;
L'écho la re**d**it.
C'est comme la clo**ch**e
D'un couvent maudit;

(Victor-Hugo)

J, ʒ

TONGUE
- TIP: wide, raised toward front palate far forward.
- SIDE-EDGES: touching ridge of pre-molars and molars.
- MUSCLES: tense (pressure of tongue very strong).

LIPS
- Play important part in articulation of j, ʒ; pushed far forward, forming small megaphone.
- CORNERS OF MOUTH: more or less far apart or close together, depending on accompanying vowel.

RESONANCE
There are three different places where sound is amplified:
1. Between tip of tongue and back of mouth.
2. Between tip of tongue and upper incisors.
3. Between lips and teeth.

MECHANISM
J, ʒ, is a gentle consonant.
As larynx is caused to vibrate, tip of tongue is raised toward front part of hard palate, and side-edges come in contact with ridge of pre-molars and molars; at same time, lips are pushed very far forward and form small megaphone. The different parts of this composite position must be taken simultaneously and before sound is uttered. Volume of air, small. Muscles, tense.

AVOID

1. Pressing side-edges of tongue insufficiently against pre-molars and molars.
2. Lowering tip of tongue instead of raising it.
3. Bringing tip of tongue too far back.
4. Keeping lips inactive.
5. Pronouncing j, ʒ, on too low a note.
6. Stopping vibrations of larynx partly or completely at end of word (whence sound of ch, ʒ).

FOR PRACTICE. Before mirror.

Do not pronounce while moving tongue, lips, or jaw. Pronounce only when in position.

I. TO TRAIN TONGUE AND LIPS, AND TO FORCE VIBRATIONS OF LARYNX: 1. $ʒa, ʒe, ʒi, ʒo, ʒu$
Keep tip of tongue raised toward front part of hard palate. Side-edges of tongue must be brought into very firm contact with part of hard palate just above pre-molars and molars. Throw lips forward. Cause larynx to vibrate as soon as side-edges come in contact with hard palate, and as soon as lips are thrown forward. Test vibrations of larynx by placing fingers on it.
  2. $a:ʒ, ɛ:ʒ, i:ʒ, o:ʒ, u:ʒ$
Do not stop vibrations between vowel and consonant; at first, one may even add a mute e, ə, to consonant to force vibrations of larynx.

II. TO TRAIN LIPS: 1. $ʒa, ʒo, ʒa, ʒo, ʒa, ʒo$
  2. $a:ʒ, o:ʒ, a:ʒ, o:ʒ, a:ʒ, o:ʒ$

READING LESSON

J'ai, j'eus. J'avais. Joue. Jeanne| joue avec le joujou. Jacques est là-bas. Juge-la. Jouer est bien,| jurer est mal. Dans la loge du général. Le chien a la rage. Sur la plage. Le livre est jaune. Il fait le siège. Il est agile. Sur ses genoux. Elle agit bien. Elle s'agite. Elle est majeure. Elle nage. Je ne joue jamais| avec Jeanne. L'agile et joli petit Georges| joue à genoux sur la plage. La loge du concierge| est jolie. Georgette| est jeune et jolie. Dans la neige. En ai-je? Irai-je la voir? A son âge. Elle est Belge. Il a dit un mensonge. Il voit un singe. L'esclavage.

-Eh bien! écoute, Jan, si tu la veux tout de même, nous te la donnerons...Le père, rouge de honte, baissait la tête...Jan fit signe que non et il sortit....A partir de ce jour, il changea sa façon de vivre, affectant d'être toujours gai, pour rassurer ses parents.

(Daudet)

Levez, les gens, la barre en fer,
Ouvrez, les gens, je suis la Neige,
Mon manteau blanc se désagrège
Sur les routes du vieil hiver.

(Verhaeren)

M, m

TONGUE Inactive.

LIPS
- LIPS: slightly pressed against each other just inside visible part.
- CORNERS OF MOUTH: more or less far apart or close together, according to accompanying vowel.
- MUSCLES: not very tense.

MECHANISM
M is a gentle consonant.
As larynx is caused to vibrate, lips are slightly pressed against each other just inside visible part; at same time, soft palate is lowered so that part of air passes out through nose. Volume of air very small. Muscles not very tense.

AVOID
1. Pressing lips together too firmly or too weakly.
2. Bringing external part of lips together.
3. Making m insufficiently audible at end of word.
4. Confusing m, mark of nasalization of a vowel, with m, consonant.

N, n

TONGUE
- TIP: against upper incisors.
- SIDE-EDGES: touching pre-molars and molars and their ridge.
- MUSCLES: fairly tense.

LIPS Inactive for n, itself, but in position of accompanying vowel.

MECHANISM
N is a gentle consonant.
As larynx is caused to vibrate, tip of tongue is placed behind and against upper incisors, and side-edges of tongue come in contact with upper pre-molars, molars and their ridge, while soft palate is lowered, so that part of air passes out through nose. Volume of air, very small. Muscles not very tense.

AVOID
1. Pressing tip of tongue against upper incisors too firmly or too weakly.
2. Bringing tongue insufficiently forward.
3. Relaxing muscles.
4. Making n insufficiently audible at end of word.
5. Confusing n, mark of nasalization of a vowel, with n, consonant.

FOR PRACTICE. Before mirror.
Do not pronounce while moving tongue, lips, or jaw. Pronounce only when in position.
I. TO TRAIN LIPS AND TO FORCE VIBRATIONS OF LARYNX:
1. ma, me, mi, mo, mu
Cause larynx to vibrate as soon as lips are closed.
2. am, εm, im, om, um
Do not stop vibrations between vowel and consonant.
II. TO TRAIN BACK OF TONGUE TO REMAIN MOTIONLESS:
a::m, a::m, a::m
Make a decided effort to refrain from raising back of tongue during whole vowel and consonant.
III. TO TRAIN LIPS: 1. ma, mo, ma, mo, ma, mo
2. am, om, am, om, am, om

READING LESSON

Ma robe. Mes enfants. Mot à mot. Maman. Moi, je viens. Mon enfant. Mari et femme. Mourir sans souffrir. Son âme. Il aime Marie. La grosse pomme. La jeune femme. C'est tout comme. Il s'amuse. Un mammifère. La minute. Enorme, immobile, assis sur son train de derrière, il était là regardant la petite chèvre blanche et la dégustant par avance. Comme il savait bien qu'il la mangerait, le loup ne se pressait pas...(Daudet)

FOR PRACTICE. Before mirror.
Do not pronounce while moving tongue, lips, or jaw. Pronounce only when in position.
I. TO TRAIN TIP OF TONGUE AND TO FORCE VIBRATIONS OF LARYNX:
na, na, na
Cause larynx to vibrate at very beginning of consonant.
II. TO TRAIN BACK OF TONGUE TO REMAIN MOTIONLESS:
a::n, a::n, a::n
Make a decided effort to refrain from raising back of tongue at any time during emission of vowel and consonant.
III. TO TRAIN LIPS: 1. na, no, na, no, na, no
2. an, on, an, on, an, on

READING LESSON

Non, non. Ni moi ni toi. Notre livre. Naître et mourir. Nier la vérité. J'ai un âne. La haine. La pleine lune. La jeune personne est bonne. Elle a bonne mine. Il ne s'ennuie pas. La nuit noire. Le nouveau venu n'est pas né en novembre. Quelle influence, l'ennui, chez nous? Mais énorme!... mais considérable! Le Français, vois-tu, a pour l'ennui une horreur poussée jusqu'à la vénération. Pour lui, l'ennui est un dieu terrible qui a pour culte la tenue.

(Pailleron)

GN, ɲ

TONGUE { TIP: behind and against lower incisors.
TOP SURFACE: almost completely raised against hard palate.
MUSCLES: fairly tense.

LIPS { Inactive for gn, ɲ, itself, but in position of accompanying vowel.

MECHANISM

Gn, ɲ, is a gentle consonant.
As larynx is caused to vibrate, tip of tongue is placed behind and against lower incisors, and top surface of tongue is raised in a single movement against hard palate, while soft palate is lowered so that part of air passes out through nose. The different parts of this composite position must be taken simultaneously; otherwise consonant is decomposed and loses its essential characteristic of being a simple consonant. Volume of air, small. Muscles, fairly tense.

AVOID

1. Raising tip of tongue toward hard palate.
2. Making too lax contact between top surface of tongue and hard palate and doing it too slowly.
3. Establishing contact at two different times or at two different places.
4. Causing larynx to vibrate too late.
5. Making gn, ɲ, insufficiently audible at end of word.
6. Confusing g+n, gn and gn, ɲ:
    magnifique   *magnifik*   for   *maɲifik*
    signification   *signifikasjɔ̃*   "   *siɲifikasjɔ̃*
    ignorance   *ignorɑ:s*   "   *iɲorɑ:s*

FOR PRACTICE. Before mirror.

Do not pronounce while moving tongue, lips, or jaw. Pronounce only when in position.

I. TO TRAIN TIP AND BACK OF TONGUE AND TO FORCE VIBRATIONS OF LARYNX:

ɲa, ɲa, ɲa

Keep tip of tongue behind lower incisors. Raise remainder of tongue in a single movement against hard palate. Cause larynx to vibrate as soon as tongue and palate are in contact.

II. TO TRAIN BACK OF TONGUE TO REMAIN MOTIONLESS TILL END OF PRECEDING VOWEL:

a::ɲ, a::ɲ, a::ɲ

Make a decided effort to refrain from raising back of tongue before end of vowel. After finishing vowel, and not before, pronounce ɲ. When you have repeated this drill some time, try to pronounce syllable more rapidly. Same with: iɲ and oɲ.

III. TO TRAIN LIPS:
1. ɲa, ɲo, ɲa, ɲo, ɲa, ɲo
2. aɲ, oɲ, aɲ, oɲ, aɲ, oɲ

READING LESSON

Gnangnan. Gnognote. Je vais à la montagne. Tu es à la campagne. J'ai une compagne. Les belles vignes. Le roi règne en Pologne. En Gascogne. Elle ment sans vergogne. Le bon compagnon. Le campagnard. Il est soigné et soigneux. Charlemagne eut un règne magnifique. Les montagnards vivent dans les montagnes et les campagnards à la campagne. Le hargneux compagnon. La signification. Son compagnon va à la campagne. Il va en Allemagne. La Champagne et la Bretagne sont des provinces de France. Une ligne. Un peigne. La vigne. Il signe. Un ivrogne. Le cygne.

Quand la chèvre blanche arriva dans la montagne, ce fut un ravissement général...Les châtaigniers se baissaient jusqu'à terre, pour la caresser du bout de leurs branches...Toute la montagne lui fit fête...
...Jan couchait avec Cadet, tout près de la Magnanerie; la pauvre vieille se fit dresser un lit à côté de leur chambre...Les magnans pouvaient avoir besoin d'elle, dans la nuit.

(Daudet)

L, l

TONGUE
- TIP: wide, forming wall, behind and against upper incisors.
- FRONT: lower than tip, not touching hard palate.
- SIDE-EDGES: touching last molars and their ridge.
- MUSCLES: tense.

LIPS
- Inactive for l itself, but in position of accompanying vowel.

MECHANISM

L is a gentle consonant.

As larynx is caused to vibrate, tip of tongue, widened, and forming a wall, presses behind and against four upper incisors, contact being established more firmly between tongue and two outer incisors. At same time, front part of tongue rises, but remains lower than tip and thus does not touch hard palate; front part of tongue seems to throw tip of tongue to a level higher than where it lies itself (this position is very important). At same time, too, side-edges are raised and come in contact with molars and their ridge; air passes out on both sides between front part of tongue and canines. All these movements are simul- taneous, and in order to avoid any extra or parasite sound, these positions are taken very rapidly, especially when l is placed after vowel at end of word. Resonance is in most forward part of mouth; l is pronounced on a sharp note.

AVOID

1. Bringing tip of tongue insufficiently forward.
2. Making contact insufficiently firm between tip of tongue and incisors.
3. Making contact of side-edges of tongue and hard palate too extensive.
4. Raising front part of tongue insufficiently.
5. Pronouncing l on too low a note.
6. Lowering larynx.
7. When l is at end of word or placed before another consonant, taking position for l too slowly, thus adding parasite sounds to preceding vowel and making a diphthong.

FOR PRACTICE. Before mirror.

Do not pronounce while moving tongue, lips, or jaw. Pronounce only when in position.

I. TO TRAIN TIP OF TONGUE, AND TO FORCE VIBRATIONS OF LARYNX:

$$la, la, la$$

Bring tip of tongue into contact with upper incisors. Cause larynx to vibrate from very beginning.

II. TO TRAIN TONGUE TO A GREATER SPEED AFTER PRECEDING VOWEL IS PRONOUNCED AND TO FORCE RESONANCE FORWARD:

$$al, \varepsilon l, il, ol, ul$$

1. Pronounce vowel very clearly, then throw tip of tongue rapidly against upper incisors, thus avoiding any extra or parasite sound.
2. Do not lower larynx or base of tongue so as to prevent a resonance in throat or in back of mouth. Pronounce l on a sharp note, bring resonance as far forward as possible.

III. TO TRAIN LIPS:
1. la, lo, la, lo, la, lo
2. $al, \varepsilon l, al, \varepsilon l, al, \varepsilon l$

READING LESSON

Les enfants. Là, sur la chaise. L'eau est froide. L'un et l'autre. L'an prochain. L'année commence. J'ai un animal. Je joue à la balle. A la ville. J'ai du fil. La foule. Elle est folle. La Ligue des Nations. Elle a lu deux lignes| dans le journal. Le long conciliabule| de Lili et de Léon. La belle Isabelle| a lu le journal. Elle a lutté loyalement. Il mêle l'utile| à l'agréable. Je vais au bal. A Noël. Un cil. Il en a mille. Guillaume Tell. Dans un bol. Le calcul. C'est nul. Elle est pâle. Une balle. Tu appelles Estelle. Il est tranquille.

Puis e_lle _lui par_la tout bas, en montrant _le ma_lade. _L'homme s'inc_lina sans répondre, sortit, siff_la son chien et _le voilà parti, _le fusil sur _l'épau_le, sautant de roche en roche avec ses _longues jambes. (Daudet)
I_l _les raille, i_l _les hait, i_l _les fuit comme peste, mais i_ls ont seu_ls son admiration secrète et sa confiance abso_lue.

Fort	E_lle	Sort	Que_lle
Be_lle,	Dort.	Frê_le!	Mort!

(de Rességuier)

FRONT LINGUAL ROLLED R, r
(French: R ROULÉ).

LOWER JAW AND LIPS: Completely motionless; in position of accompanying vowel.

TONGUE:
- BACK: flat.
- TIP: raised toward front part of hard palate; must be very free and should not touch teeth or ridge.

MECHANISM

R is a gentle consonant.

As larynx begins to vibrate, tip of tongue rises toward front part of hard palate, and as vibrating air is released through mouth, tip of tongue gives rapid succession of taps, usually not more than three. During r plus whole accompanying vowel, lower jaw and lips remain absolutely motionless.

AVOID

1. Moving lower jaw or lips.
2. Making r partly or completely voiceless, that is to say, without vibrations of larynx.
3. Bringing tip of tongue insufficiently forward.
4. Exaggerating taps in number or in intensity.
5. Making r insufficiently audible at end of word.

UVULAR R, r
(French: R UVULAIRE).

LOWER JAW AND LIPS: Completely motionless; in position of accompanying vowel.

TONGUE:
- TIP: behind lower incisors, completely motionless.
- BACK: slightly raised toward hard palate.

SOFT PALATE: Lowered; uvula vibrates or rather gives several taps in succession.

MECHANISM

R is a gentle consonant.

As larynx begins to vibrate, back of tongue rises slightly, soft palate is lowered, and as vibrating air is released through mouth, uvula gives a rapid succession of taps. During emission of r and whole accompanying vowel, lower jaw, lips, and tip of tongue remain absolutely motionless.

AVOID

1. Moving lower jaw, lips, or tip of tongue.
2. Raising tip of tongue toward hard palate.
3. Making r partly or completely voiceless (thus resembling German ch).
4. Exaggerating taps.
5. Making r insufficiently audible or even silent at end of word.

FOR PRACTICE. Before mirror.
Do not pronounce while moving lips or jaw. Pronounce only when in position.

I. TO TRAIN BACK OF TONGUE, LIPS, AND JAW TO REMAIN MOTIONLESS WHILE TIP OF TONGUE IS RAISED BEHIND UPPER INCISORS AND VIBRATES: ra, ra, ra
Have mouth open. Keep lower jaw motionless. Keep lips motionless. Keep back of tongue motionless. Then cause larynx to vibrate, and at same time raise tip of tongue behind upper incisors and cause it also to vibrate--but very gently and only once or twice.

II. TO TRAIN LARYNX TO VIBRATE: aːr, ɛːr, iːr, oːr, uːr
Do not stop vibrations between vowel and r.

III. TO TRAIN LIPS: 1. ra, ro, ra, ro, ra, ro
                      2. aːr, ɛːr, iːr, oːr, uːr

READING LESSON

Rire et pleurer. Rarement. Répéter sa leçon. Retourner à sa place. Rapide comme l'oiseau. Retirer sa plainte. Rayons X. Redire la poésie. Etre à l'heure. J'ai peur. Son père. Ma mère prend du beurre. Il est tard. Il est mort. L'erreur. Ils font une ronde. Le ronron du chat. Elle porte la lettre. Deux artistes. Il est paternel. Il travaille. C'est drôle. Le sourire aux lèvres, Bernard réapparaît. La robe de brocart|de Renée.

(The student will find on p. 81 selections for reading from Daudet and Victor-Hugo).

FOR PRACTICE. Before mirror.
Do not pronounce while moving tongue, lips, or jaw. Pronounce only when in position.

I. TO TRAIN TONGUE, LIPS, AND JAW TO REMAIN MOTIONLESS WHILE UVULA VIBRATES, AND TO FORCE VIBRATIONS OF LARYNX:
   1. ra, ra, ra
Have mouth wide open. Keep lower jaw motionless. Keep lips motionless. Keep tip of tongue behind lower incisors. Then cause larynx to vibrate just before uvula begins to vibrate; release of this vibrating air causes uvula to vibrate and produces uvular r.
   2. aːr, ɛːr, iːr, oːr, uːr
Do not stop vibrations between vowel and r.

II. TO TRAIN LIPS: 1. ra, re, ri, ro, ru
                     2. aːr, ɛːr, iːr, oːr, uːr

PARISIAN R r
(French: R PARISIEN or GRASSEYÉ).

LOWER JAW AND LIPS {Completely motionless. In position of accompanying vowel.

TONGUE {TIP: behind lower incisors and remaining completely motionless.

MECHANISM

R is a gentle consonant.

As larynx is caused to vibrate, back of tongue rises toward back of soft palate without touching it; the release of vibrating air through narrow passage formed by back of tongue and soft palate, produces the gentle Parisian r. During emission of r and accompanying vowel, lower jaw, lips, and tip of tongue remain absolutely motionless. A person may at one and the same time pronounce both Parisian and uvular r.

AVOID

1. Moving lower jaw, lips, or tip of tongue.
2. Raising tip of tongue toward hard palate.
3. Making r partly or completely voiceless, that is to say, without vibrations of larynx, especially before consonant and at end of word.
4. Making r insufficiently audible or even silent at end of word.

SUPPLEMENTARY READING

Déjà s'éteint ma lam_pe_,
Et l'ombre de la ram_pe_,
Qui le long du mur ram_pe_
Monte jusqu'au pla_fond_.

D'étranges sylla_bes_
Nous viennent encore;
Ainsi des Ara_bes_
Quand sonne le cor,...

C'est la plain_te_
Presque é_teinte_
D'une sain_te_
Pour un mort.

Leur essaim gron_de_
Ainsi, profon_de_,
Murmure une on_de_
Qu'on ne voit pas.
(Victor-Hugo)

Une grenouille vit un boeu_f_
Qui lui sembla de belle taille.
Elle, qui n'était pas grosse en tout comme un oeu_f_,
Envieuse, s'étend, et s'enf_le_, et se travaille
Pour égaler l'animal en grosseur...
(La _F_ontaine)

FOR PRACTICE. Before mirror.
Do not pronounce while moving lips or jaw. Pronounce only
when in position.
I. TO TRAIN TIP OF TONGUE, JAW, AND LIPS TO REMAIN MOTION-
LESS WHILE BACK OF TONGUE RISES TOWARD HARD PALATE; TO
TRAIN LARYNX TO VIBRATE: *ra, ra, ra*
Have mouth wide open. Keep lower jaw motionless. Keep lips
motionless. Keep tip of tongue behind lower incisors. Then
raise back of tongue toward back part of soft palate with-
out touching it. Then drop tongue for next vowel. The re-
lease of vibrating air through narrowed passage formed be-
tween back of tongue and soft palate produces the gentle
Parisian r.
II. TO TRAIN LIPS: 1. *ra, ro, ra, ro, ra, ro*
                      2. *a:r, o:r, a:r, o:r, a:r, o:r*
READING LESSON
(The student will find a reading lesson for r on p.79).

-Mais, malheureuse tu ne sais pas qu'il
y a le loup dans la montagne...Que fe-   Murs, ville
ras-tu quand il viendra?...   Et port,
-Je lui donnerai des coups de cornes,   Asile
Monsieur Seguin.   De mort
-Le loup se moque bien de tes cornes. Il   Mer grise
m'a mangé des biques autrement encornées   Où brise
que toi... Tu sais bien, la pauvre vieil-   La brise
le Renaude qui était ici l'an dernier?   Tout dort.

SUPPLEMENTARY READING

Un chant sur la grève   Elle brame
Par instants s'élève,   Comme une âme
Et l'enfant qui rêve,   Qu'une flamme
Fait des rêves d'or.   Toujours suit.
    (Victor-Hugo)   (Victor-Hugo)

C'est bien la pire peine
De ne savoir pourquoi
Sans amour et sans haine,
Mon coeur a tant de peine.
        (Verlaine)

Dans le verger et dans la vigne,
Il s'en va, furtif perruquier,
Avec une houppe de cygne.
Poudrer à frimas l'amandier.
            (Gautier)

SUPPLEMENTARY READING EXERCISES

P, p

L'époux. L'apôtre. Il va l'épouser. L'époux|fait du tapage. Papa|part pour Paris. Les petites poupées|de la pauvre petite Paulette|sont perdues. Pensez-vous|qu'il passe par la Pologne? Père,| passe-moi le pain,| je te prie. Il l'attrape. Une guêpe. Elle anticipe. La tulipe. Il fume la pipe. Il allume la lampe. Il va en Europe. Le chien jappe. Il s'en occupe. La soupe. C'est un cap. "Hop!| la voilà partie". Houp! Le pape. Ils attrapent. Il dissipe. Ils campent. Il trompe. Ils les frappent. Elles enveloppent.

B, b

Buvez |le bon vin de la bonbonne. Les beaux bébés blonds| babillent. La bonne| berce les bébés. Le bambin balbutie. L'arabe. L'éphèbe. Le scribe. Il imbibe. Il est ingambe. De belles jambes. Le feu flambe. La colombe. La bombe. Une trombe. La rhubarbe est bonne. Bêtement|est un adverbe. Le beau Danube bleu.

T, t

Il termine le tableau. Quand elle entra. C'est une enfant. Ton thé| t'a-t-il ôté ta toux? L'attentat| a attristé toute la cité. L'entêté| n'entend rien aux statistiques. Tienstoi tranquille. Tout vient à point| à qui sait attendre. Le riz tâté| tenta le rat;| le rat tenté| tâta le riz tentant. Il a hâte. Du tact. C'est direct. Le verdict. C'est net. Ils en ont huit. Une dot. Ils sont sept. Une sonate. Un acte. Ils achètent. Elle est parfaite. La révolte. Un alpiniste. Une patte. Une trompette. La lutte.

D, d

Didon dîna,| dit-on,| du dos d'un dodu Dindon. Daniel | dédaigne la dot d'Adèle. Dora|a dédommagé le descendant du duc. Bagdad. Alfred. Le Cid. David. Au sud. De la marmelade. En Suède. Il est candide. Tu te décides. Une bande. Ils répondent. Une ode. Ils tardent. Elle est lourde. La tarte est chaude.

F, f

Le froufrou| des fanfreluches de Florence. "Un frais parfum| sortait des touffes d'asphodèles". Il fait des fautes. Il a fumé. Les cheveux frisés. En relief. Il est naïf. Commémoratif. C'est positif. Ils sont vifs. Ouf! Une carafe. La girafe. Elle se coiffe. De l'étoffe. Tartufe. Il se chauffe. Tu te chauffes. Ils étouffent. Un golfe. Joseph. Adolphe. Tu triomphes. Une nymphe.

V, v

Servez vivement la verveine. L'avocat| avoue avoir volé. Vivette va venir. Yvonne l'a vue. Avez-vous vu| la vitrine? Elle est vive. Elle est Slave. Il est brave. Je vais à Genève. Elle est naïve. Une initiative. Une valve. Il se conserve. Elle est mauve. Il l'approuve. Eve. Un élève. Geneviève. Il l'énerve. Le fleuve. Il cultive.

M, m

La mémoire. La marine marchande. Menez-moi au monument des morts. "Mais,| me mèneras-tu|au mémorable monument? "Le mur murant Paris." A Amsterdam. Il va à Jerusalem. Un beau géranium. C'est un maximum. Un post-scriptum. De la crème. Ils s'aiment. La victime. Il se calme. Une gamme. Un télégramme. Un dilemme. Il charme. Un psaume.

N, n

N'a-t-elle pas ennuyé| la bonne Nanette? "Non,| il n'est rien|que Nanine n'honore." N'as-tu ni haine|ni envie? Ni Janine ni Jeannette|ne sont venues. Un specimen. Il dit amen. Il joue du Beethoven. Les Djinns. Un âne. La cabane Il imagine. Il ne parle pas à Antoine. Une héroïne. C'est l'automne. La Marne.

(The following passage contains examples of all the consonants).

"C'était un long sentier tout pavé de braise rouge. Je chancelais comme si j'avais bu; à chaque pas je trébuchais; j'étais tout en eau, chaque poil de mon corps avait sa goutte de sueur, et je haletais de soif...Mais, ma foi, grâce aux sandales que le bon saint Pierre m'avait prêtées, je ne me brûlai pas les pieds.
"Quand j'eus fait assez de faux pas clopin-clopant, je vis à ma main gauche une porte...non, un portail, un énorme portail, tout bâillant, comme la porte d'un grand four. Oh! mes enfants, quel spectacle! Là, on ne demande pas mon nom; là, point de registre. Par fournées et à pleine porte, on entre là, mes frères, comme le dimanche vous entrez au cabaret.
"Je suais à grosses gouttes, et pourtant j'étais transi, j'avais le frisson. Mes cheveux se dressaient. Je sentais le brûlé, la chair rôtie, quelque chose comme l'odeur qui se répand dans notre Cucugnan quand Éloy, le maréchal, brûle pour la ferrer la botte d'un vieil âne. Je perdais haleine dans cet air puant et embrasé; j'entendais une clameur horrible, des gémissements, des hurlements et des jurements."

C'est sur ma petite colline verte qu'il est venu rêver aujourd'hui...Il est là, debout contre un pin, son tambour entre ses jambes et s'en donnant à coeur joie...Des vols de perdreaux effarouchés partent à ses pieds sans qu'il s'en aperçoive. La férigoule embaume autour de lui, il ne la sent pas.

Il ne voit pas non plus les fines toiles d'araignées qui tremblent au soleil entre les branches, ni les aiguilles de pin qui sautillent sur son tambour. Tout entier à son rêve et à sa musique, il regarde amoureusement voler ses baguettes et sa grosse face niaise s'épanouit de plaisir à chaque roulement.

(Every consonant with the exception of gn, ɲ is contained in the following poem).

Chanson

On est venu dire
(Mon enfant, j'ai peur)
On est venu dire
Qu'il allait partir...

Ma lampe allumée,
(Mon enfant, j'ai peur)
Ma lampe allumée,
Me suis approchée...

A la première porte
(Mon enfant, j'ai peur)
A la première porte
La flamme a tremblé...

A la seconde porte
(Mon enfant, j'ai peur)
A la seconde porte
La flamme a parlé...

A la troisième porte
(Mon enfant, j'ai peur)
A la troisième porte
La lumière est morte.
   (Maeterlinck)

Chapter IX.
SYLLABIFICATION

A consideration of syllabification is important because on it depends not only the question of the nasal vowel and in part that of the mute e, but also because the <u>clear-cut</u> effect so characteristic of French speech is the result of a system of syllable division differing in many respects from the English.

The phonetic or spoken syllable is the articulation of one or several sounds in a single effort of the voice. Every syllable must contain one and <u>only one</u> vowel sound and may contain one or more consonant sounds.

I. The phonetic syllable begins when possible with a consonant:

        ca-pa-ci-té, dé-li-ca-tesse, etc.
        EXCEPTIONS:
          a. When the word begins with a vowel sound: then the first syllable begins with this vowel:

              en-fant, é-lé-phant, a-do-rer, etc.

          b. When two vowel sounds are not separated by any consonant:

              a-né-an-tir, cru-el, Ca-ïn, fa-ïence, etc.

        NOTE: The e which is inserted after g, before a, o, u, in order to produce a soft sound, does not count:

              nous man-geons, ils ju-geaient, etc.

The above phonetic division corresponds to the written syllable division.

II. In words having a written double consonant, syllables are divided before the double consonant, which in fact is pronounced as only one consonant:

        a-ller, a-nnée, te-rrain, etc.
        NOTE: A written double consonant followed by a mute e is considered as one consonant belonging to the preceding syllable and the mute e is disregarded:

              belle, telle-ment, etc.

The above phonetic division does not correspond to the written division. In the latter, the division occurs between the two letters of the double consonant:

        al-ler, an-née, bel-le,

III. In words having a group of two inseparable consonants, the division comes before the group of consonants.

The groups of inseparable consonants are: b̲l̲, b̲r̲, c̲l̲, c̲r̲, d̲r̲, f̲l̲, f̲r̲, g̲l̲, g̲r̲, p̲l̲, p̲r̲, tr, vr:
        a-gré-men-té, con-flu-ent, etc.

The above phonetic division corresponds to the written division.

  IV. When b̲, c̲, d̲, g̲, k̲, l̲, p̲, r̲, or s̲ precede:
     a. another single consonant except l or r
     b. any two consonants
        they belong to the first syllable, while the following consonant or group of consonants belongs to the second syllable:
            ab-di-quer, Ab-ner, ac-ti-vi-té, ad-mi-rable, cel-tique, mis-tral, per-du, res-plen-dir, somp-tueux, spec-tral, ver-tu, etc.

The above phonetic division corresponds to the written division.

  V. When a word contains a written mute e which disappears in the pronunciation, the consonant that precedes the written mute e belongs to one syllable and the consonant or consonants that follow written mute e, to another syllable:
            env(e)-lo-pper, $\tilde{a}v$-lo-pe ; él(e)-ver, el-ve ; am(e)-ner, am-ne; dév(e)-lopper, dev-$lope$, etc.

The above phonetic division does not correspond to the written division. In the latter, the division may occur before either of these consonants, but the mute e which does not exist in pronunciation must be written with the consonant that precedes it:
            en-ve-lopper, é-le-ver, a-me-ner, dé-ve-lopper, etc.

  VI. When a written x̲ is placed between two vowels, it represents either k̲s̲ or g̲z̲. The first consonant belongs to one syllable and the second consonant to the following:
            examen, εg-za-$m\tilde{\varepsilon}$; paradoxal, pa-ra-dok-sal ; etc.

The above phonetic division does not correspond to the written division. In the latter, the division occurs before x:
            e-xa-men, pa-ra-do-xal, etc.

  VII. When x̲ precedes one or more consonants, it represents the two sounds k̲s̲. In that case, the consonants represented by x belong to the first syllable and the consonant or consonants which follow to the second syllable:
            ex-tra-or-di-naire, ex-plo-rer, etc.

The above phonetic division corresponds to the written division.

  VIII. When the group b̲s̲ precedes a group of two inseparable consonants, it belongs to the first syllable, and the group of inseparable consonants, to the second:

    abs-trac-tion, obs-tacle, etc.

The above phonetic division corresponds to the written division.

 IX. All the consonants which follow the stressed vowel belong to the stressed syllable:

    bel, arbre, I-sa-belle, pé-destre, terre, monstre, dé-montre, etc.

    NOTE: Of course all the principles which I have described above apply not only to the grammatical but also to the phonetic word:

Tu ne-sais-pas.	tyn-se-pɑ
Job-a-sou-ffert.	ʒo-ba-su-fɛːr
La-gro-sse en-fant.	la-gro-sɑ̃-fɑ̃
Tu-vois le-ta-bleau.	ty-vwal-ta-blo
Un-mons-tre a-ffreux.	œ̃-mɔ̃s-tra-frø
Elle-sy-son-ta-llées.	ɛl-zi-sɔ̃-ta-le
Ma-me-illeu-re a-mie.	ma-mɛ-jœ-ra-mi
La-vi-lle é-ter-nelle.	la-vi-le-tɛr-nɛl
L'en-fant-a-é-té-ma-lade.	lɑ̃-fɑ̃-a-e-te-ma-lad
L'ad-mi-ra-ble (h) é-ro-ïne.	lad-mi-ra-ble-ro-in
La-f(e)-nê-tre es-tou-ver-te.	laf-nɛ-tre-tu-vɛrt
De-sa-mis mon-ta-por-té-de-grande-si-mages.	de-za-mi-mɔ̃-ta-por-ted-grɑ̃d-zi-maːʒ

Chapter X.
INTONATION

 For a correct French intonation one must group those units which are known grammatically as words but which are closely related in idea, and treat them phonetically as only one word (Fr. mot phonétique). These phonetic words are of two kinds:

  1. Stress-group
  2. Breath-group

 1. STRESS-GROUP. In this case, since the individual words lose their independence, the last syllable, not of the grammatical word but of the <u>phonetic</u> word is stressed, and for this reason such a group is called a stress-group, (groupe rythmique). These stress-groups may consist of many words, of few words, or even of only one word:

    'Viens.
    Regarde 'bien.
    C'est très impor'tant
    Elle est devant les en'fants.

The first thing for a student to do is to determine the different stress-groups of a sentence. This is not difficult, as the student has already discovered from Chapter IV, and the subsequent reading lessons.

2. BREATH-GROUP. A breath-group is a group that may be pronounced in only one breath. There is always a noticeable pause between such groups; this pause may be long or short according to the more or less close relation existing between breath-groups. Although usually consisting of several stress-groups, a breath-group may contain only one. A single upright line, |, is used in this book to separate stress-groups; double upright lines, ‖, to separate breath-groups.

The majority of sentences may be treated in more than one way:

I.
   a. Mon 'père‖qui est géné'ral‖a passé la re'vue‖'hier.‖

First breath-group, one idea:	Mon 'père
Second breath-group, one idea:	qui est géné'ral
Third breath-group, one idea:	a passé la re'vue
Fourth breath-group, one idea:	'hier.

   b. Mon père|qui est général‖a passé la revue|hier.‖

First breath-group, two ideas:	Mon 'père qui est géné'ral
Second breath-group, two ideas:	a passé la re'vue 'hier.

In a., the speaker, being particularly desirous of bringing out every idea of his sentence, makes each stress-group correspond to a breath group.

In b., the more natural and normal division, there are only two breath-groups for four stress-groups.

II.
   a. A l'âge de vingt-deux, 'ans|en allant de Nevers à Mou'lins,‖il avait eu le bonheur de sau'ver|au péril de sa 'vie,‖un homme et un cheval|qui se noyaient|dans la 'Loire.‖

First breath-group, two ideas, age of the subject and location of the action:	à l'âge de vingt-deux 'ans, en allant de Nevers à Mou'lins,
Second breath-group, two ideas, the action and the circumstances under which the subject accomplishes the action:	il avait eu le bonheur de sau'ver, au péril de sa 'vie,
Third breath-group, three ideas, the person and the animal for which the subject accomplishes his action, the state in which they were, the place where the accident occurred:	un homme et un che'val qui se no'yaient dans la 'Loire.

b. If the speaker wishes to give, however, still more emphasis to the circumstances under which the subject accomplishes the action, he may arrange his groups as follows:
A l'âge de vingt-deux 'ans,‖ en allant de Nevers à Mou'lins,‖ il avait eu le bonheur de sau'ver‖au péril de sa 'vie,‖un homme et un che'val|qui se noyaient|dans la 'Loire.‖

Third breath-group, one idea:	il avait eu le bonheur de sau'ver
Fourth breath-group, one idea:	au péril de sa 'vie,

c. And if the speaker wishes to give more emphasis to the idea of the accident, he may group his words differently, make each group shorter, as follows:
A l'âge de vingt-deux 'ans,‖ en allant de Nevers à Mou'lins,‖il avait eu le bonheur de sau'ver‖au péril de sa 'vie,‖un homme et un che'val‖qui se noyaient‖dans la 'Loire.‖

Fifth breath-group, one idea:	un homme et un che'val

Sixth breath-
group, one idea: { qui se no'yaient

Seventh breath-
group, one idea: { dans la 'Loire

The division as given in a., would be the normal one.
It is evident from the above examples that, in French as in English, the same sentence may be read or spoken differently according to the ideas which seem, at the moment, important to the reader or speaker. One may read or speak a sentence a first time, giving more importance to certain facts; the next time he may be more impressed by other facts and bring them out more conspicuously.

In order to give a stress-group or a breath-group its full value, the two following points must be taken into consideration:
  a. The normal stress
  b. The stress for emphasis

a. NORMAL STRESS. (Fr. accent tonique). The normal French stress is marked by:
    1. Intensity (force) and duration
    2. Musical pitch

1. INTENSITY. The intensity of a sound varies with the degree of force with which it is produced. For example, if one plays on the piano a given note, he may play it gently by touching the key lightly; or, on the contrary, he may play it heavily by touching the same key with force. The sound is the same in both cases; it is neither higher nor lower, but in the second case it is stronger...bigger, so to speak. Its intensity is greater.

2. MUSICAL PITCH. The musical pitch of the voice varies with the number of vibrations of the vocal chords in a given time. The greater the number of vibrations, the higher the pitch; the smaller the number of vibrations, the lower the pitch.

In English, nearly every word in a group receives a stress on one of its syllables, and many words receive two. The syllable on which the stress falls is invariable--the word is stressed in the same way under whatever circumstances it occurs.

In French, however, only the last syllable of the stress-group receives the stress; usually all the other syllables, although clearly pronounced, are unstressed. So it is that the same grammatical word, used in two different stress-groups, may be stressed in one instance and not in

the other, according to the place it occupies:
>Ta soeur est pe'tite.
>Ta petite 'soeur.
>J'ai une 'robe
>J'ai une robe 'rouge.
>J'ai une robe rouge et 'blanche.

When the stressed syllable is not the last of the sentence, a rise in the pitch of the voice is combined with the special intensity. At the end of the last stress-group of the sentence, a lowering of the pitch of the voice is usually combined with the special intensity given the syllable.

>b. STRESS FOR EMPHASIS. In any stress-group, to the normal stress, characterized by greater intensity and change in musical pitch, may be added another, the stress for emphasis, so called because it marks a word the speaker wishes to emphasize. We have seen that the normal stress falls on the last syllable (especially on the vowel of the last syllable) of the word. The stress for emphasis usually falls on the <u>first consonant</u> of the word to be emphasized, lengthening it, and at the same time, often raising it to a higher pitch. In this case, it is called a consonant stress.
>>Imbécile.
>>La*jolie robe.
>>*Quelle surprise!
>>La*douceur de vivre.

However, when the emphasized word begins with a vowel and more generally when it stands alone, the stress for emphasis may fall on the first vowel of the word. In this case, the stress is marked by a rise in pitch of the voice, a greater intensity, and also by a lengthening of the vowel.
>*E:pouvantable!
>*A:troce!
>*I:nique!

NOTE: It must be added that in French there are fewer accents for emphasis than in English. Whereas the latter may, without changing the construction of a sentence, emphasize the importance of almost any word by special stress, the former frequently prefers to produce the same effect, not so often by special stress as by constructing the sentence in such a way as to bring the word under consideration into a place where, by coinciding with the last syllable of a stress-group, it receives the normal stress.

>For instance, in the sentence, "I want to-speak to you", in English any one of five of the six

words may be emphasized in speaking without changing the written form. The French would vary the construction.

There are three types of sentences:
    1. The declarative
    2. The interrogative
    3. The exclamatory

In the treatment of this subject, I have relied chiefly on the admirable little book of Maurice Grammont, La Prononciation française, Paris, 1926, and on the inspiring teaching of M. Pierre Fouché from which I have greatly benefited this last year in Paris.

DECLARATIVE SENTENCES

A declarative sentence is composed of two parts:
    1. A rising part.
    2. A falling part.

1. THE RISING PART. The rising part, which usually arouses curiosity and makes the mind expectant of something to follow, may consist of one or more stress-groups (groupes rythmiques).

However that may be:
    a. The note at the beginning is in general lower than in English.
    b. The highest note is that on which the speaker pronounces the last syllable of the rising part.
    c. In the interior of a stress-group, the rise of the voice seldom follows a perfectly straight line, but proceeds by means of modulations which may be represented in either one of the following ways:

En allant de Nevers à Moulins
    1.

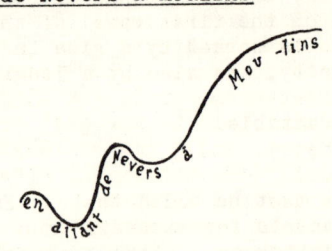

    2.

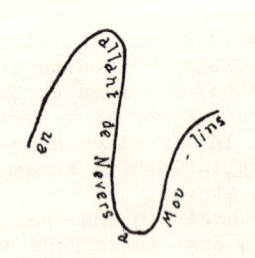

1 is more often heard than 2. The latter is
rather difficult to imitate, but for one who has
thoroughly mastered the former, the study of 2 is
well worth while, since its use enables one to
avoid monotony in reading and speaking. It may be
heard over and over again in phonograph records
made by Madame Bara de Tovar, (Installation, from
Daudet's Lettres de mon moulin, Institut de Phonétique, Paris). For example, in the clause:

<u>La nuit de mon arrivée</u>

the musical pitch of the voice is higher on <u>nuit</u>,
an unstressed syllable, than on -<u>vée</u>, the stressed
syllable, but <u>nuit</u> receives no added intensity or
length, whereas -<u>vée</u> receives intensity. Of the
three elements discussed--change in musical pitch,
increased intensity and length--<u>nuit</u> is marked by
only one:

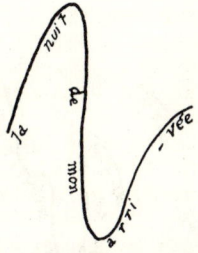

When the rising part is composed of several
stress-groups, the ascent is usually progressive
and regular in the sense that the last syllable of
each successive stress-group is generally spoken
on a note somewhat higher than that of the preceding stress-group until the highest is reached. I
repeat that this is the last syllable of the entire
rising part, and I cannot insist too often that
the modulations within the stress-group are numerous, varied and delicate.

One might represent as follows the rising part
of the sentence already studied:

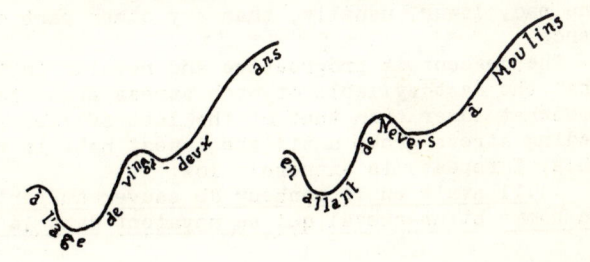

d. The musical note at the beginning of a stress-group is always much lower than that of the stressed syllable which immediately precedes. I can never overemphasize this fact or too often call the student's attention to it. Notice in the following illustration the drop of the voice between -lées and co-, between bleu and et, between -lant and l'une, between l'autre and pour:
Comme le fond des vallées│ commencait à devenir bleu ‖ et que les bêtes se serraient en bêlant│ l'une contre l'autre│ pour rentrer au parc, ‖ j'entendis qu'on m'appelait│ dans la descente ‖

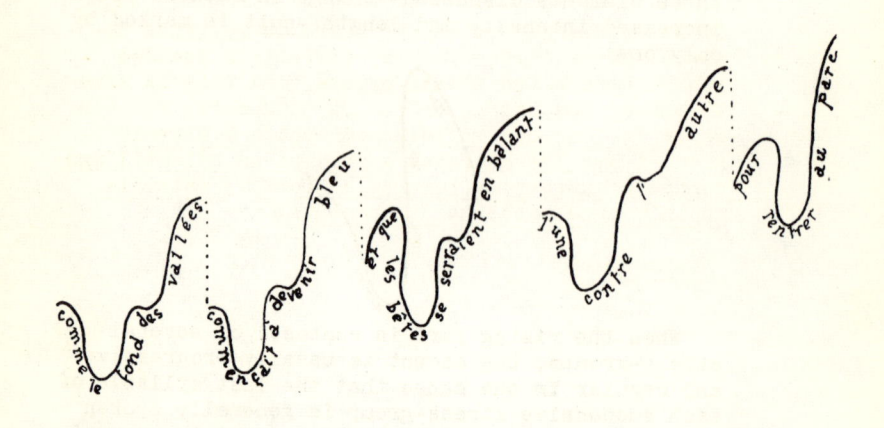

2. THE FALLING PART. The falling part, which corresponds to the satisfaction of curiosity, the knowledge for which the mind was waiting during the rising part of the sentence, follows the general laws for the rising part, as far as the modulation and the drop of the voice between a stressed-syllable and the following syllable are concerned. The last group only of the falling part falls very low at the end, lower, usually, than any other part of the sentence.

The descent is progressive and regular in the sense that the last syllable of each stress-group is on a note somewhat lower than that of the last syllable of the preceding stress-group until the lowest note is reached; and this, I repeat, is extremely low:
...il avait eu le bonheur de sauver│ au péril de sa vie ‖ un homme et un cheval│ qui se noyaient dans la Loire ‖:

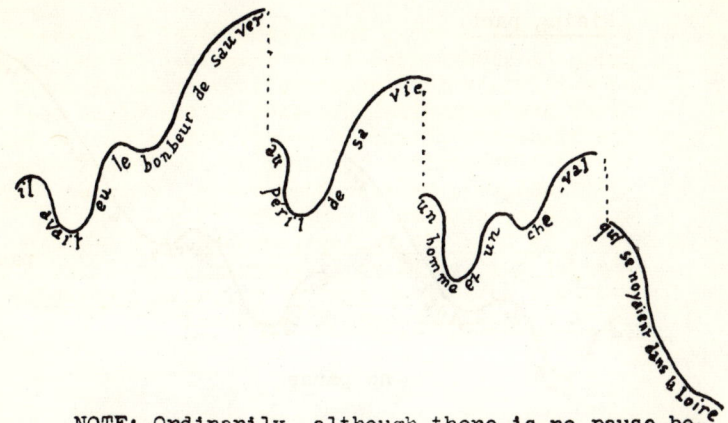

NOTE: Ordinarily, although there is no pause between simple stress-groups, there is a decided pause between two breath-groups, and this is true in either the rising or the falling part.
Comme le fond des vallées|commençait à devenir bleu‖et que les bêtes se serraient en bêlant|l'une contre l'autre|pour rentrer au parc,‖j'entendis qu'on m'appelait|dans la descente.‖

Rising part:

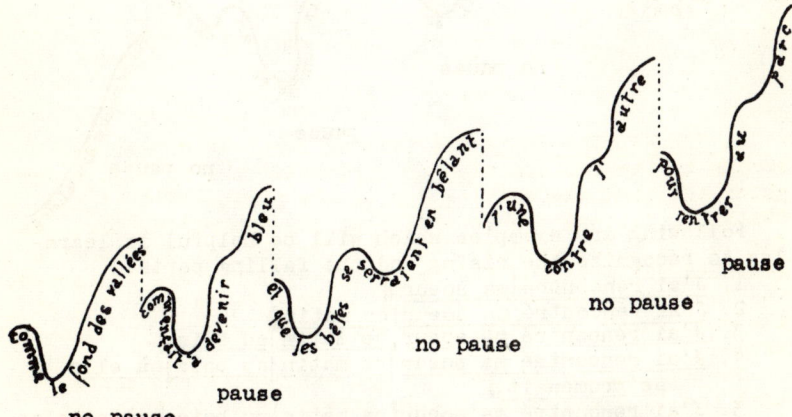

A l'âge de vingt-deux ans,| en allant de Nevers à Moulins,‖il avait eu le bonheur de sauver|au péril de sa vie,‖un homme et un cheval|qui se noyaient dans la Loire.‖

Rising part:

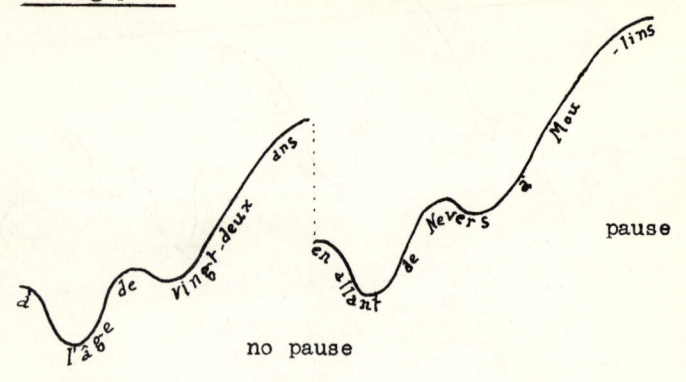

à l'âge de vingt-deux ans (no pause) *en allant de Nevers à Moulins* pause

Falling part:

il avait eu le bonheur de sauver (no pause) *au péril de sa vie* pause *un homme et un cheval* (no pause) *qui se noyaient dans la Loire*

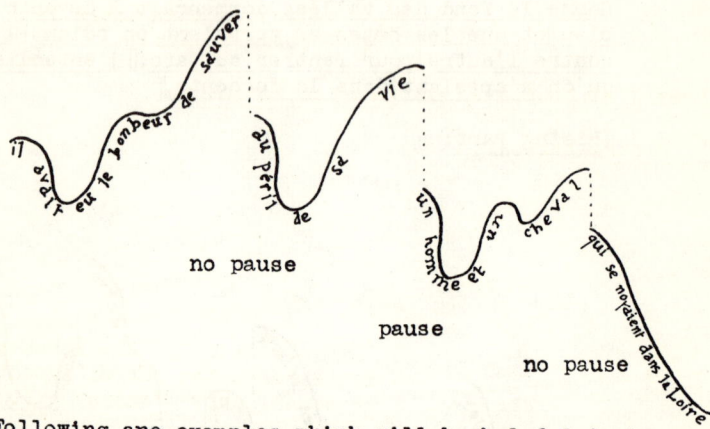

Following are examples which will be helpful in learning to recognize the rising and the falling parts:
1. J'ai rencontré | ma soeur.‖
2. J'ai rencontré ma soeur | ce matin.‖
3. J'ai rencontré ma soeur | ce matin | au bois.‖
4. J'ai rencontré ma soeur | ce matin | au bois ‖ où elle se promenait.‖
5. J'ai rencontré ma soeur | ce matin | au bois, ‖ où elle se promenait | avec ses enfants | et sa jeune bonne.‖
6. J'ai rencontré ma soeur, ‖ celle dont je vous ai parlé ‖ ce matin, au bois, ‖ où elle se promenait | avec ses enfants ‖ (qui entre nous sont adorables) ‖ et sa jeune bonne.‖

1. J'ai rencontré│ma soeur.‖

Rising part:

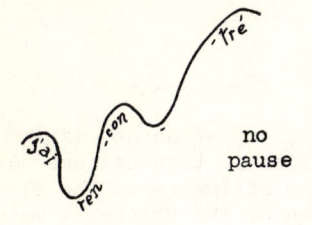

(The elevation of the speaker's voice makes the hearer expect something more, something definite. He asks himself "Who? What?").

no pause

Falling part:

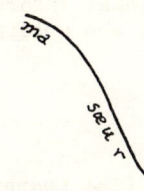

(The dropping of the voice indicates that there is nothing to add).

2. J'ai rencontré ma soeur│ ce matin.‖

Rising part:

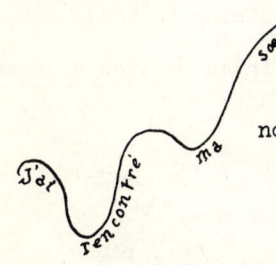

no pause

(The elevation of the speaker's voice makes the hearer expect something more: "Where? etc.).

Falling part:

(Curiosity is satisfied. By the dropping of the voice the speaker has indicated that he has given all his information. This drop shows that there is nothing to add).

3. J'ai rencontré ma soeur│ce matin│au bois.‖

Rising part:

no pause

no pause

(The group of words adding the idea of time belongs now to the rising part. The elevation of the speaker's voice keeps the hearer in suspense and makes him expect additional information in answer to the question: "Where?").

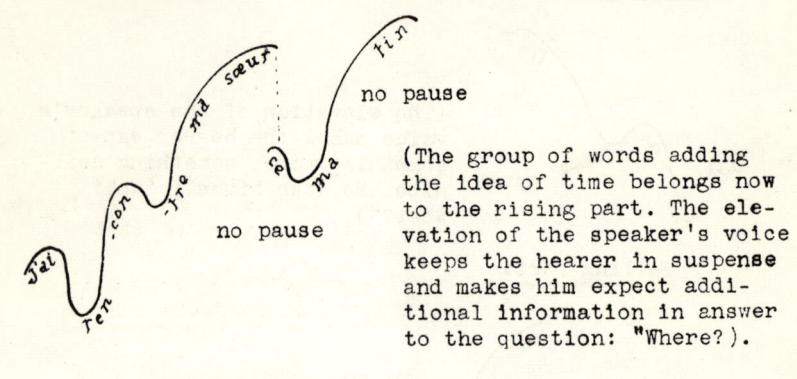

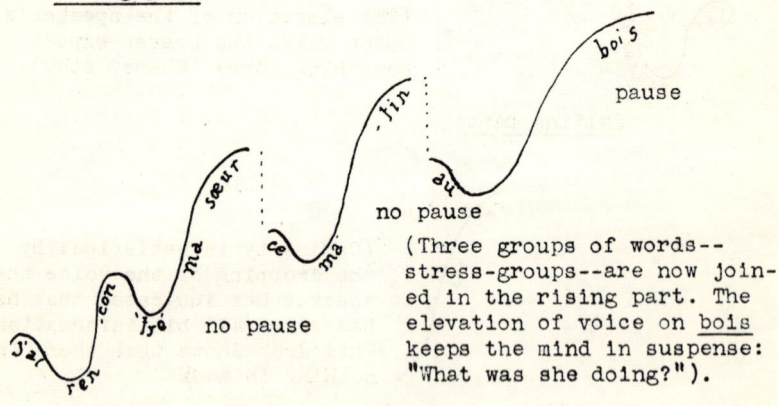

Falling part:

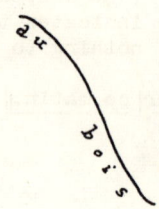

(The hearer is satisfied. He knows now where the meeting took place; and the speaker, by lowering his voice, indicates that he has nothing to add).

4. J'ai rencontré ma soeur│ce matin│au bois‖où elle se promenait.‖

Rising part:

pause

no pause

no pause

(Three groups of words--stress-groups--are now joined in the rising part. The elevation of voice on *bois* keeps the mind in suspense: "What was she doing?").

Falling part:

où elle se promenait

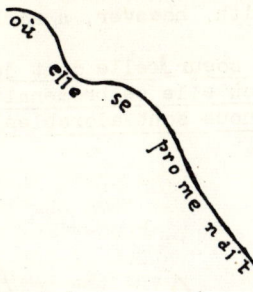

(By dropping his voice, the speaker shows that he has no further information to give).

5. J'ai rencontré ma soeur | ce matin | au bois ‖ où elle se promenait | avec ses enfants | et sa jeune bonne. ‖

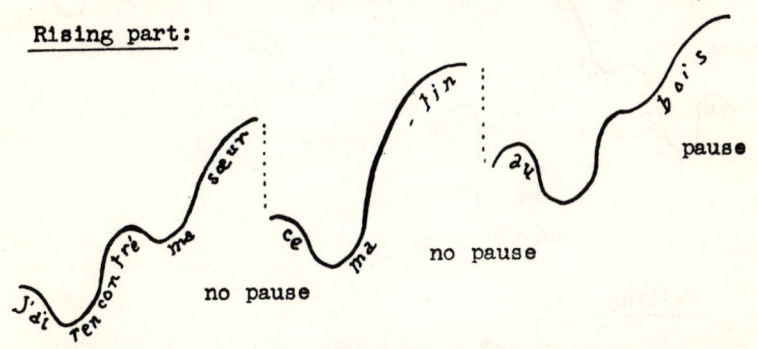

Rising part:

J'ai rencontré ma soeur — no pause — *ce matin* — no pause — *au bois* — pause

Falling part:

où elle se promenait — no pause

(Answers the question: "What was she doing?" But the elevation of the voice keeps the mind in suspense: "With whom?", etc.)

avec ses enfants — no pause

(Answers only part of remaining question since the voice is still raised).

et sa jeune bonne — pause

(The speaker shows that he has replied completely to the last unasked question: "With whom?" by dropping his voice. Curiosity is entirely satisfied).

6. When a sentence contains a parenthetical clause, whether or not enclosed by parentheses, this clause is spoken on a lower note with, however, a marked rising inflection at the end:

J'ai rencontré ma soeur,∥celle dont je vous ai parlé∥ ce matin, au bois,∥ où elle se promenait∣avec ses enfants,∥(qui entre nous sont adorables)∥et sa jeune bonne.∥

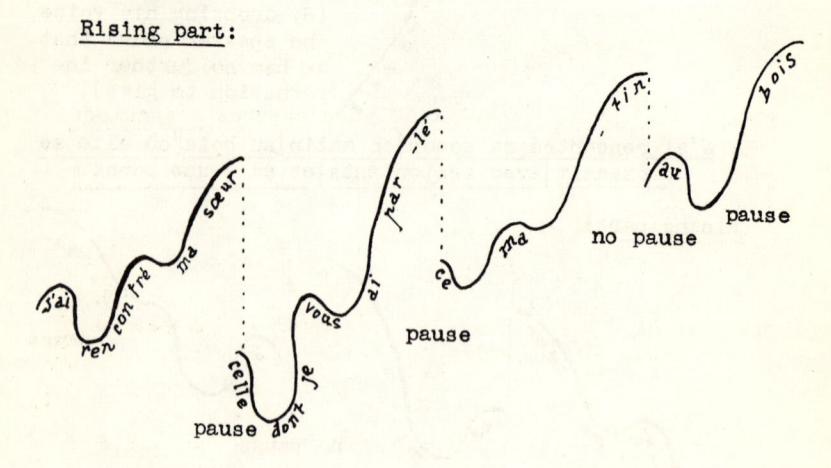

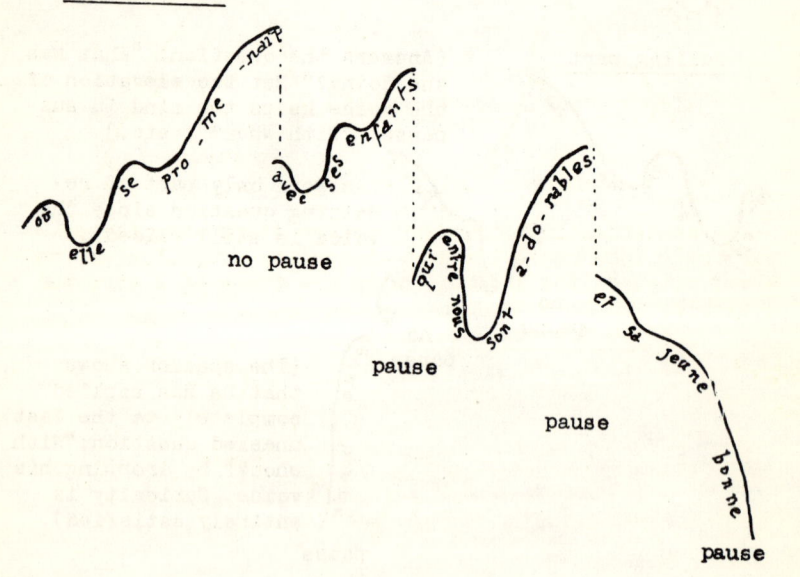

Rising part:

Falling part:

7. A phrase or clause introducing a direct quotation often ends on a very low note, corresponding generally to the end of the falling part.

Elle me dit:‖ "J'ai rencontré ma soeur, ce matin."‖

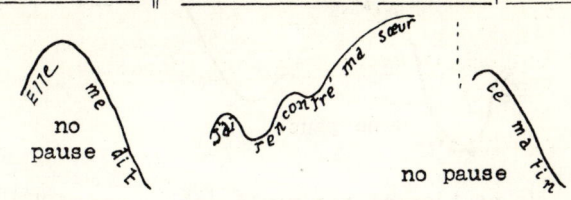

Il disait: ‖"C'est fini.‖ Les chèvres s'ennuient chez moi."

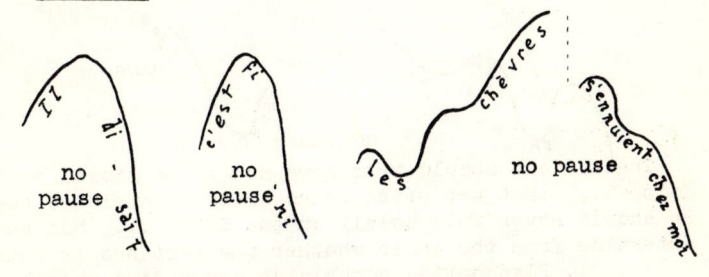

Elle lui dit en riant:‖ "J'ai besoin de toi."

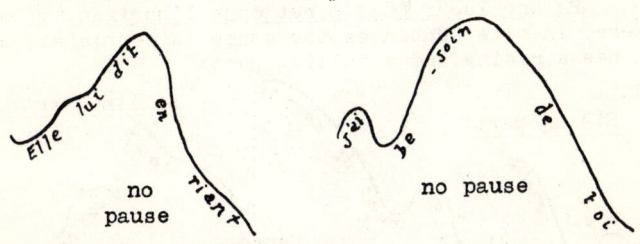

In sentences in which the speaker stops abruptly or purposely interrupts himself--intensity, duration and musical pitch of the last syllable are those of a stressed syllable:

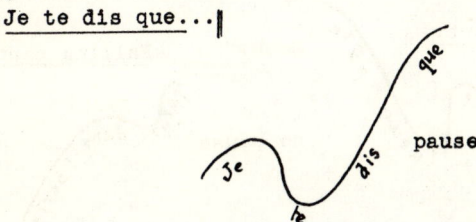

Je te dis que...‖

Tu viendras, | sinon... ‖

[intonation diagram: "tu viendras" rising then "sinon" — no pause / pause]

Je ne t'en ai pas parlé, | parce que... ‖

[intonation diagram: "je ne t'en ai pas parlé" then "parce que" — no pause / pause]

The student should take care not to be misled by the dots, ..., that are often found after a completed sentence. He should never rely solely on the dots, ..., but should determine from the sense whether the sentence is completed:
1. Blanquette | redoubla de coups de cornes, ‖ le loup | de coups de dents... ‖
2. Une lueur pâle | parut dans l'horizon... ‖ (Daudet)

Here, in both sentences the sense is completed, and each has a **rising** and a **falling** part:

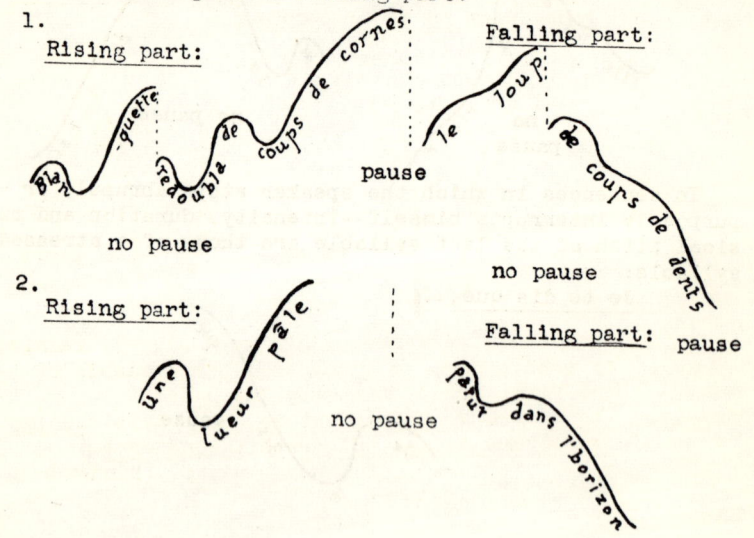

1.
Rising part: *[diagram: Blanquette redoubla de coups de cornes]* — no pause / pause
Falling part: *[diagram: le loup de coups de dents]* — no pause

2.
Rising part: *[diagram: Une lueur pâle]* — no pause
Falling part: *[diagram: parut dans l'horizon]* — pause

IMPORTANT NOTE: For the sake of variation, the
student who has perfected himself in the use of
more usual intonation may follow the model of
other forms sometimes employed by French people.
The ability to do this correctly requires not only
intelligence and taste, but also skill. It should
not be attempted by a beginner.
Some possibilities are:
a. To begin the stress-group on a very high note
   and finish on a very low one:
   Quelquefois l'hiver, ‖ quand les troupeaux ǀ
   étaient descendus dans la plaine ‖ et que je
   rentrais le soir ǀ à la ferme pour souper... ‖
   (Daudet).

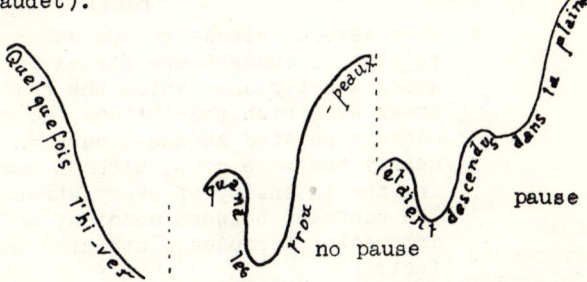

b. Or, having begun on a very high note, to drop
   the voice to a very low one near the middle of
   this stress-group and raise it at the end to a
   note as high as that of the beginning:
   Ni les caresses de leur maître, ‖ ni la peur du
   loup, rien ne les retenait. ‖

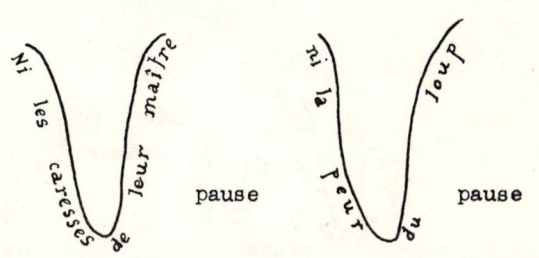

c. When two stress-groups are very closely related
   to each other, to place the last syllable of
   the first group on a very low note:
   Le pauvre M. Seguin ǀ qui ne comprenait rien ǀ au
   caractère de ses bêtes ‖ était consterné. ‖
   (Daudet)

104

[intonation curve: le pauvre monsieur Seguin — no pause — qui ne comprenait rien — no pause — au caractère de ses chèvres — pause]

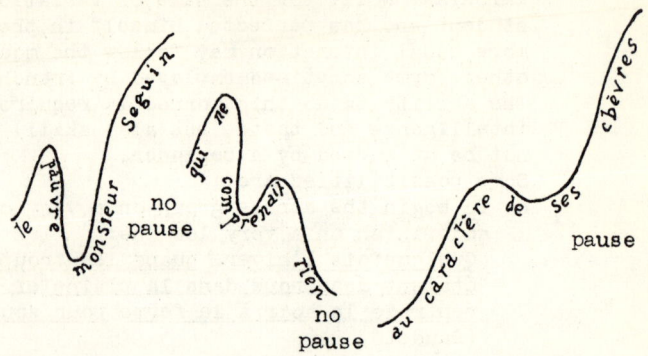

d. When several stress-groups which are <u>closely related</u> in thought are placed in a sentence among shorter ones which the reader intends to speak with rich modulations, to pronounce these closely related stress-groups on the same or nearly the same note, without however diminishing the intensity of every stressed syllable. The contrast between monotony and variety of intonation produces a striking and pleasing effect:

<u>Enfin sur les trois heures,</u> ‖ le ciel étant lavé, la montagne | luisante d'eau et de soleil, ‖ j'entendis | parmi l'égouttement des feuilles | et le débordement | des ruisseaux gonflés, ‖ les sonnailles de la mule, ‖ aussi gaies, ‖ aussi alertes ‖ qu'un grand carillon de cloches | un jour de Pâques. ‖ (Daudet)

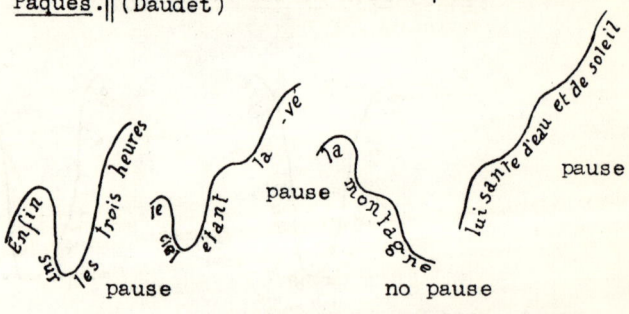

[intonation curve: Enfin sur les trois heures — pause — le ciel étant la-vé — pause — la montagne — no pause — luisante d'eau et de soleil — pause]

[intonation curve: j'entendis parmi l'égouttement des feuilles — no pause — no pause — et le débordement — no pause — des ruisseaux gonflés — pause]

e. When a stress-group, particularly at the beginning of the sentence, really <u>stands out</u> to mark the time or place of the event or scene which follows, to place the last syllable of that group on a higher note than the last syllable of the subsequent groups but rarely higher than, or even as high as, the last syllable of the entire rising part:

<u>Quelquefois l'hiver</u>,‖ quand les <u>troupeaux</u> | étaient descendus dans la <u>plaine</u>‖et que je rentrais le <u>soir</u> | à la ferme pour <u>souper</u>...‖
(Daudet)

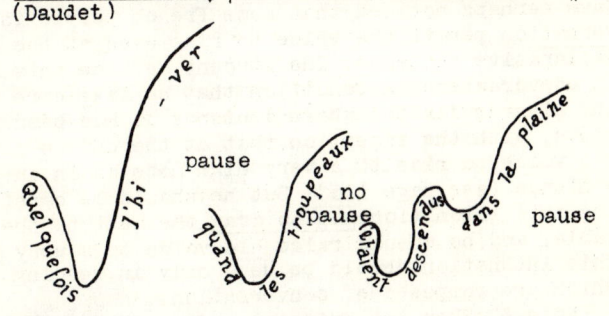

[intonation diagram: Quelquefois l'hiver — pause — quand les troupeaux — no pause — étaient descendus dans la plaine — pause]

(Compare e. with a., p.103).

f. To transfer the high musical pitch, generally associated with the last syllable, to the next-to-the-last, while taking great care that the greater intensity still falls upon the last syllable:

<u>Pas un sac</u>,‖ <u>pas un grain de blé</u>,‖ <u>pas la moindre farine</u>‖

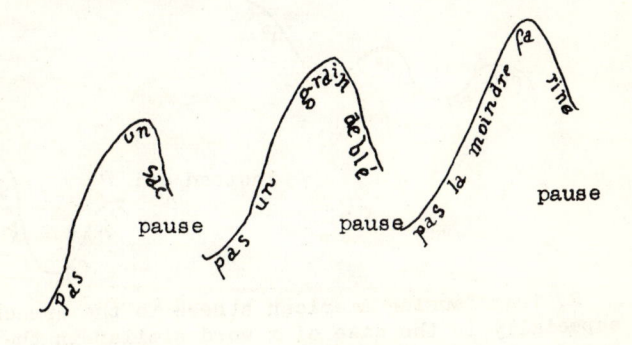

[intonation diagram: Pas un sac — pause — pas un grain de blé — pause — pas la moindre farine — pause]

(To transfer <u>intensity</u> and <u>duration</u> as well as the higher musical pitch from the last to the next-to-the-last syllable is to use an intonation characteristic of the speech of the uneducated Parisian, and constitutes an error against which the foreigner should be constantly on his guard).

Note 1. It is evident that the student should not attempt any one of the six variations of French intonation described above, if he has not already learned to recognize and dissociate the three elements of intonation--intensity, duration, and musical pitch.

Note 2. My readers who have spent some time in France have perhaps noticed that some French people in rapid conversation permit the voice to rise even at the end of a declarative sentence. The student may use this intonation in conversation on condition that he take care to follow the diagram for the whole sentence as has been indicated above, with the exception that at the end he may permit his voice to rise to a very high note as in an exclamatory sentence (see page 116). But he should be careful when using this intonation not to drag the next-to-the-last syllable, and he should raise his voice to a very high note. This intonation should be used only in reading passages which are composed of conversation.

Note 3. When the principles described above have been thoroughly mastered, let the student add, in his reading and speaking, color, life, life, and still more life.

MISTAKES TO AVOID.

Americans should avoid:

1. Beginning the sentence on a note which is insufficiently low:

Elle est venue me voir

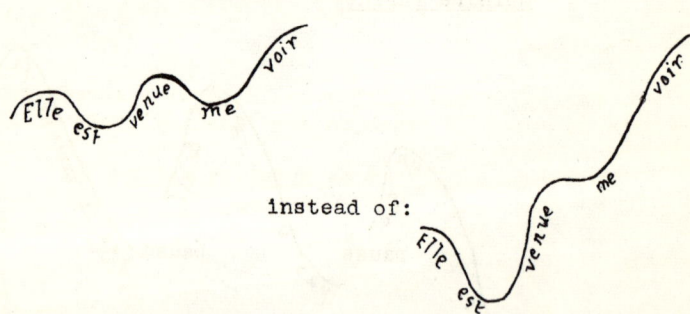

instead of:

2. Transferring American stress to the French sentence, especially in the case of a word similar in the two languages, by giving intensity, length and high pitch to the wrong syllable:

Elle est arrivée

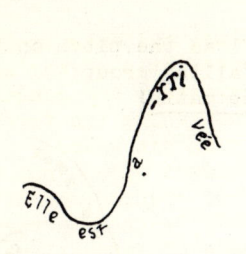

[diagrams: "Elle est a-rri-vée" curves]   instead of: *[diagram: "Elle est arri-vée"]*

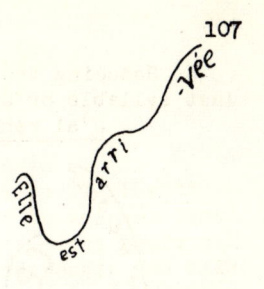

3. "Wavering" in a monotonous manner between two musical notes far less widely separated than in French, and insufficiently marking the modulations:
    <u>J'ai rencontré ma soeur</u>

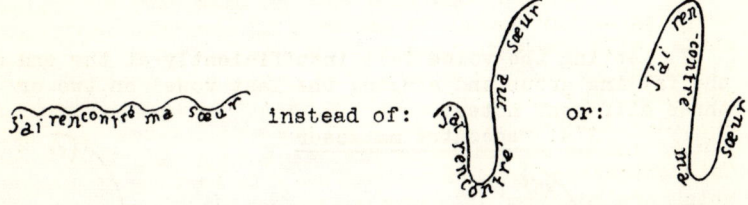

[diagram: flat "J'ai rencontré ma soeur"]   instead of: *[curve diagram]*   or: *[curve diagram]*

4. Raising the voice and at the same time giving intensity to the highest note of the rising group on the next-to-the-last-syllable instead of on the last only:
    <u>J'ai rencontré ma soeur</u>

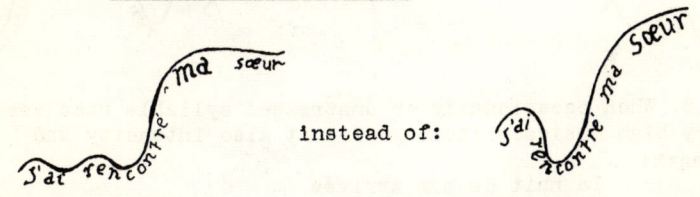

[diagram with peak on "ma"]   instead of: *[diagram with peak on "soeur"]*

5. Beginning the initial syllable of a stress-group on a note too near in pitch to the final syllable of the preceding stress-group:
    <u>J'ai rencontré ma soeur│ce matin ‖</u>

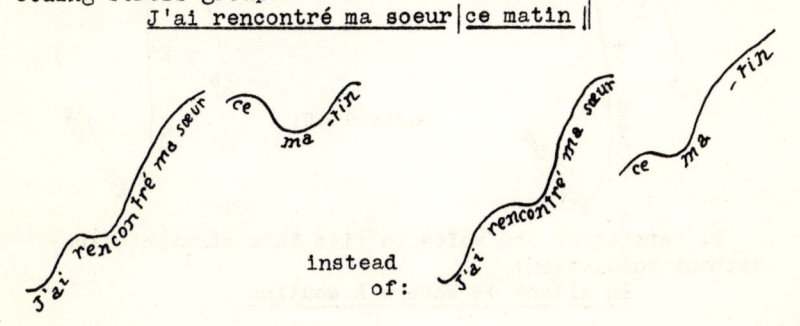

[diagram: "J'ai rencontré ma soeur ce ma-tin" with small dip]   instead of: *[diagram: "J'ai rencontré ma soeur ce ma-tin" with larger drop]*

6. Reducing the intensity as well as the pitch on the last syllable or syllables of the falling group:
J'ai rencontré ma soeur | ce matin

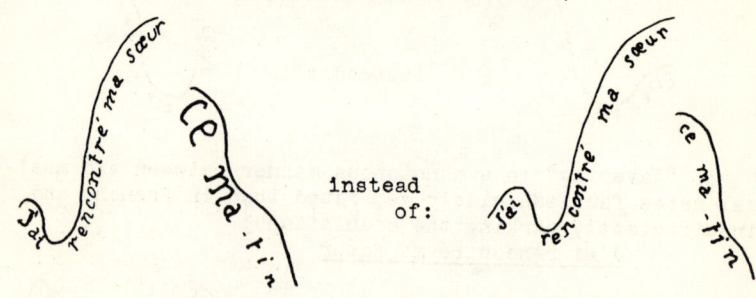

instead of:

7. Letting the voice fall insufficiently at the end of the falling group and singing the last vowel on two or three different notes:
J'ai rencontré ma soeur

instead of:

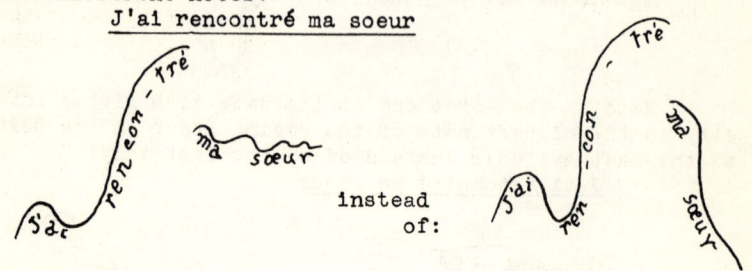

8. When occasionally an unstressed syllable receives very high musical pitch, giving it also intensity and length:
La nuit de mon arrivée

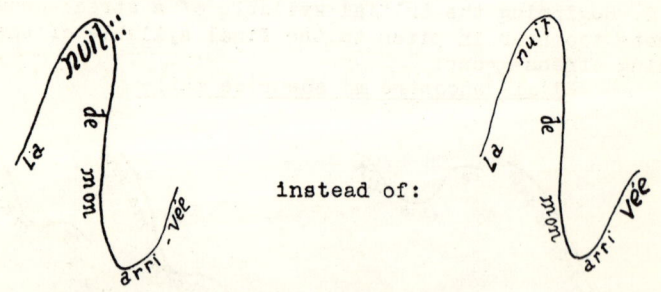

instead of:

9. Permitting the voice to rise in a straight line, without modulation:
En allant de Nevers à Moulins

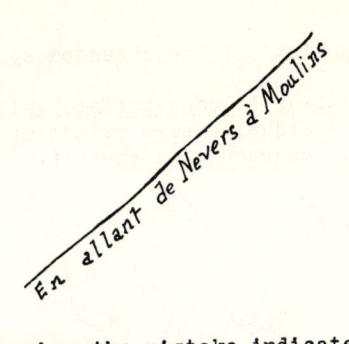

En allant de Nevers à Moulins

NOTE: If one makes the mistake indicated above he obtains a melody--if melody it may be called!--which is opposed to the true music of the French sentence. The diagram above is one artificially created by some teachers of French intonation in order "to simplify" the subject. The result is double--the music of our language is incorrectly represented, and the student acquires, in his so-called French intonation, an unbearably monotonous delivery, of which later he finds it difficult to rid himself.

10. Always pronouncing the unstressed syllables on the same note and raising the voice only on the stressed syllable. Although it is true that some French people employ this intonation under certain circumstances, it is not sufficiently customary to justify its constant use (p.104).

A l'âge de vingt-deux ans, | en allant de Nevers à Moulins ‖

A l'âge de vingt-deux ans   en allant de Nevers à Moulins

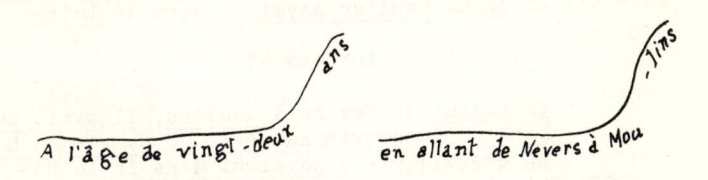

instead of:

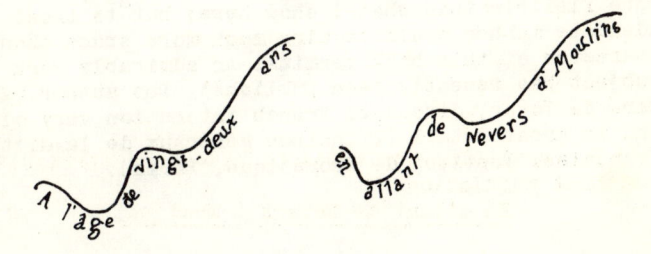

A l'âge de vingt-deux ans   en allant de Nevers à Moulins

11. Pronouncing all the stressed syllables on the same note:

Monsieur le sous-préfet, ‖ grisé de parfums, ‖ ivre de musique, ‖ essaye vainement de résister ‖ au nouveau charme qui l'envahit ‖

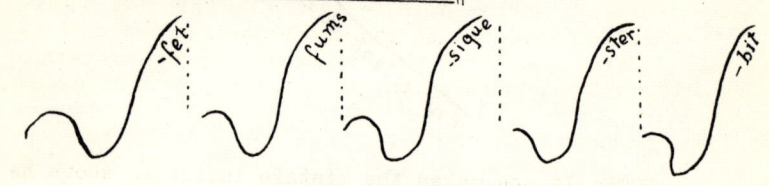

instead of:

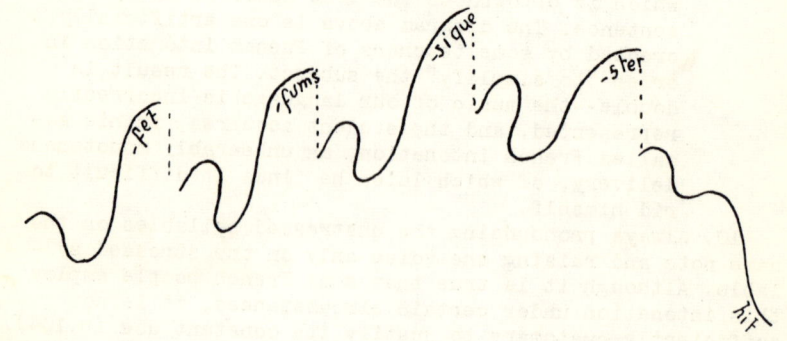

12. Making too many breath-groups, that is to say, too many pauses:

En allant de Nevers à Moulins, ‖ il avait eu le bonheur ‖ de sauver au péril de sa vie ‖ un homme ‖ et un cheval ‖ qui se noyaient ‖ dans la Loire ‖

instead of

En allant de Nevers à Moulins, | il avait eu le bonheur de sauver | au péril de sa vie ‖ un homme et un cheval | qui se noyaient dans la Loire ‖

NOTE: This is a mere sketch of the rhythm of the sentence. French intonation is far more varied, more subtle, more flexible than what I show here; but to treat it in an adequate manner would require much more space than the character of this book permits. An admirable work on this subject has recently been published. The author, Madame Bara de Tovar, discusses French intonation very clearly and in great detail (Principes généraux de la diction française, Institut de Phonétique, Paris).

INTERROGATIVE SENTENCES

The interrogative sentence corresponds, in general, to the rising part of the declarative sentence, for it arouses curiosity; but, although a complete sentence, it does not satisfy it, as is the case in the declarative sentence.

The highest syllable of the interrogative sentence is generally the same as in the corresponding rising part of the declarative sentence, but as a musical note it is much higher.

This highest note may be:
  a. At the end of the question, on the last syllable:
     1. **Est-elle ici?**   2. **Tu iras là-bas?**

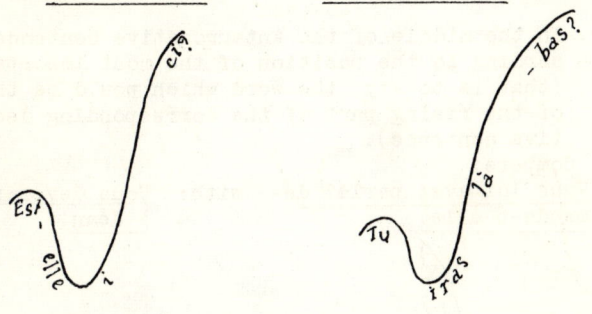

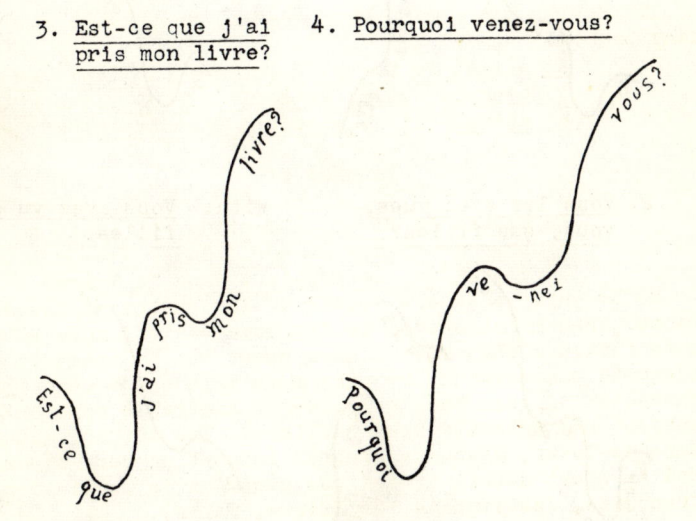

     3. **Est-ce que j'ai pris mon livre?**   4. **Pourquoi venez-vous?**

5. N'est-elle pas venue nous voir? 6. Est-elle partie ce matin?

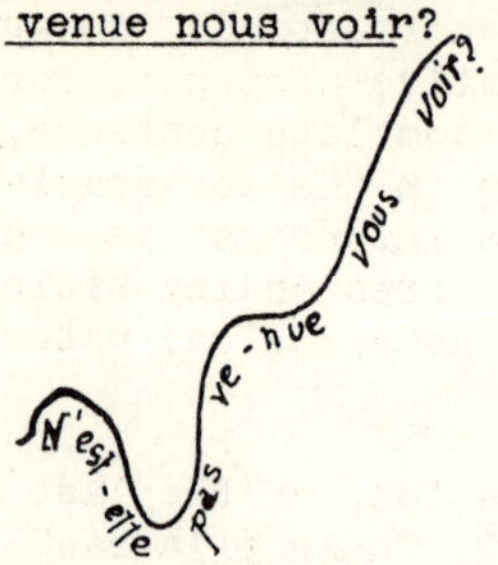

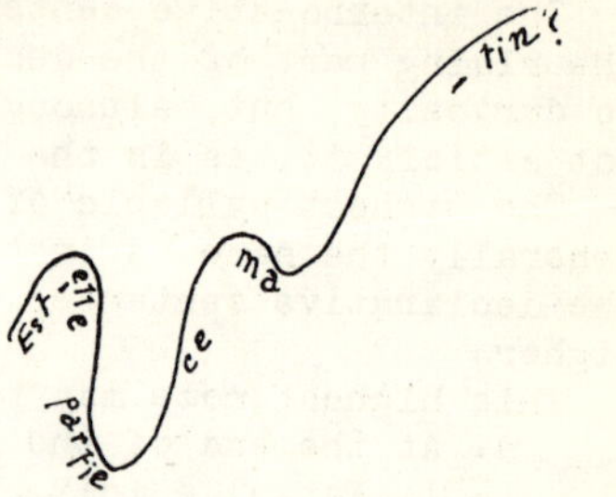

b. In the middle of the interrogative sentence, according to the position of the most important word (that is to say, the word which would be the last of the rising part of the corresponding declarative sentence).
   Compare:
1. Vous lui avez parlé? demanda-t-elle.   with: Vous devez parler à Jean.

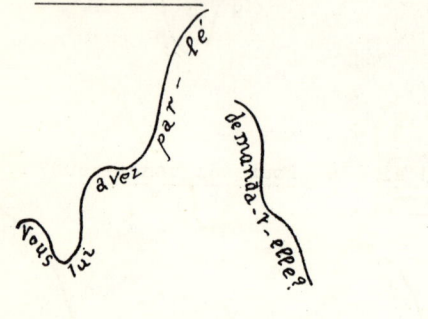

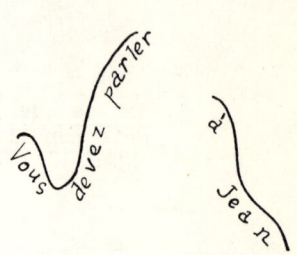

2. Vous les avez vues, vous, ses filles?   with: Vous avez vu ses filles.

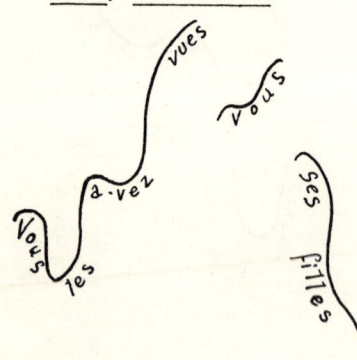

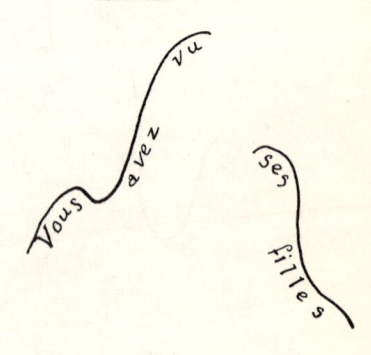

113

3. Que va-t-il faire là bas, cet enfant?   with: Il va là-bas, cet enfant.

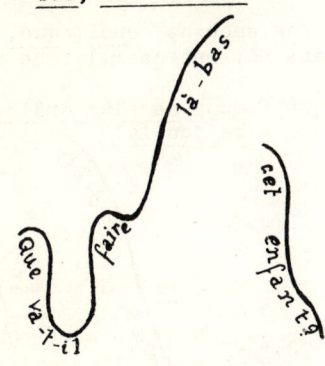

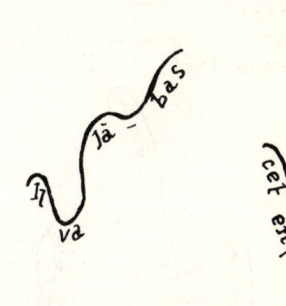

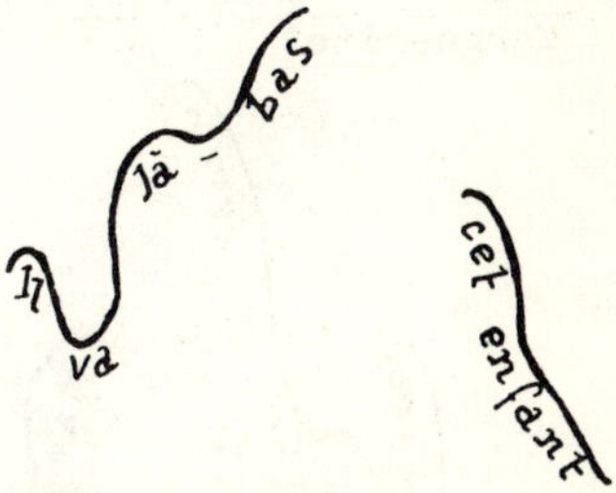

4. Est-ce à lui que tu as parlé?   with: C'est à lui que tu as parlé.

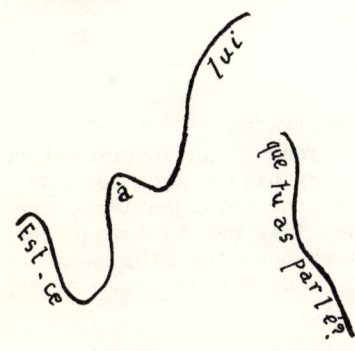

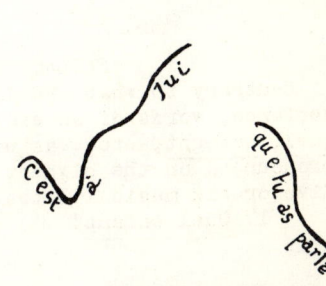

5. A qui ont-elles écrit?   with: C'est à eux qu'elles ont écrit.

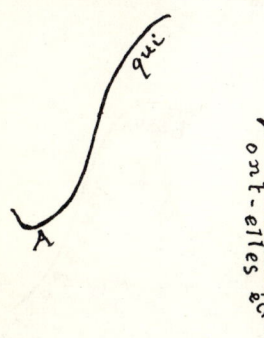

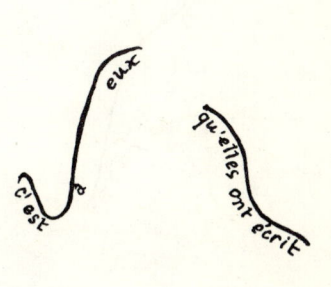

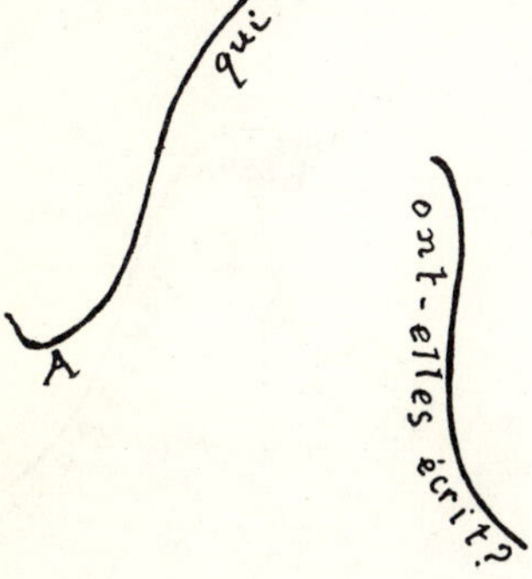

Note 1. The part of the interrogative sentence which immediately follows the highest note is pronounced on relatively low notes.

Note 2. The interrogative words such as: <u>quoi</u>, <u>que</u>, <u>qui</u>, <u>comment</u>, <u>pourquoi</u>, etc...are not necessarily the most important:

<u>Pourquoi venez-vous ce soir, Marguerite?</u>

<u>Quoi de plus drôle, que ce jeu-là?</u>

EXCLAMATORY SENTENCES

Contrary to what usually happens in an interrogative sentence, words of an exclamatory nature such as: <u>que</u>, <u>quel</u>, <u>comment</u>, etc...as well as the interjections, are pronounced on the highest note. This may be as many as five or six musical notes higher than the others.

1. <u>Quel enfant!</u>   2. <u>Que de beaux paysages!</u>

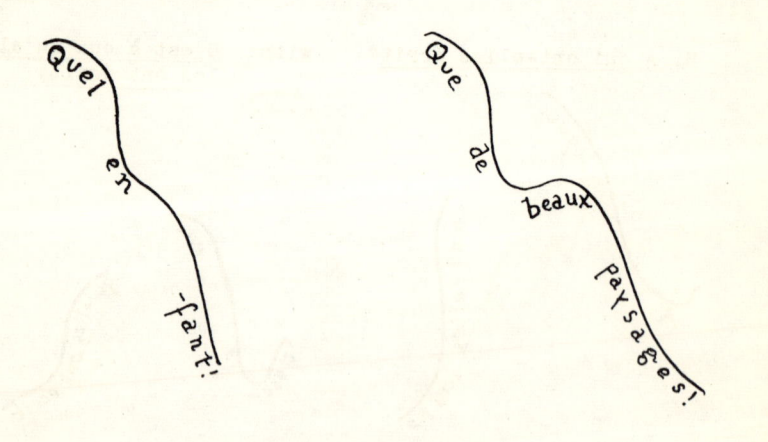

3. Comment!

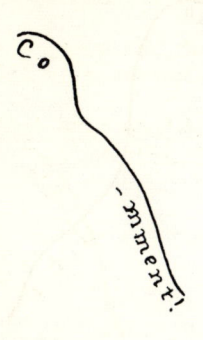

4. Combien j'ai douce souvenance!

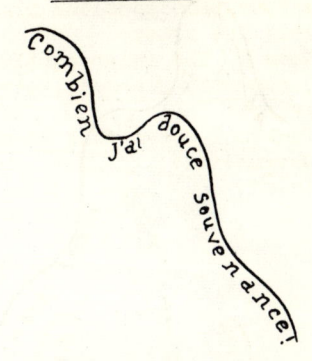

5. Oh! l'amour chéri!

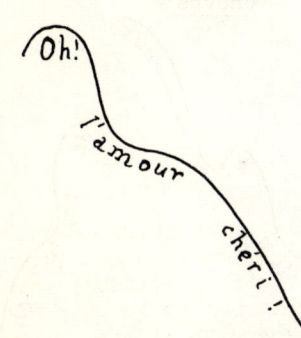

6. Ah! qu'elle était belle!

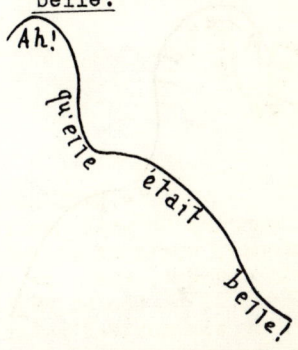

But more often than not, the exclamation is connected with the stress for emphasis (the most important word in the sentence):
1. L'imbécile qui s'est perdu!
2. Merveilleux!

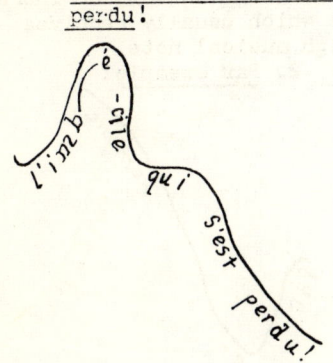

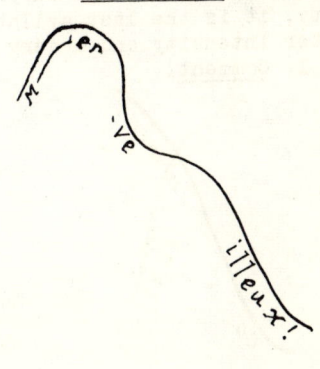

3. <u>Admirablement beau!</u>   4. <u>Bandit!</u>

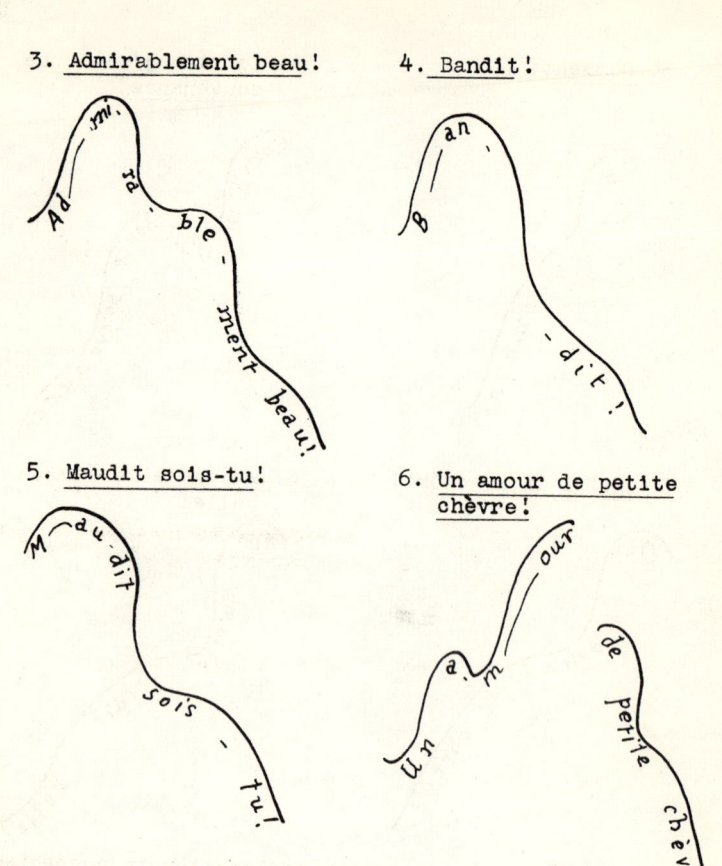

5. <u>Maudit sois-tu!</u>   6. <u>Un amour de petite chèvre!</u>

Unlike the examples already given, in those exclamatory sentences which express surprise, astonishment, or incredulity, it is the last syllable which usually receives greater intensity and a very high musical note.

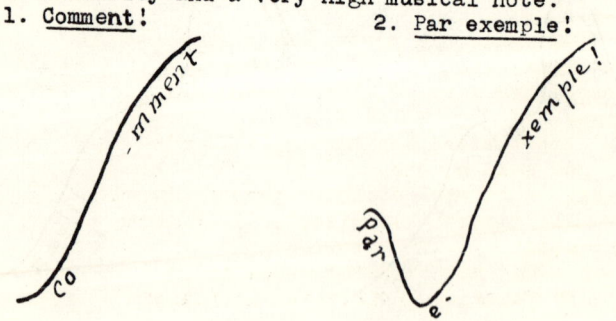

1. <u>Comment!</u>   2. <u>Par exemple!</u>

3. C'est fort!

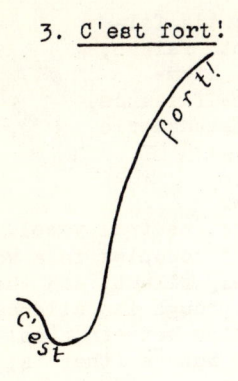

4. Elle n'est pas venue!

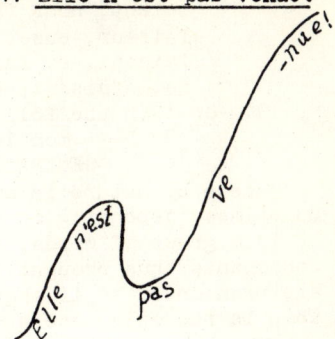

5. C'est impossible!

6. Je ne le crois pas!

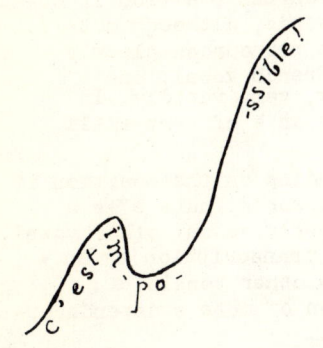

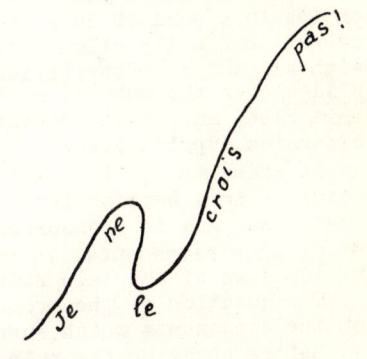

Chapter XI.
MUTE E, ə

SPELLINGS:
1. -e-, -e:
    la table, la porte, une chaise, tellement, etc.
2. -es: when mark of plural or of personal verb endings:
    les tables, les portes, tu parles, que tu sentes, etc.
3. -ent: when mark of third person plural:
    ils aiment, ils disent, ils paient, elles aimaient, etc.
4. -ai-: in the following words only:
    je faisais, tu faisais, il faisait,

nous faisions, vous faisiez, ils faisaient, nous faisons, faisant; faisan, faiseur,-euse, bienfaisance, bienfaisant,-e, malfaisant,-e, malfaisance, satisfaisant,-e, faisandé, faisanderie.

5. -on-: in the following word only:
monsieur

GENERAL CONSIDERATIONS

Mute e by nature is a vague, obscure, neutral vowel. Sometimes, depending on the position it occupies in a word or in a group of words, it is completely silent, and the consonants thus brought into contact through its silence are pronounced as if there were no letter between them. This is the only case when the name of mute e (that is, silent e) is justifiable. In this, there is no phonetic symbol to represent this letter, since it does not exist as a sound.

At other times, still depending on the position it occupies in a word or in a group of words, although mute e is not completely silent, it is not pronounced clearly with all the characteristics of a French vowel: one slides over the mute e, so to speak, very rapidly. In this case, mute e is represented by an e of very small dimension, upside down: ᵊ .

At other times, too, still depending on the position it occupies in a word or in a group of words, mute e is a real vowel and is pronounced as clearly as any other vowel. It is then represented in phonetic transcription by an e upside down of the same size as the other vowels: ə .

The question of the pronunciation of mute e depends upon the consonants which surround it.

Before studying the rules themselves, the following questions must be considered:

1. <u>WHICH CONSONANTS ARE TO BE TAKEN INTO CONSIDERATION?</u>
It is understood that only <u>pronounced</u> consonants are to be considered; silent consonants are never counted, for pronunciation deals with <u>sounds</u> and not with mere letters.

Tu me di*s̸* de partir
Il me ser*t̸* de bureau

The <u>s</u> of <u>dis</u> and the <u>t</u> of <u>sert</u> are not to be counted because they are silent.

II. <u>HOW SHOULD THE CONSONANTS BE COUNTED?</u>
When determining whether a mute e is to be pronounced or not, the consonant should be counted beginning with the first after the preceding vowel, to and including the last before the following vowel:

a. Tu veu*x̸* <u>le</u> <u>finir</u>

First consonant after the preceding vowel: <u>l</u>(preceding vowel: <u>eu</u>).

119

Last consonant before the following vowel: f (following vowel: i).
In the above example there are **two** consonants to deal with, and to determine whether mute e is to be silent or not, one must understand the rules concerning a mute e between two consonants.
b. Edit̸h me l'a dit
First consonant after the preceding vowel: t (preceding vowel: i).
Last consonant before the following vowel: l (following vowel: a).
In the above example there are **three** consonants to deal with; and to determine whether mute e is to be silent or not, one must understand the rules concerning mute e with three consonants.

III. IS MUTE E IN THE SAME WORD ALWAYS SILENT OR ALWAYS PRONOUNCED?

From the rules which will be explained later, it will be evident that in many words the same mute e may be silent or pronounced, depending on the position of the word and its surroundings.

MUTE E IS COMPLETELY SILENT:
I. At the end of a breath-group:

Sur la chais̸e Jean l'ouvr̸e
Tu mets la rob̸e Il parl̸e
Il prend des not̸e̸s La pest̸e
Tu chant̸e̸s La maison vert̸e
Il dans̸e   J'ai vu le chantr̸e
Elle est bell̸e C'est la nôtr̸e
Tu l'appell̸e̸s Ce sont les vôtr̸e̸s
Sur la terr̸e C'est un monstr̸e
Voici la tabl̸e Un bel arbr̸e

II. Between two consonant sounds, and only two. (That is to say, when preceded by one consonant only):

Voici l̸e chien
La ch̸eminée fume
Il es̸t d̸evant la f̸enêtre
On l̸e dit
On n̸e veut pas
Vous v̸enez m̸e voir
Nous sommes dans l̸e salon
Il a trois ans d̸e moins qu̸e moi
Enfin, j̸e suis là
Vous donn̸erez l̸e livre au p̸etit garçon
Il a enl̸evé les env̸eloppes et l̸e papier
Il est bien él̸evé et vous l'aim̸erez
Bien qu̸e tu n̸e sois pas allé l̸e voir, Jean
 n̸e t'en veut pas l̸e moins du monde.

EXCEPTIONS:
a. At the beginning of a breath-group, mute e between two consonants usually is pronounced:
Compare:
{ Le tableau noir
{ J'ai vu l∅ tableau noir
{ Ne dis rien
{ Tu n∅ dis rien
{ Tenez; le voilà
{ Vous t∅nez
{ Venez avec moi
{ Vous v∅nez avec moi
{ Toi, le père, tu dois lui parler
{ Tu es l∅ père tu dois lui parler
{ Depuis huit jours, il est là
{ Il y est d∅puis huit jours
{ De loin, il l'a vu
{ Il l'a vu d∅ loin
{ Serez-vous prêt à temps
{ Vous s∅rez prêt à temps
{ De toi, ça m'étonne
{ Il rit d∅ toi
{ Remettez-vous
{ Il faut vous r∅mettre

b. When the stress for emphasis falls on the syllable containing the mute e, mute e is pronounced, and it is pronounced as clearly and with as much intensity as any other vowel:
Compare:
{ Debout les morts
{ Je suis d∅bout
{ Il faudra recommencer
{ Tu r∅commences demain
{ L'auteur s'appelle Lenormand
{ C'est l∅ Normand
{ Je vous en prie, de la tenue
{ Elle n'a pas d∅ tenue
{ Restons-nous dedans ou dehors?
{ Il est d∅dans
{ Il jura devant Dieu et devant
{   les hommes
{ Je suis d∅vant vous
{ Savez-vous la différence entre
{   recommander et raccommander?
{ Je lui ai r∅commandé de venir

c. In a few words of which the first syllable contains a mute e, this

mute e is always pronounced. Following is the list of the more usual words of this type:
besace
celui
devers
menu
menuet
menuisier and words of same family
pelouse
peser and words of same family
querelle
sedan
vedette
d. In the first and second persons plural of the conditional, mute e is always pronounced:
nous danserions
vous chanteriez
nous ferions
vous feriez, etc.
e. -elier. In the words ending in -elier, mute e is always pronounced:
atelier
bâchelier
chancelier
chandelier
coutelier
ficelier
hôtelier, etc.
f. Before the word **rien**:
Tu ne manges̸ rien
Il ne demande rien

III. With three consonant sounds:
a. When the second and third belong to the same syllable and are inseparable. The groups of inseparable consonant sounds are:
1. **bl, br, cl, cr, dr, fl, fr, gl, gr, pl, pr, tr, vr**.
2. **ks, sk, ps, sp, ts, st, sf, sm, sn**.

Then, it may be said that mute e is silent with three consonants when they are grouped 1+2, that is to say, when the syllable-division is after the first, leaving the inseparable consonants together:
Dans le̸ clair-obscur
Un amas de̸ glace
J'en ai de̸ plus belles
Donnez-lui le̸ bras

　　　　Il fait l≠ snob
　　　　Saluez l≠ drapeau
　　　　Vous êtes dans l≠ vrai
　　　　Prends l≠ gros crayon
　　　　Vous mettez l≠ smoking?
　　　　Elle a des yeux d≠ sphynx
　　　　Rien d≠ spécial, aujourd'hui?
　　　　On dansait beaucoup chez l≠ tsar
　　　　Il travaillait l≠ xylophone (x=ks)
　　　　Vous n'avez pas r≠trouvé vos gants?
　　　　Nous irons d≠ préférence en autobus
　　　　C'est l≠ scandale qui lui fait peur
　　　　Cette expression est dans l≠ psaume 37
　　　　Vous n≠ frémissez pas à cette idée-là?
　　　　Les coureurs entrèrent dans l≠ stade
　　　　Prends l≠ flambeau
　　　　Préférez-vous l≠ blanc ou l≠ bleu?
　　　　Elle a l≠ gros chien
　　　　Elle étudie l≠ pluriel des adjectifs, etc.
b. When the first and second consonant sounds belong to the last syllable of a word and the third is the initial consonant of a following word. It is to be noted that the consonants are grouped --in two different grammatical words--2+1.(In such cases the second consonant becomes partly or completely voiceless, p.141):
　　　2+1 Les Chevaliers de la Tabl≠ Ronde
　　　2+1 Elle a un immeubl≠ neuf
　　　2+1 L'inaccessibl≠ sommet
　　　2+1 Il ronfl≠ fort
　　　2+1 C'est un célèbr≠ savant
　　　2+1 C'est un vrai diabl≠ noir
　　　2+1 C'est du sabl≠ jaune
　　　2+1 Il a un cartabl≠ noir
　　　2+1 C'est la port≠ verte
　　　2+1 Il voit l'oncl≠ Pierre
　　　2+1 Le gest≠ du chanteur
　　　2+1 La gard≠ du malade
　　　2+1 Presqu≠ pas
　　　2+1 Inculp≠-la
　　　2+1 Crisp≠-les
　　　2+1 Désax≠-la
　　　2+1 L'éclips≠ du soleil
　　　2+1 Le tors≠ nu, etc.
Note 1. But one must take care to pronounce the three consonants **very distinctly**; if at first this is too difficult, the student should insert a slight mute e after the second consonant sound. Even some French people, in such expressions,

sometimes pronounce not only a slight but even a complete mute e, although this practice is infrequent.

Note 2. When such words as those given in the above examples precede one of the eight monosyllables in which there is a mute e (ce, de, je, le, me, ne, que, te), the mute e of the monosyllable is very clearly pronounced:

    La tabl*e* de Jean
    L'immeubl*e* que tu possèdes
    Son oncl*e* ne voit rien, etc.

MUTE E IS PRONOUNCED:

I. With three consonants, if the first and second precede a mute e, even though in spelling there may be another mute e, between the first and second consonants. This is called the "Rule of the three consonants", because with the omission of both the mute e's, three consonants would come together. These consonants are grouped either 2+1--that is, in a single grammatical word--or 1+1+1--that is, in three consecutive grammatical words--but not in two consecutive grammatical words (page 122):

    2+1 Il sort librement
    2+1 Elle est dans l'appartement
    2+1 Il est du Parlement
    2+1 Il agit noblement
    2+1 C'est terriblement triste
    2+1 Il l'a fortement soutenu
    2+1 Il l'avait préalablement regardé
    2+1 Il fait partie du gouvernement
    1+1+1 Elle jouait avec le chat
    1+1+1 Il me l'a dit
    1+1+1 Ell*e* te voit
    1+1+1 Il me parle
    1+1+1 Il ne peut pas attendre
    1+1+1 Pouss*e* le verrou
    1+1+1 Il est arrivé sur le sommet
    1+1+1 Il reparlera
    1+1+1 La cur*e* de silence
    1+1+1 Des aiguill*es* de cette grosseur-ci
    1+1+1 Madam*e* de Sévigné
    1+1+1 Madam*e* de Maintenon
    1+1+1 Professeur de littérature
    1+1+1 Encor*e* de la soupe
    1+1+1 Toujour*s* de la viande

II. Between two consonants, and only two, in the following cases only:
1. At the beginning of a breath-group.
2. When the stress for emphasis falls on the syllable containing the mute e.

3. In a few words of which the first syllable contains a mute e.
4. In the first and second persons plural of the conditional.
5. In the ending -elier.
   (Examples have been given in the exceptions to rule II on pages 119 and 120).

MONOSYLLABLES

I.
   1. When, at the beginning of a stress-group, there are two monosyllables in succession, each containing a mute e, the first mute e usually is retained and the other dropped. However, in the combinations ce que and je te, the first mute is dropped and the second kept:
   Ne m/ dis rien
   Que c/ fut lui, je n/ le croyais pas
   Que d/ toi je m'éloigne et c'en est fait
   Que j/ parte ou non
   Que l/ soleil luise ou non, je partirai
   Que m/ fait ton récit?
   Que t/ dirai-je encore?
   Te l/ dire et mourir
   Se l/ répéter
   Ce m/ semble parfait
   Ce n/ peut pas être vrai
   Ce t/ paraît gai, n'est-ce pas?
   Je n/ veux pas
   Que n/ lui en parles-tu?
   Ne t/ mets pas en route
   De c/ beau jour je me souviendrai
   Je m/ suis fait mal
   Je l/ ferai volontiers
   Me l/ faut-il vraiment faire?
   Ne l/ prends pas
       BUT
   C/ que tu as dit
   C/ que j'aime
   J/ te parle
   J/ te raconterai une histoire
   2. When, within a stress-group, there are two monosyllables in succession, usually either one may be retained and the other dropped:
   Et je le lui donnai   je l/   or   j/ le
   André ne se rase pas   ne s/   "   n/ se
   Qu'on se le dise   se l/   "   s/ le
   Et je me suis fait mal   je m/   "   j/ me
   Il veut me le faire faire   me l/   "   m/ le
   Tu ne le prends pas   ne l/   "   n/ le

```
Vous ne me dites rien      ne mé  "  né me
Léon te le dira            te lé  "  té le
Jean ne te verra pas       ne té  "  né te
```
Note the three following exceptions:
  a. If one of the monosyllables is que
     or de, this monosyllable rather than
     the other retains the mute e:
     Que fais-tu de cé tableau
     Tu as besoin de lé dire
     Il vient de mé parler
     Il oublie de sé taire
     Il essaie de sé voir
     Tu feras bien de né pas la voir
     Tu as dit que cé livre était à toi
     Il n'a parlé que dé géographie
     Tu ne veux que lé sien
     Il ne veut que mé parler
     Marie ne fait que té louer
     Il ne faut que sé coucher. etc.
  b. In the following combinations begin-
     ning with ce: ce me, ce te, ce ne,
     ce le, and in the combination je ne,
     the first mute e is kept and the sec-
     ond dropped:
     Mais ce mé semble parfait
     Et ce té paraît très gai
     Mais ce né sera rien
     Et ce lé semblera ainsi
     Et je né sais rien de plus
  c. And in the combinations: ce que, que
     je, the first mute e is dropped and the
     second kept:
     Tu sais cé que tu veux
     Il veut qué je lui donne ma réponse
     Mais jé te parle

II. When there is a group of more than two monosyllables, usually it is the mute e of the first that is kept,
then the second dropped, the third kept, and so forth:
     Jean me lé demande
     Tu me lé redémandes
     Tu ne lé reféras pas
     Tu ne lé reféras qué si tu té souviens
     de cé que jé te dis
     Et je né le réverrai plus
     Ne parlé pas de cé que lé devin t'a dit
EXCEPTIONS:
  a. When the combination ce que occurs
     in a long group of monosyllables, the
     e of que is kept, the e of ce dropped,

and the other mute e's are suppressed alternately on either side:
Je suis content de cé que lé professeur dit
Parcé que tu la démandes
Parcé que jé me lé redémande
Et cé que cé salon est sombre!
C'est cé que jé te rédis dépuis longtemps. etc.

b. When the combination je te occurs in a long group of monosyllables, the e of te is kept, the e of je dropped: and the other mute e's are suppressed alternately on either side:
Quand jé te lé dis
Si jé te lé redonne
Et jé te lé redémande
Mais jé te lé redémandérai

NOTE: Although other pronunciations of groups of monosyllables containing mute e are sometimes heard, the rules explaining them are very complicated. A foreigner who follows those given above may be sure that his treatment of the mute e will always be considered correct by a French person.

SPECIAL OBSERVATIONS

I. The mute e of le, pronoun, when the last syllable of a phonetic group placed after the affirmative imperative, is always pronounced:

Prends-le   Attrapez-le
Dis-le   Rendez-le
Redis-le   Chantons-le, etc.

II. When one of the eight monosyllables containing mute e, or one of the conjunctions ending in -que is stressed, the mute e is pronounced very clearly--as a real vowel:
Et ce,
Parce que, étant donné---
Sur ce, elle partit.

III. Mute e is always pronounced, and very clearly pronounced when it is placed before an aspirated h or a word which does not permit liaison (p.131) or linking (p.140):

le héros   Elle parle haut
le hameau   Qu'elle dise oui
le houx   Le oui de Juliette
le haut perron   Presque onze heures
se hausser   Puisque Hortense le dit.

IV. From the preceding rules it may very easily be understood that the pronunciation of a given mute e may depend on its position in a word or group of words:

{La p̸etite fille {C'est à moi qu'il parl̸e
{Un̸e p_etite fille {Il parle͡ haut
{Je suis d̸ebout {Je n'ai pas d̸e papier
{Il chant̸e d_ebout {Le professeur de littérature

N_ote 1: These rules apply to delivery of medium speed--
neither very slow, as in the oratorical style, nor very
fast, as is apt to be the case in familiar speech. As the
general tone of a single conversation changes, the foreigner will find variations. Let him not be surprised,
however, for French is a <u>living</u> language, and as such,
subject to change. At the present time a real evolution is
taking place, especially with regard to liaison and mute e.

N_ote 2: The student will do well not to ask his French
friends for rules with regard to the omission or retention
of the mute e, for unless a French person has studied the
phonetics of his own language, he will stoutly assert and
maintain that he pronounces mute e's which in reality he
omits. Of this fact phonograph records, which may be retarded at will, furnish irrefutable proof.

Chapter XII.
LIAISON

Liaison is that phenomenon by which a final consonant
silent in the isolated word, is sounded before a word beginning with a vowel or mute h. In pronunciation, this
consonant then loses its connection with the first word
and becomes the <u>first consonant of the second word</u>. <u>Petit
enfant</u> is pronounced as if it were <u>peti</u> <u>tenfant</u>. Liaison
is indicated as follows: petit‿enfant.

GENERAL CONSIDERATIONS

Liaison takes place only between words <u>closely connect-
ed</u> in thought.

Some liaisons are obligatory; but in rapid speech, the
liaison has a tendency to disappear. Thus in many cases, a
liaison which in oratorical and formal speech is optional,
is avoided in conversation.

It is not that the succession of two or more vowel
sounds is disagreeable in French. Within a word or within
a stress-group, if two or more vowels are in contact,
there is always something which approximates a liaison
from vowel to vowel, and this is shown by the inflexion of
the voice as well as in the continuity of the vibrations
of the vocal chords. The sentence: "<u>Papa a à aller à Paris</u>"
is not shocking to a French ear, if the vibrations of the
vocal chords are not interrupted after each <u>a</u>; even a
short cessation of the vibrations however will at once re-
veal the foreigner.

Failure to make an obligatory liaison shocks the ear of

an educated Frenchman therefore, not because of the succession of two vowel sounds but because of usage, which demands the combination of a consonant and a vowel in that special case.

Liaison is unusual between two stress-groups and consequently between two breath-groups. Even within a stress-group, liaison occurs only between words closely related in thought. "Dans la prononciation courante d'aujourd'hui les mots accessoires, articles, pronoms, adjetifs ~~possessifs et démonstratifs~~, prépositions, conjonctions, adverbes, se lient toujours quand ils sont préposés et ne se lient pas quand ils sont postposés." M. Grammont, La Prononciation française, page 130.

Within a stress-group, liaisons are either:
1. obligatory
2. prohibited
3. optional

OBLIGATORY LIAISONS

I. ARTICLES
   a. Between the definite articles les, and the following noun, adjective, pronoun:
      Les enfants
      Les adorables bébés
      Les uns et les autres
   b. Between the indefinite articles, un, des, and the following noun, adjective, or pronoun:
      Un autre   Des hirondelles
      Un oiseau   Des enfants
      Un heureux mélange   Des immenses espaces

II. ADJECTIVES
   a. Between the possessive adjectives (mon, ton, son, mes, tes, ses, nos, vos, leurs) and the following noun or adjective:
      Ses autres filles   Vos immortels poèmes
      Leurs images   Ses admirables livres
   b. Between the demonstrative adjective ces, and the following noun or adjective:
      Ces usages
      Ces autres livres
   c. Between a qualitative, indefinite, or numeral adjective and a following noun:
      Les grands animaux   Vingt enfants
      Les belles histoires   Tout homme
      Le grand enfant   Second acte
      Le petit homme   Plusieurs histoires
      Cent hommes   Deux cents hommes

NOTE: There are only three adjectives ending in -ier which may be placed before the noun: premier, dernier, singulier. After them liaison always takes

place:
    Son dernier atout   Premier avril
    Un singulier ami   Au premier étage

III. PRONOUNS
  a. Between the indefinite pronoun <u>tout</u> used as subject and the following <u>verb</u>:
        Tout est dit
        Tout a disparu
  b. Between a personal pronoun used as subject and the following <u>verb</u>:
        Nous avons   Ils aiment
        Vous avez   Elles amusent l'enfant
  c. Between the <u>personal pronoun</u> used as direct or indirect object and its <u>verb</u>:
        Il vous écrit   En a-t-elle?
        Elle vous aime   Il y en a
  d. Between the relative pronoun <u>dont</u>, and the following <u>word</u>:
        Ce dont il parle
        Les tableaux dont elle est fière

IV. VERBS
  a. In an <u>interrogative</u> sentence between the <u>verb</u> and a following <u>pronoun used as subject</u>:
        Voit-il?   Parleront-elles?
        Peut-on?   Ont-elles parlé?
        Peuvent-ils?   avaient-elles dansé?
  b. Between the auxiliary <u>avoir</u>, in the <u>third person</u> of the plural, and a following <u>past participle</u>:
        Ils ont eu
        Ils ont augmenté leurs prix
  c. Between the <u>third person</u> singular or plural of the verb <u>être</u> (in every tense and mode) and the <u>following word</u>:

Il est en voyage   Elle était ici
Ils y sont encore   Ils seraient entre eux
Ce sont eux   Qu'il soit ici avant midi!
Ce furent eux   Qu'elle soit à Paris demain!

  d. Between any verb used as an <u>auxiliary verb</u> and a following <u>infinitive</u>:
        Il faut aller le voir
        Je dois être à New-York demain
        Ils pourraient entendre
        Nous voudrions entendre cet artiste

VI. PREPOSITIONS
  Between a <u>preposition</u> and a <u>following word</u>:
    Avant eux   Dans une salle
    Sous une étagère Après elle
    Devant elle   Pendant un mois
    Chez elle   Sans eux

EXCEPTION: No liaison is made after the
following prepositions:
selon┐   nonobstant┐
dès┐   vers┐
moyennant┐ hors┐

VI. CONJUNCTIONS
  a. Between the conjunction <u>quand</u> and the following word:
      Quand elle entra   *kãtelãtra*
      Quand on perd la tête *kãtõperlatɛt*
  b. Between the conjunctions <u>soit</u>...<u>soit</u>, <u>tant</u>...<u>que</u>, and the following word:
      Elle ira le voir soit à Paris soit à Londres.
      Elle est heureuse tant ici qu'à la ville.
  c. Between <u>plural nouns</u> or <u>plural adjectives</u>, used without articles or other determinatives, and the conjunction <u>et</u> or <u>ou</u>.
      Ponts et chaussées   Beaux au laids
      Forts et faibles   Gras ou maigres
      Grands ou petits   Contes et légendes

VII. ADVERBS
  a. Between adverbs ending in <u>-ment</u> and the word they modify:
      Tendrement aimé
      Admirablement écrit
  b. Between the adverbs <u>tout</u>, <u>très</u>, <u>fort</u>, and a following adjective or <u>past participle</u>:
      Il est tout autre   Ils l'ont fort applaudi
      Il est très heureux   Elle l'a fort apprécié
  c. Between <u>two adverbs</u> in the same stress-group:
      Pas encore
      Mieux encore
  d. Between <u>quant</u> and <u>à</u>:
      Quant au jour   Quant à cette enfant
      Quant à vous   Quant aux autres
  e. Between <u>comment</u> and the verb <u>aller</u>, in the expression used to inquire about <u>health</u>:
      Comment allez-vous?
      Comment alliez-vous?
  But in all other cases, there is no liaison between comment and the next word.

VIII. IDIOMATIC PHRASES AND EXPRESSIONS
  With some words, in idiomatic phrases and in certain other expressions, there are no rules; usage alone prevails. The student should learn such expressions by heart.
  Accent aigu   Dos à dos   Pot-au-feu
  Avant-hier   D'un bout à l'autre   Pot au lait

131

Bout à bout	Franc-alleu	Pot-aux roses
But à but	Franc-archer	Respect humain
De but en blanc	Franc-étrier	Sang impur
De fond en comble	Le fait est	Suer sang et eau
De haut en bas	Les Champs-Elysées	Tout à coup
De mieux en mieux	Les Etats unis	Tout à fait
De moins en moins	Le Tiers-Etat	Tout à l'égout
De pied en cap	Mot à mot	Tout à l'heure
De plus en plus	Pas à pas	Un croc-en-jambes
De temps en temps	Petit à petit	Un guet-apens
Deux à deux	Pied à terre	Un pis-aller
Deux ou trois	Pot à eau	Vis-à-vis

NOTE: These rules concerning obligatory liaisons are based on the every day speech of the majority of cultured Frenchmen, but one will occasionally discover some variations in usage among equally cultured French people. As I have said, the phenomenon of liaison is in evolution, and will be as long as French is a living language. However, if a foreigner observes the rules given herewith he will be certain neither to make incorrect liaisons, nor to omit those that are indispensable.

PROHIBITED LIAISONS

I. PRONOUNS

Between the personal pronouns elles and ils used as subject, when placed after the verb, and the following word:

    Ont-elles | étudié?   Vont-elles | y aller?
    Ont-ils | appris?   Apprendront-ils | une fable?

II. NOUNS

a. Between a noun or word used by exception as a noun in the singular and a following qualitative adjective:

    Un chat | étique   Un front | adorable
    Un lit | immense   Un nez | épaté
    Un cas | inouï   Un garçonnet | étrange

EXCEPTIONS: In the following expressions, liaison takes place:

    Accent aigu
    Sang impur   sãkɛ̃py:r

b. Before the word uhlan or ululer, and words derived from ululer:

    Des | uhlans   Les affreux | ululements
    Les | uhlans   Les grands | uhlans

c. Before a word beginning with y + a vowel:

    Des | yachts   Des | yes
    Des | yatagans   Des | yoles

EXCEPTIONS:

    des yeuses
    des yeux

d. Between a <u>noun</u>, a <u>pronoun</u> (with the exception of nous, vous, ils, elles, on, tout) or any word used as subject, and a <u>following verb</u>:
  Ces cahiers⌐ ont une jolie couleur
  Ces personnes⌐ iront vous voir
  Ce jouet⌐ a besoin de réparation
  Le tout⌐ est de savoir (<u>tout</u> here used as noun)
  Le fermier⌐ est parti
  D'autres⌐ ont dansé
  Trois⌐ est son nombre favori
  Deux⌐ est la moitié de quatre
  Aimer⌐ est un joli verbe

e. With the <u>s of the plural</u>, within <u>compound words</u>:
  Des arcs-en-ciel Des salles à manger
  Des pots-au-feu Des chambres à coucher

f. Before <u>oui</u>:
  Mais⌐ oui   Pour un⌐ oui ou pour un non
  Elle t'a dit⌐ oui Les⌐ oui qu'elle t'a dits

III. CONJUNCTIONS
 a. Between the conjunction <u>et</u> and the following word:
Marguerite et⌐ Yvonne Des roses et⌐ une violette
Une robe et⌐ un manteau Elle est grande et⌐ élevée

IV. INTERJECTIONS
 Before an <u>interjection</u>:
  Les⌐ oh! et les⌐ hi! de Jean
  Elle faisait des⌐ ah! et des⌐ oh! très amusants

V. ADVERBS
 Between <u>comment</u> and the <u>next word</u>--except in the expression used to inquire about health:
  Comment⌐ iras-tu à l'école?
  Comment⌐ a-t-il fait?
  Comment⌐ allons-nous au théâtre?
  Comment⌐ êtes-vous?
    but
  Comment‿allez-vous?
  Comment‿allait-il?

VI. NUMERALS
 Before the numerals <u>un</u>, <u>huit</u>, and <u>onze</u>:
  Quatre-vingt-huit Les numéros⌐ un et deux
  Tous les⌐ huit   Louis⌐ onze
  Tous les⌐ onze   Ils sont⌐ onze
  Les⌐ onze enfants Quatre-vingt-un
 NOTE: In the following numerals, liaison occurs:
  dix-huit   soixante-dix-huit
  vingt-huit quatre-vingt-dix-huit

VII. ASPIRATE H
Before a word beginning with an aspirate h:
    Un⁊ héros   Les⁊ huit de coeur
    Un⁊ héron   Ces⁊ hauts murs
    De grands⁊ héraut   Deux⁊ homards

VII. TO AVOID LACK OF HARMONY IN SOUND
    Vous êtes⁊ aisée   Six heures⁊ et demie
    Comment⁊ êtes-vous? Nous sommes allés⁊ aux eaux

IX. IN CERTAIN EXPRESSIONS:
    Au doigt⁊ et à l'oeil Nez⁊ à nez
    Chaud⁊ et froid   Riz⁊ au lait
                           Pot⁊ à tabac

All cultured people strictly observe the preceding rules in oratorical, formal and every day speech.

OPTIONAL LIAISONS

I. ADJECTIVES
  Between an **adjective** and a following **preposition**:
        Prêt⌣à parler
        Haut⌣en couleur
  But in rapid speech, this liaison is usually avoided.

II. NOUNS
  a. Between a **plural noun** and a following **preposition**:
        Des appartements⌣à louer
        Des petites filles⌣à élever
        Les héros⌣en question
    But in rapid speech, this liaison is usually avoided.

  b. When **two plural** nouns that are determinated are united by the conjunctions **et** or **ou**, the liaison is optional between the first noun and the following conjunction:
        Des filles⌣et des garçons
        Des fleurs⌣et des feuilles
        Des livres⌣et des cahiers

  c. Between **a plural noun** and a following **adjective**:
        Des personnes⌣aimables
        Des bouquets⌣exquis
        Des chapeaux⌣adorables
    NOTE: When in either the singular or the plural the noun ends with a consonant sound or sounds especially in rapid speech, linking (p.140) may take place:
            Des person̸n̸e̸s̸ aimables
            Des livr̸e̸s̸ ennuyeux
    But the liaison is correct also.

  d. Before **proper names**:
        Chez⁊ Yvonne
        Chez⌣ Médiard
  But this liaison is more and more avoided.

III. PRONOUNS

Between personal pronoun **eux** placed at beginning or in middle of a stress-group and the following word:

　　　　Eux‿aussi
　　　　Eux‿et moi

But in rapid speech, this liaison is usually avoided.

IV. VERBS

a. Between the auxiliary verbs **avoir**, **être**, and the following **past participle** (exception: with the third person the liaison is obligatory):

Nous avons‿eu
Vous l'aviez‿abandonné　　Je suis‿allé en ville
Tu eus‿aimé à le faire　　Nous sommes‿allés les voir
Tu l'avais‿organisé　　　 Nous serions‿enchantés

But in rapid speech, this liaison is usually avoided.

b. Between the **verb** and a following **object**:

　　　　Nous avons‿un beau livre
　　　　Nous jouons‿une sonate

But in rapid speech, this liaison is avoided more and more often.

c. Between **infinitives** ending in -er and the following word:

　　　Aimer‿à parler　　　Jouer‿aux cartes
　　　Aimer‿et chanter　　Jouer‿aux échecs
　　　Monter‿à cheval　　 Se promener‿en auto

But in rapid speech, this liaison is avoided more and more often.

d. Between the **verbal ending -ent** (mark of the third person plural) and the following word:

　　　　Elles aiment‿à parler
　　　　Ils dansent‿un tango

But in rapid speech, this liaison is usually avoided.

e. Between a **past participle** and a following **preposition**:

　　　　Mis‿en demeure
　　　　Remis‿à neuf

f. Between a **present participle** and a following **preposition**:

　　　　En allant‿à Paris
　　　　En venant‿au moulin
　　　　En répondant‿à Marguerite

V. CONJUNCTIONS

Between the conjunction **mais** and the following word:

　　　　Mais‿il viendra
　　　　Mais‿aujourd'hui même
　　　　Mais‿encore plus

REMARK: Liaison never takes place between mais and oui.

VI. ADVERBS
  a. Between the adverbs **beaucoup**, **trop**, or **jamais**, and a following past participle, adjective, or the preposition à.
      Elle a beaucoup‿appris
      Elle a trop‿à dire
      Elle n'en a jamais‿eu
    But in rapid speech, this liaison is more and more avoided.

  b. Between an **adverb** placed at the beginning of a stress-group and the following word:
      Aussitôt‿arrivé
      Cependant‿on le lui répétait
      Partout‿où elle ira
      Elle ne pense à rien, tant‿elle est sotte
      Elle ne part plus, tellement‿elle se plaît ici
    But in rapid speech, this liaison is more and more avoided.

  c. When **two adverbs** are united by the conjunctions **et** or **ou**, the liaison is optional between the first adverb and the following conjunction.
      Rapidement‿et lestement
      Longuement‿ou rapidement

NOTE: Most of these liaisons are avoided in rapid speech but observed in oratorical and formal speech.

CHANGES OF SOUND IN LIAISON

I. **C=K**. In the following expressions:
      Franc-alleu
      Franc-archer
      Franc-étrier

II. **CT=K**. In the following expression only:
      Respect humain

III. **D=T**:
      Il prend une pomme
      Quand il viendra
      Son second enfant
      Grand homme

IV. **G=K**. In the following expressions:
      Suer sang et eau
      Sang impur
      NOTE: With all other words ending in **-g**, and with **sang** placed before words other than the two above, there should be no liaison:
        Un long exorde
        Il perd du sang en quantité

V. -RC, -RD, -RF, -RG, -RS, -RT=R.
    Un clerc intelligent   Vers elle
    Un abord aimable   Envers eux
    Sourd et muet   Vert et jaune
    Un cerf aux abois   Il part au matin
    Un iceberg énorme   Toujours immense
    EXCEPTIONS:
      1. -RD, -RT = RT.
        In the interrogative verbal forms before a pronoun used as subject.
          Perd-il?
          Sert-elle?
        Usually with the adverb fort.
          Fort heureusement
          Fort adroit
          Fort habile
          Fort intelligent
      2. -RS=RZ:
        With the following indefinite adjectives:
          Plusieurs enfants
          Divers autres

NOTE: Final s, mark of the plural, placed after an r pronounced in the isolated word, may form the liaison instead of the r. Either is correct, unless s is required to indicate plural (in case the context is not clear).

      Des airs ingénus   (With or without liaison,
      Des ports étendus   since the plural is indicated by des).
          BUT
      Airs ingénus   (With liaison, since there
      Ports étendus   is no other way of indicating plural).
      Mers immenses

VI. S=Z:
      Vas-y   Gros homme
      Perds-en   Dans un mois
      Donnes-en   Sans elle
      Bas étage

VII. X=Z:
      Dix hommes   Tu peux aller la voir
      Je veux y être   De mieux en mieux

Chapter XIII.
LIAISON OF THE N OF THE NASAL VOWELS

GENERAL RULE: Liaison <u>never</u> takes place between a noun in the singular or a word used by exception as a noun and the following word. Therefore, between such a noun when ending with a nasal vowel and the initial vowel of the following word, liaison **never** occurs:

    Adam⁊est le premier homme   Le marchand⁊est parti
    Aucun⁊est un pronom   Le mien⁊est plus joli
    C'est un parfum⁊enivrant   Le second⁊est parti
    C'est un rien⁊auquel il   On⁊est un pronom
     faut penser   Quelqu'un⁊a dit
    Chacun⁊en voulait   Quelqu'un⁊en voulait
    Combien⁊a coûté ce livre?   Sottement⁊est un adverbe
    En⁊est une préposition   Un⁊a pour pluriel des
    En voulez-vous chacun⁊un   Une conversation⁊agréable
    Il a faim⁊et soif   Une leçon⁊admirable
    Il est à Caen⁊ou à Rouen   Un⁊est un article
    Jean⁊est venu   Un nom⁊agréable
    Jean⁊et Jacques sont sortis   Un ruban⁊orange
    Le bien⁊et le mal   Un son⁊affreux

    NOTE: Unless otherwise indicated, the nasal vowel **retains** its nasal quality.

I. AN, $\tilde{a}$

1. **EN**, préposition. Liaison always takes place after **en**, préposition:

    Nous sommes en‿Autriche
    Il est en‿Europe
    En‿avant, marche

2. **EN**, pronoun. Liaison takes place after **en**, pronoun, when it is placed before the verb:

    S'en‿est-il allé?
    Il en‿a pris trois
    Tu en‿apportes deux

    NOTE: When **en** pronoun, is placed after the verb, no liaison takes place:

        Allez-vous-en⁊ailleurs
        Donnez-m'en⁊un peu
        Parlez-lui-en⁊un peu

After all other words ending with the nasal vowel $\tilde{a}$, whatever its spelling, no liaison takes place.

II. ON, $\tilde{o}$

1. **MON, TON, SON**. Liaison takes place after any of these three words, and the vowel may either retain its nasal quality or be pronounced like an open o:

    Mon‿école
    Ton‿enfant

2. **ON**. When **on** is the subject of a declarative sentence, liaison takes place:

    On‿aime la tranquillité
    On‿espère une amélioration
    On‿y va souvent

    NOTE: In other cases, no liaison takes

place after on, pronoun:
  a. When on follows the verb and is placed before either the past participle or another word:
   A-t-on eu des nouvelles?
   Est-on arrivé à le voir?
   A-t-on envoyé la lettre?
  b. When on is used to take the place of a noun:
   On est un mot vague
   On est un pronom indéfini
   On a plusieurs significations

3. BON. When bon is placed before the noun, liaison takes place. In this case, the vowel loses its nasal quality and is pronounced like an open o (as if it were the feminine form: bonne):
   Un bon ami   Un bon enfant
   Un bon exercice   Bonheur
   NOTE: In expressions where bon precedes the preposition à no liaison takes place and the vowel retains its nasal quality:
   Bon à tirer
   Bon à prendre

After all other words ending with the nasal vowel $\tilde{o}$, (whatever its spelling) no liaison takes place.

III. IN, $\tilde{\epsilon}$

1. RIEN, indefinite pronoun. Liaison takes place after rien, indefinite pronoun:
   Vous n'avez rien à faire?
   Il n'a rien obtenu
   Rien à penser

2. BIEN, adverb. Liaison takes place after bien, adverb.
   Nous sommes bien à plaindre
   Vous êtes bien en retard
   Est-il bien arrivé?
   NOTE: After bien used as an adjective no liaison takes place:
   Ils sont bien ensemble

3. BIEN ENTENDU. In this expression, liaison takes place:
   Bien entendu

4. ANCIEN, CERTAIN, HAUTAIN, HUMAIN, LOINTAIN, MOYEN, PLEIN, PROCHAIN, SOUDAIN, SOUVERAIN, VAIN, VILAIN. When these adjectives are placed before a noun, liaison takes place, but the vowel loses its nasal quality and is pronounced like an open e, thus giving the sound of the feminine form:
   C'est un ancien amiral   En plein air
   Une dame d'un certain âge Au prochain arrêt

Un hautain accueil   Un soudain éclat
L'humain espoir   Un souverain empire
Dans un lointain avenir   Le vain espoir
Au moyen âge   Quel vilain oiseau

5. DIVIN. When this adjective is placed before a noun, liaison takes place and the vowel loses its nasal quality and is pronounced i, thus giving the sound of the feminine form:
   Divin enfant
After all other words ending with the nasal vowel ɛ̃, (whatever its spelling) no liaison takes place.

IV. UN, ŒS

1. AUCUN, adjective. Liaison takes place after aucun, adjective:
   Aucun homme ne l'a jamais vu
   Pourquoi n'a-t-il aucun ami?
   NOTE: No liaison takes place after aucun, pronoun:
   Je n'en ai vu aucun ici

2. UN, article. Liaison takes place after un, article:
   Un heureux caractère
   Un enfant très sage
   NOTE: No liaison takes place after un, pronoun:
   En veut-il un aussi?
   J'en ai un orange

3. UN, numeral. Liaison takes place with un, numeral, if un multiplies the following noun:
   Vingt et un arbres
   Trente et un hommes
   Quarante et un élèves
   Cet homme a cinquante et un ans
   Note 1. In dates before a noun beginning with a vowel, liaison is optional:
   vingt-et-un avril
   Note 2. In other cases, there is no liaison:
   un Hollandais
   un et un font deux

4. D'UN COMMUN ACCORD. In this expression, liaison takes place:
   D'un commun accord

5. OPTIONAL LIAISONS. In all expressions beginning with un or l'un, except those already noted, liaison is optional:
   Un à un
   L'un ou l'autre
   L'un avec l'autre

L'un~~t~~ et l'autre
L'un~~t~~ auprès de l'autre
After all other words ending with the nasal vowel œ̃ (whatever its spelling), no liaison takes place.

Chapter XIV.
LINKING

In some words the final consonant or group of consonants is always pronounced whatever the position of the word. When it appears before a word beginning with a vowel or mute h, such a final consonant or final group of consonants is not only pronounced but also linked with the initial vowel of the following word. This phenomenon, called <u>linking</u>, is similar to liaison in that it has the effect of producing that smoothness of sound so characteristic of spoken French.

It is by his failure to observe this phenomenon that the foreigner is easily detected. He inserts a slight mute e which often exists in the spelling but never in the spoken word.

Linking is usually required <u>within a breath-group</u>:

Cet~~te~~ idée-là   Naîtr~~e~~ et mourir
Chèr~~e~~ enfant   Nobl~~e~~ enfant
Cher enfant   Paraîtr~~e~~ et disparaître
Entr~~e~~ eux   Pour avoir
Heureus~~e~~ et confiante   Quatr~~e~~ hommes
Le beau lys en fleur   Sain~~e~~ et solide
La bel~~le~~ amie   Se mettr~~e~~ au lit
La fleur en bouton   Tout~~e~~ à toi
La grand~~e~~ enfant   Un arbr~~e~~ en fleur
La petit~~e~~ Isabelle   Un brav~~e~~ homme
Légèr~~e~~ ironie   Victor-Hugo
Modest~~e~~ auberge   Votr~~e~~ ami

Note 1. In the following expressions in which liaison does not occur, linking takes place:
de par~~t~~ et d'autre
de par~~t~~ en part
bor~~d~~ à bord
mor~~t~~ ou vif
à tor~~t~~ et à travers
corp~~s~~ a corps

Note 2. In the following expressions either linking or liaison may take place:
nor~~d~~-est
nor~~d~~-ouest
But linking is used more and more.

EXCEPTIONS: The only exceptions are the
following:
1. NUMERALS
    Before the numerals <u>un</u>, <u>huit</u>, and
    <u>onze</u>:
        Le nombre⌐ un
        Le nombre⌐ onze
        Le nombre⌐ huit
2. OUI, UHLAN, ULULEMENT
    Before <u>oui</u>, <u>uhlan</u>, or <u>ululement</u>:
        La particule⌐ oui
        Ce seul⌐ oui
        D'admirables⌐ uhlans
        L'effroyable⌐ ululement
3. Y+VOWEL
    Before a word beginning with <u>y+
    vowel</u>:
        Une belle⌐ yole
        Un superbe⌐ yacht
            EXCEPTIONS:
                des‿yeuses
                des‿yeux

4. ASPIRATED H
    Before a word beginning with <u>aspi-
    rated h</u>:
        L'horrible⌐ honte
        Le fidèle⌐ héros
        La belle⌐ housse
        Quelle⌐ haute⌐ haie
5. INTERJECTIONS
    Before an interjection:
        De terribles⌐ ah! s'échappaient
            de sa poitrine
        D'admirables⌐ oh!

IMPORTANT NOTE: A consonant or a group of consonants
used in linking, belong not to the vowel that precedes but
to the vowel that follows, thus forming a normal French
syllable: consonant plus vowel. Linking is usually required
between stress-groups. It is even heard, at times between
breath-groups.

Chapter XV.
ASSIMILATION
(CONSONANT HARMONY)

Assimilation is the phenomenon involving the modification of a voiced consonant by a voiceless consonant, or

vice versa.

This modification occurs whenever the two consonants are in complete contact, that is to say, when they are not separated by a sounded vowel. A mute e, in case it is not pronounced, does not prevent the complete contact of two consonants.

This modification may take place between consonants that are in the same word or between consonants that are in different words.

Assimilation does not occur between stress-groups.
There are two kinds of assimilation:
1. Regressive, which is the more usual.
2. Progressive, which does not often occur.

I. REGRESSIVE ASSIMILATION

1. When a voiced consonant occurs before a voiceless consonant the voiced consonant, through the influence of the voiceless becomes partly voiceless itself:

absolument, abcès, médecin, je tiens, grande table

2. When a voiceless consonant occurs before a voiced consonant, the voiceless consonant, through the influence of the voiced consonant, becomes partly voiced itself:

cette jeune fille, petite violette, une pêche verte

la puissante dame, un vif bavardage

In rapid pronunciation, the assimilation occurs naturally. In slow pronunciation it very seldom occurs.

Assimilation does not completely transform the nature of the assimilated consonant. One cannot say, for instance, that the t of puissante dame becomes a real d: the beginning of the consonant remains voiceless, that is to say, without vibrations, and part only of the consonant becomes voiced through the influence of the following voiced consonant. It is a voiced t and not a veritable d.

PROGRESSIVE ASSIMILATION

When voiceless s is placed before voiced m, m through the influence of s becomes voiceless too:

enthousiasme, journalisme, romantisme,
scepticisme, cataplasme, sarcasme, spasme,
judaïsme, catholicisme, paroxysme, organisme,
égoïsme, schisme

>Note 1. In English the inverse is true.
>Note 2. Some French people make the inverse assimilation here, that is to say, they permit voiced m to influence voiceless s so that it sounds nearly like z. But this pronunciation should be carefully avoided by the foreigner.

Chapter XVI.
VOWEL HARMONY
(Fr: HARMONIE VOCALIQUE)

Vowel harmony is the result of the influence of one vowel, (usually stressed) on the closing or opening of the preceding vowel.
Vowel harmony occurs in the following cases:
I. A <u>closed e closes an open e</u> which precedes:
   a. When the two vowels are separated by only one consonant:
      ailé, *ele*, aider, *ede*, démêler, *demele* , vous aimez, *vuzeme*, fêté, *fete*
   b. When the two vowels are separated by a double consonant (only one sound):
      guettez, *gete*, mettez, *mete*
   c. When the two vowels are separated by two inseparable consonants of which the second is <u>l</u> or <u>r</u>: Such groups are <u>bl</u>, <u>br</u>, <u>cl</u>, <u>cr</u>, <u>dr</u>, <u>fl</u>, <u>fr</u>, <u>gl</u>, <u>gr</u>, <u>pl</u>, <u>pr</u>, <u>tr</u>, <u>vr</u>:
      guettrez, *getre*, mettrez, *metre*
      NOTE: In all other cases, a <u>closed e does not close</u> a preceding open e:
         chercher, *ʃerʃe*, détester, *detestɛ* perler, *perle*, pester, *peste*
II. An <u>i</u> or <u>u</u> <u>closes an open e</u> which precedes:
   a. When the two vowels are separated by only one consonant:
      aigu, *egy*, aiguë, *egy*, engrêlure, *ãgrely:r*, plaisir, *plezi:r*
   b. When the two vowels are separated by a double consonant (only one sound):
      épaissir, *epesi:r*, blessure, *blesy:r*
   c. When the two vowels are separated by two inseparable consonants: (<u>bl</u>, <u>br</u>, <u>cl</u>, <u>cr</u>, <u>dr</u>, <u>fl</u>, <u>fr</u>, <u>gl</u>, <u>gr</u>, <u>pl</u>, <u>pr</u>, tr, <u>vr</u>).
      maigrir, *megri:r*,
      NOTE: In all other cases i or u does not close a preceding open e:
         architecture, *arʃitekty:r*, lecture, *lekty:r*, Mercure, *merky:r* perdit, *perdi*, perdu, *perdy*
III. A <u>closed eu closes an open eu</u> which precedes:
   heureux, *ørø*, malheureusement, *malørøzmã*, peureux, *pørø*, valeureux, *valørø*
IV. An <u>open o</u> preceded by the sound <u>z</u> <u>opens</u> a preceding <u>closed o</u>:
   myosotis, *mjɔzotis*, philosophe, *filɔzof*, théosophie, *teɔzofi*

V. Rarely, open e opens a closed e which precedes:
j'étais, ʒetɛ, il répétait, ilrɘpete
NOTE: The foreigner will notice that many French persons use indifferently the two different pronunciations:
ʒetɛ and ʒete

IMPORTANT REMARKS
I. Vowel harmony occurs only in the cases explained above. Contrary to what is often said, closed o does not close an open o which precedes:
copeau,kɔpo , dotaux,dɔto , loto,lɔto, pommeau, pɔmo
In words of the type of roseau, the first o is closed through the influence of z and not through the influence of vowel harmony.
II. Vowel harmony is a phenomenon essentially Parisian. The speech of many cultivated French persons who are not Parisian by birth or breeding has not yet been influenced by it. Consequently one often hears with an open e words such as:
plaisir, plɛziːr, aimer, ɛme, mettez, mɛte
That is why in the selections from French authors quoted in the Reading Lessons, the sounds susceptible to modification through vocalic harmony have not been underlined. For example, the first vowel of the word peignée, occurring on page 31, may through the influence of vocalic harmony be pronounced as a closed e, peɲe, but many French people prefer to preserve the open e, without however exaggerating the sound: pɛɲe.

Chapter XVII.
THE DOUBLE CONSONANT

As has been shown in the discussion of Syllabification and elsewhere, double consonants are generally pronounced as one single consonant. Under certain circumstances, however, they are pronounced, not as two separate consonants, it is true, but as one very much prolonged. This is the case as follows:
I. In future and conditional of the verbs courir, mourir, acquérir, conquérir:
Je courrais, nous mourrons, vous acquerriez, nous conquerrons
II. When the two letters of the double consonant are separated by a mute e:
Nous n∉ nommons pas, nett∉té, mêm∉ment, un aid∉ désireux d'agir, la petit∉ terrasse, une grand∉ dame, vous l∉ lirez, écout∉-t-il?

III. When the stress for emphasis falls on the double
consonant. (In this case even a single consonant
is sounded like a double consonant):
Immense
C'est *ravissant
Elle est *jolie au possible
Et votre *fier dédain
*Vivez, si m'en croyez
Je te dis *non, *non et *non
IV. In all words beginning with ill-:
Illustre, illogique, illettré
V. In rare, scientific, or literary words having a double
consonant:
distiller, intelligence
REMARK. More and more the pronunciation of the double
consonant as such is tending to disappear except in the
three first cases.

Chapter XVIII.
PRONUNCIATION OF H

The letter h is not a sound in French. It is merely an
orthographic sign, and therefore may be pronounced only in
combination with the consonants c and p whose pronunciation is thus modified.

Placed at the beginning or in the middle of a word, it
is said to be mute when its presence does not prevent
liaison or elision:
l'homme, un homme, l'héroine, bonheur
aux hommes

It is said to be aspirate when its presence indicates
the impossibility of liaison or elision:
des héros, la haine, en haut, dehors

The presence of an aspirate h causes a mute e which
precedes to be pronounced with the value of a true vowel:
une honte, l'horrible haine, la grande hâte

There are about six hundred words in French that begin
with an aspirate h. The majority of these words are rare or
scientific and generally of Germanic origin. The most common are:
SUBSTANTIVES
la hache, la haie, le haillon, la haine,
le hâle, le hall, la halle, la hallebarde,
la halte, le hamac, le hameau, la hanche,
le hanneton, la harangue, le hareng, le
haricot, la harpe, le hasard, la hâte, La
Havane, Le Hâvre, La Haye, le héraut, le
hère, le héros, le héron, le hêtre, le hibou,

la hiérarchie, la Hollandaise, le Hollandais, La Hollande, La Hongrie, la horde, la hutte
> Note 1. Words derived from héros have mute h:
> l'héroïne, l'héroïsme
> Note 2. In the expression:
> par hasard
> linking takes place.

ADJECTIVES
hagard,-e; hardi,-e; haut,-e; hideux, -euse

VERBS
haïr, hanter, haranguer, harasser, heurter (se), hurler

MISCELLANEOUS
en haut, hors, dehors, hormis

Chapter XIX.
PRONUNCIATION OF X

I. At the beginning of a word x is pronounced:
  a. k in the two following words:
     Xérès, $keres$ Ximénès, $kimenes$
  b. gz in the following words:
     Xantippe, $gz\tilde{a}tip$, Xénophon, $gzenofõ$, Xerxès, $gzerses$
  c. z in the following word:
     Xavier, $zavje$
  d. s in the following word (often written with an s):
     Xaintonge, $s\tilde{e}tõ:ʒ$
  e. ks in the following word:
     xylophone, $ksilofon$

II. In the middle of a word, x is pronounced:
  a. gz in words containing the prefixes; ex-, hex-, inex-, before a vowel or a mute h:
     exact, $egza$, examen, $egzam\tilde{e}$, exhumer, $egzyme$
     hexagone, $egzagon$, inexorable, $inegzorabl$
  b. z in the following words and words derived from them:
     deuxième, $døzjem$, dixième, $dizjem$,
     sixième, $sizjem$, dix-huit, $dizɥit$
     as well as in liaison:
     dix ouvrages, $dizuvra:ʒ$, heureux ami, $ørøzami$, malheureux hommes, $malørøzom$
  c. s in the following words:
     Auxerre, $ose:r$, Bruxelles, $brysel$,

dextrier, *destrije*, Saulxure, *sosyːr*, soixante, *swasɑ̃ːt*, and words derived from it.
  d. <u>ks</u> in all other words:
   expatrier, *ɛkspatrije*, inexplicable, *inɛksplikabl*, paradoxal, *paradoksal*
III. At the end of a word, <u>x</u> is pronounced <u>ks</u>:
 1. In the following words only, having the terminations:
  -<u>ax</u>:
   Ajax, pax, thorax
  -<u>aix</u>, -<u>eix</u>, -<u>ex</u>:
   Aix, Aix-la-Chapelle, Aix-les-Bains, codex, index, vertex, vortex
    In all other common words ending in -<u>aix</u>, <u>x</u> is not pronounced:
     paix̸, Roubaix̸
  -<u>ix</u>:
   Cadix, Félix, phénix, préfix, Vercingétorix
    In all other common words ending in -<u>ix</u>, <u>x</u> is not pronounced:
     perdrix̸, prix̸
    For the numerals <u>six</u> and <u>dix</u>, see Chapter XXI.
  -<u>inx</u>, -<u>ynx</u>:
   larynx, linx or lynx, pharynx
  -<u>ux</u>:
   fiat lux, Pollux
  -<u>yx</u>:
   onyx, Styx
 2. In all words having the terminations:
  -<u>xe</u>:
   boxe, complexe, fixe, luxe, paradoxe
  -<u>xes</u>:
   tu boxes, tu fixes, tu luxes

Chapter XX.
PRONUNCIATION OF DONC, PLUS, SENS, TANDIS QUE, TOUS.

DONC
I. When <u>donc</u> has the meaning of <u>consequently</u>, <u>therefore</u>, or when it stands alone, <u>c</u> is pronounced (like <u>k</u>):
   Je pense, don<u>c</u> je suis
   Je vois son chapeau, don<u>c</u> il est là
   Tu iras don<u>c</u> à la poste
   Don<u>c</u>, ainsi que je vous le faisais prévoir

II. In exclamatory sentences, where <u>donc</u> loses the meaning of <u>consequently</u>, the articulation of <u>c</u>, though most people make it silent, is optional:

    Allons donç! or Allons don<u>c</u>!
    Dis donç or Dis don<u>c</u>
    Dites donç or Dites don<u>c</u>
    Comment donç or Comment don<u>c</u>
    Ne pleure donç pas or Ne pleure don<u>c</u> pas
    Finissez donç or Finissez don<u>c</u>

PLUS

I. The <u>s</u> of <u>plus</u> is pronounced:
  a. When <u>plus</u> is the sign of an addition:
    2+3+5
    C'est mille francs plu<u>s</u> dix pour cent
    Vous êtes quatre plu<u>s</u> vos cousins
  b. When <u>plus</u> meaning <u>more</u> follows the verb (to avoid confusion with the negation):
    Elle n'en veut pas plu<u>s</u>
    J'en ai plu<u>s</u>
    Il en faut plu<u>s</u>
    Elle veut plu<u>s</u>
  c. In the following expression:
    Plu<u>s</u>-que-parfait

II. The pronunciation of <u>s</u>, in plus, is optional, when <u>plus</u> meaning <u>more</u>, is not placed after the verb and is not the mark of the comparison:
    Un peu plus et vous tombiez à l'eau, *ply* or *plys*
    Il y restera tout au plus deux ans, *ply* or *plys*

III. In all the other cases, <u>s</u>, in <u>plus</u>, is not pronounced:
  a. In the negation:
    Il n'est pluş dans sa chambre
    Jamais pluş je ne vous croirai
    Je n'en ai pluş
    Il n'en faut pluş
  b. When <u>plus</u> is used to form a comparison:
    Est-elle pluş grande ou pluş petite que moi?
    Il est pluş tard que je ne pensais
  c. In the expression <u>plus de</u> and <u>plus que</u>:
    J'ai pluş de livres que vous
    Pas pluş d'une heure
    A votre place, pluş d'un accepterait
    Pas pluş que vous
  d. In the following expressions:
    Tant et pluş   Sans pluş
    Ni pluş ni moins D'autant pluş
    Bien pluş   Tout au pluş

De plus̸   Au plus̸
In the following expressions, there is a
liaison, s sounding like z:
  Qui plus est
  De plus en plus
  Plus ou moins
        SENS
I. In the following expressions the final s of sens is
   silent:
        sens̸ dessus dessous
        sens̸ devant derrière
II. In the following expressions, the pronunciation of
the final s of sens is optional:
        sens commun   or sens̸ commun
        bon sens   or bon sens̸
III. In all other cases, final s of sens is pronounced
(always like s):
        j'ai cinq sens
        le sens de l'odorat
        dans un autre sens
        sens unique
        TANDIS QUE
S should be silent in tandis̸ que. Some cultured French
people, however, sound it.
        TOUS
I. In tous, pronoun, s is pronounced (always like s):
        Tous sont venus
        Ils les ont tous invités
        Ils les veut tous.
II. In tous, adjective, s is silent.
        Tous̸ les enfants
        J'ai vu tous̸ ceux dont il parle
        PUIS, PUISQUE
Although in puis the s is silent, in puisque it is
sounded.

            Chapter XXI.
        PRONUNCIATION OF THE NUMERALS

                A

PRONUNCIATION OF THE TEN FIRST NUMBERS, ACCORDING
        TO THEIR POSITION IN THE SENTENCE
I. Un
   a. Before a noun or adjective beginning with a vowel
      or mute h, when un limits the noun, liaison takes
      place without denasalization:
        un arbre, un autre arbre, vingt et un
        arbres, quatre-vingt-un arbres, un homme

 b. In dates, before a noun beginning with a vowel, liaison is optional:
   vingt-et-un‿avril, trente et un‿août
 c. In other cases, there is no liaison:
   un͜ Hollandais, un͜ et un font deux

II. **Deux**
 a. Before a noun or adjective beginning with a vowel or mute h, when deux multiplies the noun, liaison takes place, the x being pronounced like z:
   deux‿enfants, deux‿autres enfants, deux‿hommes
 b. In dates, before a noun beginning with a vowel, liaison is optional:
   le deux‿avril
 c. In other cases, the x is not pronounced:
   deuxꬸ tables, deuxꬸ hêtres, le deuxꬸ mai, j'en ai deuxꬸ
    EXCEPTIONS: In expressions such as the following, liaison usually takes place:
     deux‿à deux, deux‿ou trois, deux‿ou quatre, deux‿et deux font quatre

III. **Trois**
 a. Before a noun beginning with a vowel or mute h, when trois multiplies the noun, liaison takes place, the s being pronounced like z:
   trois‿élèves, trois‿aimables dames, trois‿horaires
 b. In dates, before a noun beginning with a vowel, liaison is optional:
   le trois‿août, le vingt-trois‿octobre
 c. In other cases, the s is not pronounced:
   troisꬸ, troisꬸ professeurs, troisꬸ homardsꬸ, troisꬸ et troisꬸ font six, le troisꬸ mai, le troisꬸ avril, j'en ai troisꬸ, une heure troisꬸ, Henri troisꬸ
    EXCEPTIONS: In expressions such as the following, liaison usually takes place:
     trois‿à trois, trois‿ou quatre

IV. **Quatre**
 a. Before words beginning with a consonant, the r, as well as the mute e, disappears, unless the pronunciation is extremely slow, as is sometimes the case when a teacher speaks to a class. The disappearance in rapid speech of these two sounds may be compared to a similar phenomenon in the English expression, "I'll do it." Although it is frequently written, "I will do it", there are few persons who do not, when speaking, use the contracted

form:
>> quat~~re~~ tables, quat~~re~~ livres, le quat~~re~~ mai

b. In all other cases r is pronounced very distinctly, and when followed by a word beginning with a vowel or mute h it is linked very closely with the first vowel of this word, so that in pronunciation the r becomes a part of its syllable (the mute e being suppressed):
>> quatr~~e~~ oncles, quatr~~e~~ ~~h~~orloges, le quatr~~e~~ août, quatr~~e~~ et quatr~~e~~ font huit, Henri quatr~~e~~, j'en ai quatr~~e~~

c. Before a noun or an adjective beginning with an aspirate h, the r and the mute e are both pronounced:
>> quatre] homards, quatre] hautes fenêtres, quatre] hardis voyageurs

V. Cinq

a. Before a noun or adjective beginning with a consonant or aspirate h, when cinq multiplies the noun, the q is not pronounced:
>> cin~~q~~ pupitres, cin~~q~~ petites filles, cin~~q~~ hussards

b. Although the pronunciation of q is optional when cinq occurs before the expression pour cent or in date before the name of a month beginning with a consonant, the present tendency is to sound q under such circumstances:
>> cinq pour cent, le cinq mai, le vingt-cinq septembre

c. In other cases q is pronounced like k, and when preceding a word beginning with a vowel or mute h, q is linked to its first vowel:
>> cinq, cinq ans, cinq anciens professeurs, cinq ~~h~~eures, une heure cinq, j'en ai cinq, Georges cinq

VI. Six

a. Before a noun or adjective beginning with a consonant or aspirate h, when six multiplies the noun, the x of six is not pronounced:
>> si~~x~~ crayons, si~~x~~ hamacs

b. Before a noun or adjective beginning with a vowel or mute h, when six multiplies the noun, the liaison takes place, the s sounding like z:
>> six articles, six ~~h~~éroïnes

c. Although the pronunciation of x is optional when six occurs before the expression pour cent or in a date before the name of a month beginning with a consonant, the present tendency is to sound x-- like s--under such circumstances:

six pour cent, le six novembre
- d. In other cases, that is to say at the end of a stress-group or before any word which six does not multiply, the s of six is pronounced like s:
j'en ai six, le six avril, nous sommes six, nous sommes six en tout, une heure six, Charles six

VII. Sept
NOTE: p in sept is never pronounced.
- a. Before a noun or adjective beginning with a consonant or aspirate h, when sept multiplies the noun, t may or may not be pronounced:
sep̸t̸ plumes, sep̸t̸ haies
- b. Although the pronunciation of t is optional when sept occurs before the expression pour cent or in a date before the name of a month beginning with a consonant, the present tendency is to sound t under such circumstances:
sep̸t pour cent, le vingt-sep̸t septembre, le dix-sep̸t novembre
- c. In other cases, t is pronounced, and when the word which follows begins with a vowel or mute h, t is linked to its first vowel:
sep̸t, sep̸t h̸irondelles, sep̸t oracles, j'en ai sep̸t, une heure sep̸t, Alphonse sep̸t

VIII. Huit
- a. Before a noun or adjective beginning with a consonant or aspirate h, when huit multiplies the noun, t is not pronounced:
hui̸t̸ jeunes filles, hui̸t̸ haricots
- b. Although the pronunciation of t is optional when huit occurs before the expression pour cent or in a date before the name of a month beginning with a consonant, the present tendency is to sound t under such circumstances:
huit pour cent, le huit mai, le vingt-huit juin
- c. In all other cases, t is pronounced, and when the word which follows begins with a vowel or mute h, t is linked to its first vowel:
huit, huit incidents, huit h̸érésies, j'en ai huit, une heure huit, Léon huit

IX. Neuf
- a. Before a noun or adjective beginning with a consonant, when neuf multiplies the noun, f may or may not be pronounced:
neuf chiens, neuf tables, neuf livres, etc.

b. Although the pronunciation of _f_ is optional when
neuf occurs before the expression pour cent or in
a date before the name of a month beginning with a
consonant, the present tendency is to sound _f_ under such circumstances:
neuf pour cent, le neuf mai, le dix-neuf juin
c. In other cases, _f_ is pronounced and when the word
which follows begins with a vowel or mute h, _f_ is
linked to its first vowel:
neuf, neuf accidents, neuf ḥistoires,
neuf hiboux, etc.
d. In two cases only, liaison of f takes place, _f_
sounding like _v_:
neuf ans, neuf ḥeures, nœvã, nœvœ:r

X. Dix
The same rules as for six.

B

11, ɔ̃:z
12, du:z
13, trɛ:z
14, katorz
15, kɛ̃:z
16, sɛ:z
17, disɛt
18, dizɥit
19, diznœf
20, vɛ̃
21, vɛ̃teœ̃
22, vɛ̃tdø
23, vɛ̃ttrwa
24, vɛ̃tkatr
25, vɛ̃tsɛ̃:k
26, vɛ̃tsis
27, vɛ̃tsɛt
28, vɛ̃tɥit
29, vɛ̃tnœf
30, trã:t
31, trãteœ̃
32, trãtdø
33, trãttrwa
34, trãtkatr
35, trãtsɛ̃:k
36, trãtsis
37, trãtsɛt
38, trãtɥit

39, trãtnœf
40, karã:t
41, karãteœ̃
42, karãtdø
43, karãttrwa
44, karãtkatr
45, karãtsɛ̃:k
46, karãtsis
47, karãtsɛt
48, karãtɥit
49, karãtnœf
50, sɛ̃kã:t
51, sɛ̃kãteœ̃
52, sɛ̃kãtdø
53, sɛ̃kãttrwa
54, sɛ̃kãtkatr
55, sɛ̃kãtsɛ̃:k
56, sɛ̃kãtsis
57, sɛ̃kãtsɛt
58, sɛ̃kãtɥit
59, sɛ̃kãtnœf
60, swasã:t
61, swasãteœ̃
62, swasãtdø
63, swasãttrwa
64, swasãtkatr
65, swasãtsɛ̃:k

66, swasɑ̃tsis
67, swasɑ̃tsɛt
68, swasɑ̃tɥit
69, swasɑ̃tnœf

70, swasɑ̃tdis
71, swasɑ̃teɔ̃:z
72, swasɑ̃tdu:z
73, swasɑ̃ttrɛ:z
74, swasɑ̃tkatorz
75, swasɑ̃tkɛ̃:z
76, swasɑ̃tsɛ:z
77, swasɑ̃tdisɛt
78, swasɑ̃tdizɥit
79, swasɑ̃tdiznœf

80, katr(ə)vɛ̃
81, katr(ə)vɛ̃œ̃
82, katr(ə)vɛ̃dø
83, katr(ə)vɛ̃trwa
84, katr(ə)vɛ̃katr
85, katr(ə)vɛ̃sɛ̃:k
86, katr(ə)vɛ̃sis
87, katr(ə)vɛ̃sɛt
88, katr(ə)vɛ̃ɥit
89, katr(ə)vɛ̃nœf

90, katr(ə)vɛ̃dis
91, katr(ə)vɛ̃eɔ̃:z
92, katr(ə)vɛ̃du:z
93, katr(ə)vɛ̃trɛ:z
94, katr(ə)vɛ̃katorz
95, katr(ə)vɛ̃kɛ̃:z
96, katr(ə)vɛ̃sɛ:z
97, katr(ə)vɛ̃disɛt
98, katr(ə)vɛ̃dizɥit
99, katr(ə)vɛ̃diznœf

100, sɑ̃
101, sɑ̃œ̃
102, sɑ̃dø
103, sɑ̃trwa

110, sɑ̃dis
111, sɑ̃ɔ̃:z

112, sɑ̃du:z

120, sɑ̃vɛ̃
121, sɑ̃vɛ̃teœ̃
122, sɑ̃vɛ̃tdø

200, døsɑ̃
201, døsɑ̃œ̃
202, døsɑ̃dø

300, trwasɑ̃
301, trwasɑ̃œ̃
302, trwasɑ̃dø

400, katr(ə)sɑ̃, katsɑ̃
401, katr(ə)sɑ̃œ̃, katsɑ̃œ̃
402, katr(ə)sɑ̃dø, katsɑ̃dø

500, sɛ̃sɑ̃
501, sɛ̃sɑ̃œ̃
502, sɛ̃sɑ̃dø

600, sisɑ̃
601, sisɑ̃œ̃
602, sisɑ̃dø

700, setsɑ̃
701, setsɑ̃œ̃
702, setsɑ̃dø

800, ɥisɑ̃
801, ɥisɑ̃œ̃
802, ɥisɑ̃dø

900, nøsɑ̃, nœfsɑ̃
901, nøsɑ̃œ̃, nœfsɑ̃œ̃
902, nøsɑ̃dø, nœfsɑ̃dø

1000, mil
1001, milœ̃, milœ̃
1002, mildø

1,000,000, œ̃miljɔ̃

1,000,000,000, œ̃milja:r

IMPORTANT REMARKS.
1. In **dix-ɥuit**, the **x** is pronounced like **z** even before **huit**, which ordinarily does not permit liaison;

in vingt-~~h~~uit, trent~~e~~-~~h~~uit, etc., the t of vingt, trente, etc., is thrown forward to become the first letter of the following syllable.
2. In quatre-vingt~~t~~-un, cent~~t~~-un, deux cent~~t~~-un, etc., there is no liaison between t and the following vowel.
3. There is strong assimilation:
  a. In dix-neuf, which causes x to sound like z.
  b. In vingt-deux, trente-deux, etc., which causes t to become voiced (but not in 82).
  c. In vingt-neuf, trente-neuf, etc., which causes t to become voiced (but not in 89).
4. The t, though sounded in 21, 22, 23, 24, 25, 26, 27, 28, 29, is silent in 81, 82, 83, 84, 85, 86, 87, 88, 89.
5. In soixante, x, although between two vowels, is pronounced, not like z but like s.

Chapter XXII.
PRONUNCIATION OF WRITTEN OU+VOWEL, U+VOWEL, AND I+VOWEL

Written ou, u, or i plus a vowel, is pronounced in a single syllable:
  a. alouette, $alwɛt$; allouons, $alwɔ̃$; jouer, $ʒwe$; Rouen, $rwɑ̃$; silhouette, $silwɛt$; Louis, lwi.
  b. duel, $dɥɛl$; nuage, $nɥa:ʒ$; puis, $pɥi$; Ruy, $rɥi$; celui, $səlɥi$; afféctueux, $afɛktɥø$.
  c. bien, $bjɛ̃$; rien, $rjɛ̃$; siège, $sjɛ:ʒ$; pied, pje; voyage, $vwaja:ʒ$; assiette, $asjɛt$; vous alliez, $vuzalje$; nous apportions, $nuzaportjɔ̃$; Assomption, $asɔ̃psjɔ̃$; congestion, $kɔ̃ʒɛstjɔ̃$; version, $vɛrsjɔ̃$.
      EXCEPTIONS:
      1. Written ou, u, or i plus a vowel if preceded by two consonants forming a so-called inseparable group belonging to the same syllable, is pronounced in two syllables. Such groups (of which the second consonant is always l or r) are: bl, br, cl, cr, dr, fl, fr, gl, gr, pl, tr, vr.
          a. brou-ette, $bru-ɛt$; é-blou-is-se-ment, $e-blu-is-mɑ̃$; trou-er, $tru-e$.
          b. cru-el, $krɥ-ɛl$; mons-tru-eux, $mɔ̃s-trɥ-ø$; obs-tru-er, $ɔbs-trɥ-e$.
          c. cen-dri-er, $sɑ̃-dri-je$; s'é-cri-a,

se-kri-ja ; ouv-ri-er, *u-vri-je* ; en-cri-er, *ã-kri-je*; pri-ère, *pri-jɛːr* ; su-**ppli**-er, *sy-pli-je* ; tri-angle, *tri-jãːgl*.

In such cases i is pronounced twice, i in the first syllable, and yod, j, in the second.

2. In the first and second person plural of the imperfect indicative and present subjunctive, written ou, or u, plus a vowel is pronounced in two syllables:
que vous nou-iez, *kə-vu-nu-je;*
que nous allou-ions, *kə-nu-za-lu-jɔ̃;*
que vous pollu-iez, *kə-vu-pɔ-ly-je;*
que vous tu-iez, *kə-vu-ty-je*

Note 1. When u, y, is followed by the vowel i, the combination is regularly pronounced in a single syllable:
autrui, *o-trɥi*; bruit, *brɥi* ; druide, *drɥid*

Note 2. Those forms of the verbs lier and rire in which the combination in either of the above ways (one or two syllables):
nous rions, *nurjɔ̃* or *nuri-jɔ̃*
vous liez *vulje* or *vuli-je*

Note 3. Those forms of the verb nier in which the combination i plus a vowel occurs are pronounced in two syllables:
nier, *ni-je* ; nous nions, *nuni-jɔ̃*

PART III

LEXICON

As has been said before, French is not a phonetic language. Not only may different combinations of letters be pronounced in the same way (as é, -er, -ez, etc.), but the same combinations of letters may be pronounced in different ways (as -tien, $tjɛ̃$, in chrétien, but $sjɛ̃$ in Egyptien).

Naturally, inasmuch as it is usage alone which determines the pronunciation of such letters or groups of letters in different words, they often prove puzzling to a foreigner.

In the following pages will be found lists of such spellings and the indication of their pronunciation, together with exceptions in common use. Thus, when a student in his reading outside this book comes across a word containing a group of letters for which he knows that different pronunciations exist under different circumstances, he may easily find which is the correct pronunciation by reference to this condensed lexicon. Immediately below the name of the sound under consideration I have placed the spellings which represent it. Sometimes the same spelling represents two different sounds--depending on the word in which it is located, the position which it occupies in the word, etc. This spelling therefore appears on two different pages, but with sufficient explanation so that the student need never be at a loss. The order will be seen to correspond to that in Part I, with the exception that I treat first of all the four principal vowels which may be either open or closed.

In general, I have treated the various sounds according to their position in the word--the four vowels just mentioned, first, when in the last pronounced syllable, second, when in other syllables; the vowels ou, u, u, y, i, and the nasal vowels, first, when the last sound, second when not the last sound of a word; yod, first, when at the end, second, when in the middle, third, when at the beginning of a word; the consonants, first, when at the beginning or in the middle, second, when at the end of a word; the semi-vowels ou, w, and u, $ɥ$, in one way only, by spelling. The student should always remember that since I am dealing primarily with sounds, the expression "last syllable" means last <u>pronounced</u> syllable. When, in order to show the timbre of a vowel, I include among the examples the first, second, or third person singular of a regular verb, it will of course be understood that this timbre remains unchanged throughout the conjugation of the verb. Plural forms are indicated in the list of spellings immediately following the title--op(s)--but among the examples will be found only the singular form.

I have included very few scientific words, and have used phonetic symbols only when I considered them absolutely necessary.

Parts I and III are designed to be used together. By study of the former the student will be enabled to produce the sound correctly; by reference to the latter he will be able to recognize the various orthographic forms under which the sound may appear.

Chapter XXIII.
POSTERIOR A, α

A-, -A-, Â-, -Â-, -AE-, -EA-, -(O)I-; -A(S), -ACS, -ARS, -AS, -AT(S), -ÂT(S), -(O)İ(S), -(O)İD(S), -(O)İDS, -(O)İE, -(O)İES, -(O)İE(S), -(O)İS, -(O)İT(S), -(O)İT, -(O)İX.

-A-

In the last syllable of a word, a is posterior:
I. When it is the last sound of a word and is written:
  1. -a. In the three following words only:
  fa (music), la (music), bêta.
  2. -acs. In the following word only:
  lacs (Eng. net; nets).
  3. -as. In the following words and their derivatives:
  amas, ananas, appas, bas, cas, cervelas, compas, coutelas, Dumas, échalas, fatras, fracas, glas, gras, Judas, las, lilas, Nicolas, pas, patatras, plâtras, ras, repas, tas, Thomas, tracas, trépas.
  4. -ars. In the following word only:
  gars.
  5. -at. In the following words only:
  chocolat, climat.
  6. -ât:
  bât, mât, etc.

EXCEPTIONS (a). Verbal forms:
qu'il allât, qu'il parlât, etc.

7 -(o)i, -oî-, -(o)id, -(o)ids, -(o)ie, -(o)ies, -(o)is -(o)it, -(o)ît, -(o)ix. (In these combinations o represents w, i and the following silent letters, if any, represent posterior a, α; the combination oi represents wα).
  a. When preceded by r, except in the endings -roisse, -roite:
  roi, froid, je crois, trois, endroit, il croît,

croix, etc.
  b. When not preceded by r, in the following words only:
  foi, loi, poids, j'emploie, joie, que je noie,
  oie, soie, voie, courtois, mois, pois, toit,
  choix, noix, poix.
II. When it is not the last sound of the word and is written:
  1. -â-, -â-:
  âge, albâtre, plâtre, etc.
                    ONLY EXCEPTIONS (a):
                    All verbal forms:
                      nous aimâmes, vous parlâtes,
                      vous dansâtes, etc.
  2. -a-, -a-:
   a. In the following spellings:
    α. -abre, -adre, -afle, -afre, -affre, -ase, -ases,
    -avre, -az, -aze:
      candélabre, cadre, rafle, balafre, affre,
      base, Le Hâvre, gaz, topaze, etc.
    β. -able. In the three following common words only:
      diable, il l'accable, sable.
    γ. -ace. In the two following words only:
      elle lace, espace.
    δ. -acle. In the following words only:
      miracle, oracle, tabernacle.
    ε. -aille, -ailles. In nouns:
      bataille, fiançailles, Versailles, etc.
                    ONLY EXCEPTIONS (a):
                    médaille, de Noailles.
    ζ. -ame. In the following words only:
      il acclame, elle déclame, je proclame, il
      s'exclame, il réclame.
    η. -ape:
      il dérape.
    θ. -asse. In the following words only:
      basse, casse, classe, grasse, lasse, passe.
    ι. -ate. In the following word only:
      Ponce-Pilate.
   b. In the following words:
    Anne, crabe, damne, gagne, flamme, Isaac,
    Jacques.
  3. -aë-. In the two following proper names:
    Ruisdaël, Staël.
  4. -(o)i-, -(o)î-. (In this combination o represents u, i, posterior a, a; the combinations oi, oî, represent wa).
  When preceded by r, except in the endings -roisse, -roite:
    froide, roide, croître, etc.

-B-
In any syllable in a word except the last, a is posterior when it is written:
I.â-, -â-:
ânonner, bâton, pâlir, etc.
II.-a-:
1. In the following terminations:
   a. -ason, -azon:
      blason, gazon, Jason, etc.
      ONLY EXCEPTION (a):
      diapason.
   b. -assion, -ation:
      conversation, location, passion, etc.
2. In the following common words and their derivatives: baron, bazar, brasier, carré, carreau, carosse, charron, graillon, haillon, Jacob, jadis, maçon, madré, marron, masure, poulailler, quasi, sarreau, satan, scabreux.
3. In general in the words derived from those which have a posterior a in the last syllable:
   batailleur from bataille; cadrer from cadre; damner from damne; endiablé from diable; espacer from espace; gagner from gagne; passage from passe; troisième from trois, etc.

IN OTHER CASES A IN ANY SYLLABLE OF A WORD EXCEPT THE LAST IS ANTERIOR.

REMARK. Posterior a varies progressively in degree from a sound produced only slightly farther back in the mouth than anterior a to one produced as far back as possible. The degree depends upon the word, the circumstances, the speaker.

Chapter XXIV.
ANTERIOR A, a

A-, -A-, -Â-, -E-, -(o)E-, -(o)Ê-, (o)I-, -(o)Î-, -(o)Y-; -A, -A(S), -AC(S), -AP(S), -AS, -AT, -AT(S), -ÂT, -ATS, -ÂT(S), -(o)Î, -(o)Ï(S), -(o)IE, -(oIE(S), -(o)IENT, -(o)IES, -(o)ÏGT(S), -(o)ÏS, -(o)ÏT, -(o)IX.

In the last syllable of a word a is anterior:
I. When it is the last sound of a word and is written:
   1. -a:
      ça, il a, opéra, va, etc.
      ONLY EXCEPTIONS (α):
      fa (music), la (music), bêta.
   2. -ac, -ap:
      drap, estomac, tabac, etc.

3. -as. In the following common words:
 bras, cadenas, canevas, chasselas, débarras,
 embarras, galetas, maletas, taffetas.
And in all verb forms:
 tu as, tu chantas, tu feras, tu iras, etc.
4. -at:
 avocat, délicat, etc.
>> ONLY EXCEPTIONS (a):
>> chocolat, climat.
5. -ât: In verb forms only:
 qu'il parlât, qu'il chantât.
6. _ats_:
 je bats.
7. -(o)i, -(o)ie, -(o)ient, -(o)ies, -(o)igt, -(o)is, -(o)it, -(o)ix. (In this combination o represents w, i and the following silent letters, if any, represent anterior a, a; the preceding combinations represent wa).
Not preceded by r, in the majority of words:
 moi, quoi, qu'il voie, qu'ils soient, que tu voies, doigt, je dois, voix, etc.
>> ONLY EXCEPTIONS (a):
>> foi, loi, poids, j'emploie,
>> joie, que je noie, oie, soie,
>> voie, courtois, mois, pois,
>> toit, choix, noix, poix.

II. When it is not the last sound of the word and is written:
1. -a-:
 a. In the following spellings:
  α. -able:
   adorable, aimable, épouvantable, etc.
>> ONLY EXCEPTIONS (a):
>> diable, il l'accable, sable.
  β. -ace:
   il l'agace, place, surface, etc.
>> ONLY EXCEPTIONS (a):
>> espace, elle lace.
  γ. -acle:
   obstacle, spectacle, etc.
>> ONLY EXCEPTIONS (a):
>> miracle, oracle, tabernacle.
  δ. ail, -ail:
   ail, détail, travail, etc.
  ε. -aille, -ailles. In the two following nouns only:
   médaille, de Noailles.
  And in verb forms:
   tu travailles, il taille, etc.
  ζ. -am, -ame:
   Abraham, dame, drame, etc.

ONLY EXCEPTIONS (a):
déclame, elle acclame, il s'exclame, elle le proclame, il réclame.

η.-asse:
chasse, je tracasse, masse, que j'embarrasse, que tu aimasses, terrasse, etc.
ONLY EXCEPTIONS (a):
basse, casse, classe, grasse, lasse, passe.

b. Before a double consonant:
balle, bizarre, datte, gramme, nappe, etc.
ONLY EXCEPTIONS (a):
Anne, enflamme, flamme.
NOTE: Double s (ss) has already been explained.

c. Before the consonant sounds: b, d, f, g, ʒ, k, l, n, p, r, t, v, ʃ, ɲ :
arabe, salade, girafe, bague, page, bac, balle, Diane, j'attrape, art, fat, brave, vache, bagne, etc.
ONLY EXCEPTION (a):
Ponce-Pilate.

d. Before the other groups of consonants which have not yet been mentioned either for posterior a or anterior a, namely: c+consonant, g+consonant, l+consonant, p+consonant, r+consonant, s+consonant, t+consonant, x=(ks):
acte, Ajax, algue, arme, astre, calme, marbre, Marne, quatre, remarque, enthousiasme, syntaxe, valse, etc.

2. -â-. In verb forms only:
nous aimâmes, vous dansâtes, etc.

3. -e-, -ê-. In the following words:
femme, moelle, poêle.

4. (o)i-, -(o)i-, -(o)î-. (In these combinations o represents w, i and the following silent letters, if any, represent anterior a, a; the combinations oi, oî, represent wa).

a. Preceded by r in the following terminations only: -oisse, -oite:
froisse, paroisse; droite, étroite; etc.

b. Not preceded by r, in the majority of words:
oiseau, angoisse, boîte, étoile, villageoise, etc.

Note 1. In solennel and its derivatives, in the derivatives of femme, moelle, poêle, as well as in adverbs in -emment, e is pronounced like anterior a, a:
solennité, femmelette, poêllée, moelleux, évidemment,

intelligemment, etc.
Note 2.In the proper name Jeanne, a may be either posterior or anterior.
Note 3.In any syllable in a word except the last, a is usually anterior, except in the cases already mentioned (p.160).

Chapter XXV.
CLOSED O, *o*

AU-, -AU-, HO-, O-, Ô-, -O-, -Ô-; -AO, -AU, -AU(X), -AUD(S) -AULD, -AULT, AULX, -AUT, -AUT(S), -AUX, -EAU(X), -O(S), -Ô, -OC(S), -OD, -OP, -OP(S), -OS, -OST, -OT(S), -ÔT(S).

-A-
In the last syllable of a word, o is closed:
I.When it is the last sound of the word and is written:
1.-ao, -au, -aud, auld, -ault, aulx, -aut, -aux, -eau, -o, -ô, -oo, -ost, -ôt:
curaçao, Pau, chaud, La Rochefoucauld, Hérault, aulx, il faut, faux, beau, domino, Pô, Waterloo, Prévost, rôt, etc.
2.-oc.In the following words only:
accroc, broc, croc, escroc, raccroc.
3.-od.In proper names only:
Gounod, Monod, Pernod, etc.
4.-op.In the following words only:
galop, sirop, trop.
> NOTE: Some French people make the o of trop open, but this practice is not to be recommended.
5.-os.In the following common words:
à propos, campos, chaos, clos, dispos, dos, éclos, enclos, gros, héros, os (plural), nos, propos, repos, vos.
> Note 1.In the following words, s is pronounced:
> albatros, albinos, Burgos, Calvados, Carlos, intra-muros, mérinos, tétanos.
> Note 2.In the following word, o is open and s pronounced:
> os (singular), *os*.
> Note 3.In the following word, s is pronounced and o is either closed or open:
> rhinocéros, *rinoseros*, or

6.-ot:
  escargot, Margot, etc.
      rinoseros.
    NOTE: In the following words, t
    is pronounced and o is open:
      dot, Lot.
II.When it is not the last sound of a word and is written:
  1.-aô-.In the following word:
    Saône.
  2.-au-, -au-:
    autre, Paule, pauvre, saute, etc.
      EXCEPTIONS (ɔ):
        a.Before r:
          Centaure, Laure, maure, etc.
        b.In the following words:
          Faust, Paul (compare with
          Paule).
  3.-o-.In the following terminations:
    a.-ome.In the following common words:
    arome, atome, axiome, Chrysostome, idiome, tome.
      Note 1.In the following words, o
      is open:
        agronome, astronome, économe,
        métronome, Sodome.
      Note 2.In the following words, o
      may be open or closed:
        autonome, gnome, hippodrome,
        majordome, vélodrome.
    b.-one.In the following common words:
    cyclone, zone.
      Note 1.In the following words, o
      may be open or closed:
        amazone, aphone, atone, autochtone, décagone, hexagone, octogone, ozone, polygone.
      Note 2.All the other words in
      -one, have an open o.
    c.-ose:
    arrose, chose, rose, etc.
    d.-osse.In the following words only:
    adosse, désosse, endosse, fosse, grosse.
  4.-ô-:
    drôle, j'ôte, le nôtre, le vôtre, etc.
  5.-os-.In the following word:
    Vosges.

-B-

In any syllable in a word except the last, o is closed, when it is written:

I. au-, -au-:
autrement, Pauline, pauvreté, etc.
    EXCEPTIONS (ɔ):
    a. Before r:
      j'aurai, Laurence, restaurant, etc.
    b. In the following words:
      cauchemar, encaustique, mauvais.
    c. In augmenter and its derivatives:
      augmentatif, augmentation, etc.
    d. In all the words beginning with auto:
      autobus, automobile, autorité,
              BUT
      auto with closed o, *oto*, as well as compound words in which auto, as a prefix, is joined to the remainder of the word by a hyphen:
      auto-suggestion.

II. o-, -o-:
  1. Before the sound z:
    j'oserai, position, rosette, etc.
      EXCEPTIONS (ɔ):
      cosaque, losange, myosotis, philosophe and its derivatives; théosophe and its derivatives; sosie.
  2. In words derived from dos, gros, fosse, os:
    adosser, désossement, dossier, endosser, fossé, grossir, grossier, ossement, etc.
      EXCEPTION (ɔ):
      fossette.
      NOTE: In the following words, o may be open or closed:
      fossoyement, fossoyer, fossoyeur.
  3. In the termination -otion:
    devotion, notion, etc.
  4. In the following words:
    momie, odeur, odieux, vomir, etc.

III. ô-, -ô-, hô-:
  j'ôterai, drôlerie, enrôlé, hôtesse, etc.
      NOTE: In the following words, ô may be open or closed, but open o is preferred:
      côté, côtelette, hôpital, hôtel, rôti, rôtir.

IN OTHER CASES o, IN ANY SYLLABLE OF A WORD EXCEPT THE LAST, IS OPEN.

Chapter XXVI.
OPEN O, ɔ

AU-, -AU-, O-, -O-, -Ô-, U(M).

In the last syllable of a word, o is open when it is written:
1.-au-:
  a.Before the sound r:
  Centaure, Laure, maure, Minotaure, etc.
  b.In the following words only:
  Faust, Paul (but Paule with closed o).
          NOTE: In all other words, -au- in the last syllable is closed.
2.-o-:
  a.In the following terminations:
  α.-ome.In the following common words:
  agronome, astronome, économe, métronome, Rome, Sodome.
          Note 1.In the following words, o is closed:
            arome, atome, axiome, Chrysostome.
          Note 2.In the following words, o may be open or closed:
            autonome, gnome, hippodrome, majordome, vélodrome.
  β.-one.In the following common words:
  anémone, Babylone, Barcelone, carbone, madone, matrone, monotone, Simone, téléphone, etc.
          EXCEPTIONS (o):
          cyclone, zone.
          NOTE: In the following words, o may be open or closed:
            amazone, aphone, atone, autochtone, décagone, hexagone, octogone, ozone, polygone.
  γ.-osse:
  bosse, brosse, gosse, etc.
          EXCEPTIONS (o):
          In the following words and their derivatives:
            adosse, désosse, endosse, fosse, grosse.
  b.And in all other cases where o is followed by one

or several pronounced consonants:
adopte, divorce, dogme, médiocre, quatorze, porte, école, globe, féroce, os (singular), moque, code, pope, dot, etc.
3. -u(m). In this combination, m is sounded:
album, maximum, pensum, rhum, etc.

> EXCEPTION (œ̃):
> The only exception is the following word, in which um is pronounced like the nasal un, œ̃ :
> parfum, *parfœ̃*.

IMPORTANT NOTE. O is never open when it is the last sound of a word.
GENERAL REMARKS.
1. O is silent in the following words:
faøn, Laøn, Laønnois, paøn, paønne, taøn.
2. Two successive o's are pronounced in two syllables and both are open (oɔ):
co-opérative, zo-ologie, etc.

> EXCEPTION (ɔ):
> alcool and its derivatives are pronounced with only one o, and that is open: *alkɔl*

3. ao is usually pronounced in two syllables (aɔ):
a-oriste, a-orte, extra-ordinaire.

> EXCEPTIONS (ɔ):
> In the following words -ao- and -aô- are pronounced in one syllable and sound like closed o:
> curaçao, Saône.

Chapter XXVII.
CLOSED E, *e*

AI-, -AI-, -AIE-, E-, -É-, -ÉE-; -AI, -AI(S), -AIS, -AIT, -É(S), -ÉE(S), -EF(S), -ER, -ER(S), -(ERS), -EZ, ET conjunction.

-A-
In the last syllable of a word, e is closed when it is written:
1. -ai.
  a. In verb forms:
  j'ai, j'aimerai, je chantai, je donnerai, etc.
  b. In the following words:
  gai, quai.
2. -ais, -ait. In the following words only (verb forms):
je sais, tu sais, il sait, je vais.

NOTE: Some French people pronounce these verb forms with an open e.

3. -é, -ée:
bonté, clé, donné, donnée, poupée, etc.
4. -e without written accent, in all Italian or Latin words:
fac simile, tolle, etc.
5. -ed. In the following word and its derivatives only:
pied.
6. -ef. In the following word:
clef.
7. eh, -eh.
eh! nargileh, (or nargilé).
8. -er, -ers:
aimer, boucher, léger, mener, porter, etc.
and the adverb:
volontiers.

EXCEPTIONS (ε):
In the following common words, e is open and r pronounced:
amer, cancer, cher, enfer, éther, fer, fier (adjective) but fier (verb) with closed e and silent r; hier, hiver, mer, revolver, ter, ver.

9. -es. In the six monosyllables:
ces, des, les, mes, ses, tes.

NOTE: In poetry, the e of these six monosyllables is open.

10. et. In the conjunction:
et.
11. -ez:
assez, dansez, nez, parlez, vous aimez, vous chantez, voyez, etc.

-B-

In any syllable in a word except the last, e is closed when written:

I. -ae:
Maeterlink.
II. -aie-. In derivatives of gai:
gaiement, gaieté, etc.
III. é-, -é-, -ée-:
édifice, Américain, bénéfice, général, phonétique, féerie, etc.
IV. -e-, without written accent when it is the last sound of a syllable in words of Latin, Italian, or English origin:
brasero, Montenegro, revolver, vice-versa, etc.

V.-oe:
   Oedipe, oesophage, etc.
   Note 1. In case of vowel harmony, any of the spellings of open e may become closed:
   aigu, *egy*; aisé, *eze*; bêtise, *beti:z*; plaisir, *plezi:r*; etc.
   Note 2. In the following prefixes e may be open or closed:
   desc-, dess-, eccl-, eff-, ex-:
   descendre, dessiner, ecclésiastique, effacer, examen, exhumer, etc.
   IN OTHER CASES E, IN ANY SYLLABLE OF A WORD EXCEPT THE LAST, IS OPEN.

Chapter XXVIII.
OPEN E, ε

AI-, -AI-, -AIE-, -E-, -È-, -Ê-, -Ë-, -EI-, -EY-; -AI, -AID(S), -AIE, -AIE(S), -AIENT, -AIES, -AIS, -AIT, -AÎT, -AY, -AIX, -E-, -È-, -Ê-, -EI-, -EY-, -ECT(S), -EGS, -ES, -EST, -ET(S), -ÊTS, -EY, HAIE, HAIS, HAIT.

In the last syllable of a word, e is open:
I. When it is the last sound of a word and is written:
   1. -ai, -aid, -aie, -aient, -aies, -ais, -ait, -aît, -ay -egs, -es, est, -et, -ets, -êt, -ey, haie, hais, hait.
   geai, laid, baie, qu'ils aient, que tu aies, j'aimerais, il prendrait, il paraît, Charlotte Corday, legs, tu es. il est, jouet, je mets, genêt, Vevey, haie, hais, il hait, etc.
   EXCEPTIONS (e):
   a. -ai. In verb forms:
   je danserai, je parlai, etc.
   and in the following words:
   gai, quai.
   b. -ais, -ait. In the following words:
   je sais, tu sais, il sait, je vais.
   NOTE: Some French people pronounce these verb forms with an open e.
   2. -aix:
   faix, paix, Roubaix, etc.
   NOTE: In the following words x is pronounced ks:
   Aix, Aix-la-Chapelle, Aix-les Bains.

3.-e̶c̶t̶.In the following words only:
anspe¢t̶, aspe¢t̶, circonspe¢t̶, suspe¢t̶, respe¢t̶.
> Note 1.In derivatives of the preceding words, ct is pronounced:
> > respectueux, suspecter, etc.
>
> Note 2.In the following words and their derivatives, ct is pronounced:
> > abject, correct, direct, infect.

4.-ès:
expres, près, succès, très, etc.
> NOTE: In the following common words, s is pronounced:
> > Agnès, aloès, cacatoès, Cérès, Damoclès, ès, Méphistophélès, palmarès, pataquès, Périclès, Xérès.

II. When it is not the last sound of a word and is written:
1. -ai-, -aie-, -è-, -ê-, -ë-, -ei-, -ey-:
laide, paiement, zèle, bête, Ismaël, reine, Seyne, etc.
2. e without written accent, when it is followed by one or more pronounced consonants in the same syllable:
Albert, amer, avec, chef, commerce, Elizabeth, mettre, reste, romanesque, terre, etc.

Chapter XXIX.
CLOSED EU, Ø

-EU, -EU-, -EÛ-, HEU-, -HEU-; -EU(X), -EUE(S), -OEUD(S), -OEUF(S), -EUT.

-A-
In the last syllable of the word, eu is closed:
I. When it is the last sound and is written:
-eu, -eue, -oeu, -oeud, -oeufs, -eus, -eut, -eux:
adieu, queue, voeu, noeud, boeufs, je me meus, il peut, je veux. etc.
II. When it is not the last sound of a word and is written:
-eu, -eu-, -eû-, heu-:
1. Before the sound z:
creuse, heureuse, Meuse, etc.
2. In the following terminations:
a.-eude, -eudes, -euges, -eûne, -eute, -eutre:
leude, Eudes, Maubeuge, jeûne (fasting) but jeune (young) with open eu; emeute, neutre, etc.
b.-eugle.In the two following words:

il beugle, il meugle.
   c.-eule. In the two following words:
   meule, veule.
  3. In unusual or scientific words:
   Zeus, Pentateuque, etc.
                        -B-
  In any syllable of a word except the last, eu is closed:
 I. In all words derived from those in which eu is closed
in the last syllable:
   bleuir from bleu; deuxième from deux; meuglait
   from meugle; neutralité from neutre; veulerie from
   veule, etc.
 II. In the following words also:
   Eugène, Eugénie, Eulalie, jeudi, meunier, Meurice
   (Hôtel).
III. In unusual or scientific words:
   Deutéronome, eucalyptus, euphonie, leucocyte,
   thérapeuthie.
 IV. As a result of vowel harmony:
   heureux, peureux, etc.
  IN OTHER CASES EU, IN ANY SYLLABLE OF A WORD EXCEPT THE
LAST, IS OPEN.

                      Chapter XXX.
                      OPEN EU, œ

EU-, -EU-, HEU-, -HEU-, -OEU-, OEI-, -U-.

  In the last syllable of a word, eu is open:
 I. When it is written:
  1.-eu-. In the following terminations:
   a.-euble:
    meuble, etc.
   b.-euf, -oeuf:
    neuf, boeuf, but boeufs (plural) with closed eu and
    silent f, bø; oeuf, but oeufs (plural) with closed
    eu and silent f, ø.
   c.-eugle. In the following word:
    aveugle.
   d.-euil, -ueil, -euille, -ueille, oeil:
    fauteuil, accueil, feuille, cueille, oeil, etc.
   e.-eul, -eule:
    seul, aïeule, etc.
                   EXCEPTIONS (ø):
                    meule, veule.
   f.-eune:
    déjeune, jeune.
   g.-eur, -eure, -eurre, -oeur:

meilleur, meilleure, beurre, coeur, etc.
2. heu-, -heu-:
heure, malheur, etc.
3. -u-. In words borrowed from the English:
club, tub, etc.

> NOTE: All such words may also be pronounced with u, *y*:
> *klyb, tyb.*

Chapter XXXI.
OU, *u*

AOÛ-, HOU-, HOUL-, OU-, -OU-, -OÛ-, -OUE-, -OUL-, -OW-; -AOUL, -OU(S), -OU(X), -OUBS, -OUD, -OUDS, -OUE, -OUE(S), -OUENT, -OUES, -OUL, -OÛL, -OULD, -OULS, -OUP(S), -OUS, -OUT, -OUT(S), -OÛT(S), -OUX, AOÛT, HOUE, HOUX.

I. When it is the last sound of a word, ou is written:
  1. -aoul, -ou, -oubs, -oud, -ouds, -oue, -ouent, -oues, -oûl, -ould, -ouls, -oup, -ous, -out, -oût, -oux:
  saoul, sou, Doubs, elle coud, tu mouds, je joue, ils louent, tu joues, soûl, Sainte-Menehould, pouls, loup, dessous, tout, goût, Chateauroux, etc.

II. When it is not the last sound of a word, ou is written:
  1. hou-, houe-, houl-, ou-, -ou-, -oû-, -oue-, -ow-:
  hourra, houement, houlque, outrage, mouton, coûter, dévouement, clown, *klun*, etc.
  2. aoû-. In the following word only:
  aoûteron.

Note 1. The following words are pronounced as one sound only:
houe, houx.

Note 2. In the following word the pronunciation of t is optional:
août, *u or ut.*

> NOTE: For the spelling ou representing the semi-vowel *w*, see page 155.

Chapter XXXII.
I, *i*

HI-, HY-, -HI-, -HY-, I-, -I-, -Î-, -Ï-, -IE-, -IS-, -Y-; -I, -I(S), -I-, -IC(S), -ID(S), -IE, -IE(S), -ÏE, -IENT, -IES, -ÏES, -IL(S), -IS, -ÎS, -IT, -IT(S), -ÎT, -ÏT, -IX, -IZ, -Y, -Y(S), -YS, -YE(S).

I. When it is the last sound of a word, i is written:
1. -hi, -i, -î, -ie, -ïe, -ient, -ies, -ïes, -is, -ïs, -it, -ït, -ît, -iz, -y, -ye, -ys.
trahi, ceci, Sinaï, je prie, Isaïe, ils prient, que tu ries, elles sont haïes, tu fis, je haïs (preterit), il fit, il haït (preterit), qu'il dît, riz, Annecy, abbaye, pays, etc.

> NOTE: In the following common words in -it, -ït, t is pronounced:
> accessit, aconit, affidavit, Christ, but Jésus-Chri$\cancel{st}$ with s and t silent, *Ʒezykri*; granit, huit (see page 152); introït, prétérit, transit.

2. -ic. In the following word only:
cric.

> NOTE: In other words, c is pronounced and has the sound of k: alambic, sic, etc.

3. -id. In the two following words:
muid, nid.

> Note 1. In other words d is pronounced:
> Cid, crid, David.
> Note 2. In Madrid the pronunciation of d is optional.

4. -il. In the following words only:
baril, chenil, courtil, coutil, douzil, fenil, fournil, fusil, gentil, gril, nombril, outil, persil, sourcil.

> Note 1. In other words, l is pronounced:
> Brésil, cil, fil, Nil, etc.
> Note 2. In fi$\cancel{l}$s (Eng. son; sons), l is not pronounced, but s is sounded, *fis*.

5. -is.
a. In all verb forms:
tu dis, je vis, etc.
b. In the following words:
Alexis, avis, bis (color) but bis (encore) with s sounded, (*bis*); brebis, colis, coloris, commis, compromis, concis, croquis, depuis, devis, Etats-Unis, exquis, gris, hormis, logis, louis, malappris, marquis, mépris, paradis, permis, pis, précis, promis, puis, radis, Saint-Denis, souris, tapis, vernis, vis-à-vis.

6. -ix. In the three following words only:
crucifix, perdrix, prix.

NOTE: In the following common words x=ks:
Cadix, Félix, phénix, préfix, Vercingétorix.

II. When it is not the last sound of a word, i is written:
1. hi-, hy-, -hi-, i-, -î-, -i-, -î-, -ie-, -y-:
hiver, hygiène, trahison, idéal, discipline, naïf, abîme, licenciement, analyse, etc.

NOTE: ie placed before a double mm is pronounced with yod and anterior a, ja:
sciemment, sjamã, etc.

2. -is-. In the following words only:
Fismes, Vismes.

NOTE: For the spelling i representing yod, see p. 155.

Chapter XXXIII.
U, y

HU-, -HU-, U-, -U-, -Û-, -Ü-, -EÛ-; EU(S), EUE(S), EUS, EUT, EÛT, -HU, -HUE, -HUES, -HUT(S), -U, -U(S), -Û, -Û(S), -UE, -UE(S), -UE(S), -UES, -US, -UT, -UT(S), -ÛT, -ÛT(S), -UX.

I. When it is the last sound of the word, u is written:
-hu, -hue, -hues, -hut, -u, -û, -ü, -ue, -ûe, -ue, -ues, -ûes, -us, -ut, -ût, -ux:
tohu-bohu, hue, tu hues, chahut, absolu, dû, Esaü, je tue, dûe, aiguë, tu le tues, dûes, dessus, il vécut, attribut, qu'il fût, affût, afflux, etc.

II. When it is not the last sound of a word u is written:
hu-, -hu-, u-, -u-, -û-:
huguenot, inhumain, unanime, aucune, flûte, vous fûtes, etc.

IMPORTANT REMARK. In the following forms of the verb avoir only, eu is pronounced u, y:
j'eus, tu eus, il eut, nous eûmes, vous eûtes, ils eurent qu'il eût; eu, eue, eus, eues, past participle.

NOTE: For the spelling u representing the semi-vowel ɥ, see p. 155.

Chapter XXV.
AN, ã

-AEN-, AM, -AM-, AN-, -AN-, EM-, -EM-, -EMP-, EN-, -ANG-,

-AEN, -AM, -AMP, -AMP(S), -AN, -AN(S), -ANC(S), -AND,
ANDT, -AND(S), -ANG(S), -ANS, -ANT, -ANT(S), -AON, -AON(S),
-EAN, -EMPS, -EMPT, -EMPT(S), -EN, -END, -END(S), -ENDS, -ENG(S),
-ENS, -ENT, -ENT(S).

I. When it is the last sound of a word, the sound an, $\tilde{a}$, is written:
  1. -aen, -amp, -an, -anc, -and, -ang, -ans, -ant, -ean, -emps, -empt, -end, -ends, -eng:
  Caen, Fécamp, camp, océan, banc, quand, allemand, rang, dans, maintenant, enfant, Jean, temps, longtemps, exempt, il apprend, tu vends, hareng, etc.
  2. -am. In the following words only:
  Adam, dam.

  NOTE: In all other words in -am, the vowel is not nasalized and m is sounded:
  Cham, islam, macadam, etc.

  3. -aon. In the following words:
  faon, Laon, paon, taon.

  NOTE: In the following words, aon is pronounced in two syllables, anterior a+on:
  phara-on, Lyca-on

  4. -en. In the following word only:
  Rouen, $rw\tilde{a}$

  Note 1. In the following common words en is not nasalized, e is pronounced like open e and n is sounded:
  abdomen, albumen, amen, Beethoven, cyclamen, eden, gluten, hymen, lichen, pollen, Reischoffen, specimen.
  Note 2. Preceded by i, en is always pronounced like in, $\tilde{\epsilon}$.
  bien, sien, etc.
  Note 3. In all other common words, en is pronounced like in, $\tilde{\epsilon}$.
  Agen, européen, examen, etc.

  5. -ens:
  dépens, encens, j'assens, suspens, tu mens, tu sens, etc.

  NOTE: In the following words s is sounded:
  cens, sens and its derivatives (contresens, non-sens).
  EXCEPTIONS:

a.($\tilde{\epsilon}$).In verb forms:
je viens, tu maintiens, etc.
b.($\widetilde{\epsilon s}$):
Rubens, *rybɛ̃ːs*

6.-ent:
agent, bonnement, il consent, orient, etc.
EXCEPTIONS:
a.($\tilde{\epsilon}$).In verb forms, third person singular, if preceded by i, ent is pronounced in, $\tilde{\epsilon}$:
il tient, il vient, etc.
b.(ə).When ent is the mark of third person plural of verb, it represents a mute e:
ils parlent, *ilparl*, etc.

II.When it is not the last sound of a word, the sound an, $\tilde{a}$, is written:
1.-aën-.In the following proper name:
Saint-Saëns, *sɛ̃sɑ̃ːs*.
2.am-, -am-.Before b and p:
ambassadeur, ambition, lampe, etc.
NOTE: Before m, n, or a vowel, am is not nasalized. It is pronounced like anterior a, and m is sounded with the next syllable:
amener, *amne*, ammoniaque, *amonjak*, amnistie, *amnisti*, flammèche, *flamɛʃ*, ramification, *ramifikasjɔ̃*
3.an-.Before any consonant except n:
ancêtre, ange, danser, etc.
NOTE: Before a vowel or another n, an is not nasalized, and it is pronounced like anterior a; n is then sounded with the next syllable:
anecdote, *a-nɛk-dɔt*, année, *a-ne*, sanitaire, *sa-ni-tɛːr*, etc.
4.em-, -em-.Before b, p and m:
embrasser, emmener, empereur, décembre, remporter,etc.
EXCEPTIONS:
a.(a).In adverbs in -emment; as well as in femme, moelle, poêle, solennel and their derivatives, e is pronounced like anterior a; mm is then pronounced m and sounded with the next syllable:

femmelette, *famlɛt*, intelligemment, *ɛ̃-tɛl-li-ʒa-mã̃*, patiemment, *pa-sja-mã̃*, etc.
b.(ɛm).Before me at the end of a word, em (except in femme mentioned above) is pronounced like open e and mm is sounded m: dilemme, *dilɛm*, gemme, *ʒɛm*, etc.

5. en-, -en-. Before any consonant except another n: ascenseur, cens, contresens, enfer, non-sens, pentecôte, science, etc.

EXCEPTIONS: (ɛ̃). In words of Latin or foreign origin, and their derivatives, en is pronounced in, ɛ̃. The most common of these words are:
agenda, appendice, benjamin, benzine, pensum, Pensylvanie, Stendahl.

NOTE: Before a vowel or another n, en usually is not nasalized, e is pronounced like an open e. n is sounded:
doyenne, *dwajɛn*; enigme, *ɛnigm*; ennéade, *ɛnead*; ennemi, *ɛnmi*; énorme, *ɛnɔrm*; etc.

BUT in the following words and their derivatives, en is nasalized and pronounced an, ã, while n sounds also with the next syllable:
enamourer, *ã-na-mu-re*, enivrant, *ã-ni-vrã*, ennoblir, *ã-no-bli:r*, ennui, *ã-nɥi*, enorgueillir, *ã-nɔr-gœ-ji:r*.

6. -ang-. In the following word: sangsue.

7. -emp-. In forms of the following verb: exempter, j'exempte, etc.

BUT exemption has sounded p.

GENERAL NOTE. Em at the end of a word is not nasalized, and it is pronounced like an open e plus m, *ɛm*: Bethléem, hem! Jerusalem, etc.

Chapter XXXIV.
ON, ɔ̃, ɔ̃

OM-, -OM-, ON-, -ON-, -ONT-, UN-; -OM, -OM(S), -OMB,

-OMB(S), -OMPS, -OMPT, -ON, -ON(S), -ONC(S), -OND, -OND(S), -ONDS, -ONG(S), -ONS, -ONT, -ONT(S).

I.When it is the last sound of a word, the sound on, $\tilde{o}$, is written:
  1.-om, -omb, -omps, -ompt, -on, -ond, -onds, -ong, -ons, -ont.
  Riom, nom, Christophe Colomb, plomb, je romps, prompt, Didon, il répond, profond, tu confonds, long, nous allons, ils font, pont, etc.
  2.-onc.In the three following words only:
  ajonc, jonc, tronc.
                NOTE: In the following word, c is often pronounced like k: donc (see p. 147).

II.When it is not the last sound of a word, the sound on, $\tilde{o}$, is written:
  1.om-, -om-:
    a.Before b or p:
    accompagner, nombre, ombre, etc.
    b.In the following words:
    comte and its derivatives; Domrémy.
  2.-omp-.In the following words and their derivatives:
  compte, dompte, prompte.
  3.-on, -on-.Before any consonant except n:
  bonté, monde, oncle, etc.
  4.-ong-.In the following word:
  longtemps.
  5.-ont-.In words derived from mont:
  mont-de-piété, Montmartre, Montmorency, Montparnasse, etc.
  6.un-, -un-.In unusual words from Latin and in the following common words:
  de profundis, $deprof\tilde{o}dis$, punch, $p\tilde{o}{:}ʃ$, secundo, $seg\tilde{o}do$, etc.

Chapter XXXVI.
IN, $\tilde{\epsilon}$

AIN-, -AIN-, -EIM-, -EIN-, EN-, -EN-, IM-, -IM-, IN-, -IN-, -YM-, -YN-; -AIM(S), -AIN, -AIN(S), -AINC, -AINCS, -AINS, -AINT, -AINT(S), -EIN, -EIN(S), -EING(S), -EINS, -EIN(S), -EINT, -EINT(S), -EN, -EN(S), -(I)ENS, -(I)ENT, -IN(S), -INCT(S), -ING(S), -INGT(S), -INS, -INT, -INT(S), ÎNT, -YM.

I.When it is the last sound of a word, the sound in, $\tilde{\epsilon}$, is written:
  1.-aim, -ain, -ainc, -aincs, -ains, -aint, -ein,

eing, -eins, -eint, -(i)en, -(i)ens, -(i)ent, -in,
-ing, -ingt, -ins, -int, -înt, -ym:
faim, Ain, américain, il vainc, tu convaincs,
je plains, il craint, saint, hein, plein, seing,
je peins, dessein, il teint, teint, sien, maintien, je viens, il tient, Berlin, vin, poing,
vingt, j'appartins, elle vint, qu'il vînt, qu'il
tînt, thym, etc.
2.-en:
Agen, européen, examen, moyen, etc.
     EXCEPTIONS:
     a.($\tilde{a}$).In the following word:
      Rouen,
     b.(εn).In the following words, en
     is not nasalized and it is pronounced open e plus n:
      abdomen, albumen, amen, Beethoven, cyclamen, eden, gluten,
      hymen, lichen, pollen, Reischoffen, spécimen.
3.-inct.In the two following words only:
  instinct, succinct.
     Note 1.In words derived from the
     two above, ct is pronounced:
      instinctivement, succincte, etc.
     Note 2.In the following word and
     its derivatives, ct is pronounced:
      distinct, distinction, etc.
II.When it is not the last sound of a word, the sound in,
$\tilde{\varepsilon}$, is written:
  1.ain-, -ain.Before any consonant:
  ainsi, craindre, plaintivement, etc.
     NOTE: Before a vowel, ain is not
     nasalized; it is pronounced like
     open e, and n is sounded:
      aine, Bazaine, douzaine, Maine,
      vingtaine, etc.
  2.-eim-:
  Reims,
  3.-ein-:
  ceinture, peindre, teinte, etc.
     NOTE: Before a vowel ein is not
     nasalized; it is pronounced like
     open e, and n is sounded:
      peine, Seine, etc.
  4.en-, -en-:
  a.en-.In the two following words only:
   endécagone, endécasyllabe.

b.-en-. Generally in scientific, rare or unusual words of Latin or Italian origin, and their derivatives, as well as in the following more common words:
agenda, appendice, benjamin, benzine, pensum, Pensylvanie, Stendahl.

5. im-, -im-. Before b or p:
imbécile, impossible, simple, timbre, etc.

NOTE: Before a vowel or another m, im is not nasalized and m is sounded with the next syllable:
image, immobile, limite, etc.
In the three following words, and their derivatives, i may or may not retain its nasal quality: immangeable, $\tilde{\varepsilon}$-$m\tilde{a}$-$zabl$ or $m\tilde{a}$-$zabl$; immanquable, $\tilde{\varepsilon}$-$m\tilde{a}$-$kabl$ or i-$m\tilde{a}$-$kabl$; immesurable $\tilde{\varepsilon}$-$m\vartheta$-zy-$rabl$ or i-$m\vartheta$-zy-$rabl$.

6. in-, -in-, -în-. Before any consonant except n:
incapable, nous maintînmes, prince, etc.

NOTE: Before a vowel or mute h or another n, in is not nasalized and n is sounded with the next syllable:
binocle, inhumain, innocence, inutile, sinistre, etc.

7. -ym-, -yn-. Before any consonant:
larynx, lymphatique, lyncher, nymphe, etc.

GENERAL NOTE. Im at the end of a word is not nasalized and m is sounded:
interim, Joachim, $zoakim$; olim, etc.

Chapter XXXVII.
UN, œ̃

HUM-, -UN-; -EUN, -EUNG, HUN(S), -UM(S), -UN, -UN(S), -UNT(S).

I. When it is the last sound of the word, the sound un, œ̃, is written:
1. -eun, -eung, hun, un, -un, -unt:
à jeun, Jean de Meung, Hun, un, Verdun, emprunt, etc.
2. -um. In the following word only:
parfum.

NOTE: In all other words in -um, u is pronounced like open o, and

m is sounded:
album, maximum, opium, etc.
II. When it is not the last sound of the word, the sound un, $\tilde{œ}$, is written:
1. hum-:
humble.

NOTE: hum before a vowel is not nasalized, and m is sounded with the next syllable:
humanité, humilité, humour, etc.

2. -un-:
défunte, emprunte and its derivatives; pétunsé.

Note 1. Un before a vowel is not nasalized and n is sounded with the next syllable:
brunette, unanime, union, etc.

Note 2. In scientific and unusual words of Latin origin, un placed before a consonant is pronounced on, $ɔ̃$:
uncial, etc.
and also in the following more common words:
punch, $pɔ̃:ʃ$, secundo, $səgɔ̃do$.

Chapter XXXVIII.
SEMI-VOWEL OU, u

HOU(+vowel), O(+e), O(+ê), OU(+vowel), (q)U(+a), (g)U(+a), O(+i), O(+ids), O(-id)(s), O(+ie), O(+ie)(s), O(-ies), O(+igt)(s), O(+in), O(+in)(s), O(+ing)(s), O(+ins), O(+int)(s), O(+is), O(+it), O(+it)(s), O(+ix), O(+y), -OO(ing).

The sound u is written as follows:
I. hou(+vowel):
houache, houette, etc.
II. o(+e), o(+ê). In the following words and their derivatives, e is sounded like anterior a:
moelle, $mwal$; poêle, $pwal$; etc.

NOTE: In all other words oè is pronounced in two syllables, open $ɔ$, $ɔ$, and open e, $ɛ$:
po-ète, $pɔ-ɛt$; tro-êne, $trɔ-ɛn$, etc.

III. o(+i), o(+id), o(+ids), o(+ie), o(+ies), o(+igt), o(+in), o(+ing), o(+ins), o(+int), o(+is), o(+it), o(+ix):
oiseau, moitié, roi, froid, poids, que je voie,

que tu t'asseoies, doigt, loin, lointain, coing, moins, point, que tu sois, qu'il soit, exploit, choix, etc.

EXCEPTIONS: In the following words and their derivatives, oi is pronounced like open o, ɔ: encoîgnure, ãkɔɲy:r, moîgnon, mɔɲɔ̃, oignon, ɔɲɔ̃.

IV. o(y):
croyant, incroyable, loyal, loyauté, etc.

EXCEPTIONS (ɔ):
In the following words o retains its quality of open o:
boyard, bɔ-ja:r , oyant, ɔ-jã.

V. -oo(+ing): In the following word borrowed from the English:
schampooing,

VI. ou(+vowel):
louis, ouest, oui, etc.

EXCEPTIONS (u):
a. When preceded by two consonants forming a so-called inseparable group belonging to the same syllable, ou plus a vowel is pronounced in two syllables. The groups of inseparable consonants are:
bl, br, cl, cr, dr, fl, fr, gl, gr, pl, pr, tr, vr:
brouette, bru-ɛt ; éblouissement, e-blu-is-mã; trouer, tru-e , etc.

b. In the first and second person plural of the imperfect indicative and present subjunctive, ou plus a vowel is pronounced in two syllables:
vous nou-iez, vu-nu-je , que nous allou-ions, ke-nu-a-lu-jɔ̃, etc.

VII. (q)u(+a), (g)u(+a). In scientific or unusual words of which the majority are of Latin origin. The most usual are:
adéquat, aquarelle, aquarium, équateur, équation, in-quarto, loquace, quadrangulaire, quadruple, quartette, quatuor, quaternaire, square, Guadeloupe, jaguar, lingual, Nicaragua, Paraguay.

NOTE: In all other usual words qua is pronounced ka; and gua, ga:

qualité, quantité, quatre,
légua, navigua, etc.
VIII.-hu, -o(+a):In the following words:
cacahuète, ka-ka-wɛt, joaillier, ʒwa-je, Roanne,
rwan

Chapter XXXIX.
SEMI-VOWEL U, ɥ

HU(+i), U(+vowel), (q)U(+e or i), (g)U(+i).

The sound ɥ is written as follows:
I. hu(+i):
aujourd'hui, huile, huitaine, etc.
II.-U(+any vowel), -u(+any vowel)-:
affectueux, cuisine, duel, ennuyeux, juin, nuance,
nuit, puits, ruelle, vertueux, etc.
    EXCEPTIONS (y):
    a. When preceded by two consonants
    forming a so-called inseparable
    group belonging to the same syl-
    lable, u+any vowel (except i) is
    pronounced in two syllables. The
    groups of inseparable consonants
    are:
      bl, br, cl, cr, dr, fl, fr, gl,
      gr, pl, pr, tr, vr.
    cru-auté, cru-elle, monstru-
    eux, obstru-èrent, etc.
    b. In the first and second person
    plural of the imperfect indica-
    tive and present subjunctive, u
    plus a vowel is pronounced in two
    syllables:
      que nous pollu-ions, que vous
      tu-iez, etc.
III.(g)u(+i,+e,+in), (q)u(+i,+e,+in):Generally in scientific and unusual words of Latin origin; also in the following
more common words, and their derivatives:
    aiguille, aiguiser, ambiguïté, arguer, inextinguible,
    linguiste, obséquieux, quiet, quintuple.
      NOTE: In all other common words,
      qu before a vowel is pronounced
      k; gu before a vowel is pro-
      nounced g:
        acquis, a-ki, alangui, a-lã-gi,
        convainquit, kɔ̃vɛ̃ki, gui, gi,
        marquis, mar-ki, qui, ki, etc.

Chapter XL.
THE SOUND YOD, j

HI(+vowel)-, -HI(+vowel)-, HY(+vowel)-, -I(+vowel), -Ï(between vowels)-, -(vowel+)ILL-, -(I+)LL-, -LH-, Y(+vowel)-, -Y(+vowel, -(vowel+)ILLE(S), -(I+)LLE(S), -(vowel+)IL(S).

I. When it is the last sound of a word, the sound yod is written:
  1.-il, -ille, preceded by a vowel. In this case i does not combine with the preceding vowel which thus retains its own timbre:
  appareil, Auteuil, détail, soleil, travail; grenouille, merveille, tu travailles, etc.
  2.-lle, preceded by i:
  Bastille, bille, famille, etc.
          EXCEPTIONS ($i\underline{l}$):
          a. In the following words and their derivatives, -lle is pronounced like $\underline{l}$:
            il distille, Lille, mille, Millet, pupille, tranquille, ville.
          b. In scientific and rare words:
          Achille, bacille, etc.
          NOTE: In the following word, -lle may be pronounced l or j:
            scintille, $s\tilde{\epsilon}til$ or $s\tilde{\epsilon}tij$.
  3.-(a)ye, -(e)ye, in subjunctive forms. In such cases, y first combines with the preceding vowel to make it sound like open $\underline{e}$; next, it is sounded yod:
  que je paye, $k\vartheta\mathfrak{z}\vartheta p\epsilon j$; qu'il égaye, $kile g\epsilon j$;
  que tu essayes, $k\vartheta-ty-e-s\epsilon j$; que je m'asseye, $k\vartheta\mathfrak{z}-ma-s\epsilon j$; que tu grasseyes, $k\vartheta tygra s\epsilon j$; etc.

II. In the middle of a word, the sound yod is written:
  1.-hi(+vowel)-, -i(+vowel)-:
  cahier, bien, etc.
  2.-ï-, between two vowels of which the second is not mute e:
  aïeul, $a-j\oe l$; faïence, $fa-j\tilde{a}:s$; païen, $pa-j\tilde{\epsilon}$; etc.
          NOTE: When mute $\underline{e}$ follows i, i retains the characteristics of a vowel, the dieresis preventing it from combining with the preceding vowel:
            ha-ïe, $a-i$; Isa-ïe, $i-\mathfrak{z}a-i$; etc.
  3.-ill-, preceded by a vowel. In such cases, i does not combine with the preceding vowel which thus retains

its own timbre.
ba-illi, *ba-ji*; groseillier, *gro-ᴣe-jе̇* travailler, *tra-va-je* ; ve-iller, *ve-je* ; etc.
5.-ll-, preceded by <u>i</u>:
billet, fillette, etc.

        EXCEPTIONS (*il*):
        a. In the following words and
        their derivatives <u>il</u> is pronounced like l:
        Lille, mille, Millet, pupille,
        tranquille, ville, etc.
        b. In rare or scientific words <u>ll</u>
        is pronounced like double l:
        bacillaire, instiller, etc.

6.-y-, between vowels. In such cases, first, <u>y</u> combines with the preceding vowel in the following way:
ay= open <u>e</u>, ε ; ey= open e, ε; oy= ou semi-vowel plus anterior <u>a</u>, *wa*; uy=u semi-vowel plus <u>i</u>, *ɥi;* and next it has the sound of yod, *j* , in the same syllable with the following vowel:
balayer, *ba-lɛ-je* ; ennuyer, *ã-nɥi-je* ; nous croyons, *nu-krwa-jõ* ; voyager, *vwa-ja-ᴣe* ; etc.

        EXCEPTIONS. In the following common words <u>y</u> does not combine
        with the preceding vowel, but
        has only the sound of yod in
        the same syllable with the next
        vowel:
        Ba-yard, *ba-ja:r* ; bo-yard,
        bɔ-ja:r ; bru-yamment, *brɥi-ja-mã* ; bru-yant, *brɥi-jã* ;
        bru-yère, *brɥi-jɛ:r*; gru-yère,
        grɥi-jɛ:r; ma-yonnaise, *ma-jɔ-nɛ:z* ; o-yant, *ɔ-jã* .

4.-lh-, in a few names of towns in the south of France:
Milhau (often written Millau), *mi-jo* ; Nolhac, *nɔ-jak* ; Pardalhac, *par-da-jak*, etc.

III. At the beginning of a word:
1. hi(+vowel)-, hy(+vowel)-:
hier, hyène, etc.
2. y(+vowel):
yacht, yole, etc.

        Chapter XLI.
    THE SOUND AND LETTER P , *p*

P-, -P-, -PE-, -PP-, -PPE-; -P(S), -PE, -PE(S), -PES, -PPE, -PPE(S), -PPES.

I. At the beginning or in the middle of a word the sound p is written:
p-, -p-, pe-, -pp-, -ppe-:
partir, psaume, psychologie, psychée, opération, équipement, appartement, Assomption, concept, contempteur, Neptune, rapt, transept, laps, jappement, etc.

SILENT P
The letter p is silent in the following words and their derivatives:
ba*p*tême, che*p*tel, com*p*te, dom*p*te, exem*p*t, but exemption; il rom*p*t, je rom*p*s, prom*p*t, promptitu*d*e, tu rom*p*s, scul*p*ter, se*p*t, se*p*tième, se*p*tièmement, but septante, septembre, septentrion, tem*p*s.

And in nouns composed with champ:
Cham*p*lever, Cham*p*mêlé, etc.

II. At the end of a word the sound p is written:
1. -pe, -pes, -ppe, -ppes:
type, tu tapes, Dieppe, enveloppe, tu développes, etc.
2. -p:
cap, croup, Gap, hop! houp! etc.

SILENT P
The letter p is silent in the following words:
beaucou*p*, cam*p*, ce*p* (de vigne), cham*p*, cou*p*, dra*p*, Dupanlou*p*, Fécam*p*, galo*p*, Longcham*p*, lou*p*, siro*p*, tro*p*.

Chapter XLII.
THE SOUND AND LETTER B, *b*

B-, -B-, -BB-, -BE-, -BH-; -B, -B(S), -BBE, -BBES, -BE, -BE(S), -BES.

I. At the beginning or in the middle of a word the sound b is written
b-, -b-, -bb-, -be-, -bh-:
beau, abolir, table, abbé, bombement, abhorrer, etc.

II. At the end of a word the sound b is written:
1. -bbe, -bbes, -be, -bes:
je gobbe, tu gobbes, je dérobe, globe, tu dérobes, etc.
2. -b:
club, Jacob, etc.

SILENT B
The letter b is silent in the following words:
aplom*b*, plom*b*, surplom*b*, Christophe Colom*b*,

Dou~~b~~s, Lefe~~b~~vre.

Chapter XLIII.
THE SOUND AND LETTER T, *t*

T-, -T-, -TE-, TH-, -TH-, -TT-, -TTE-; -T, -T(S), -TE, -TE(S), -TES, -THE(S), -TTE, -TTE(S), -TTES; D (in liaison)

I. At the beginning or in the middle of a word the sound t is written:
  t-, -t-, -te-, th-, -th-, -tt-, -tte-:
  timbre, fatigue, lentement, thé, mythologie, flatteur, nettement, etc.
  SILENT T
  The letter t is silent:
  a. In words containing the prefixes mont- and pont:
  Mon~~t~~martre, Pon~~t~~château, Mon~~t~~parnasse, Mon~~t~~réal, Mon~~t~~pellier, etc.
  > NOTE: However, if the letter t is followed by a vowel or if mont represents the combination of mon (Eng. my), plus the t of the following syllable, the letter t is sounded:
  > Montauban, Montrésor, Montreuil, Pontoise.
  b. In the following words and their derivatives:
  as~~t~~hme, *asm*; ist~~h~~me, *ism*.

PRONUNCIATION OF THE LETTER T WHEN FOLLOWED BY I+A VOWEL:
  1. When t(i) is preceded by s or x it is pronounced t:
  bestial, hostie, mixtion, question, Sébastien, vestiaire, etc.
  2. In the following terminations t=s:
  a. -tiade, -tiaire, -tial, -tiale, -tiaux, -tiane, -tiate, -tiel, -tielle, -tience, -tieux, -tieuse, -tio, -tium, -tius:
  Miltiade, pénitentiaire, initial, initiale, initiaux, nicotiane, Spartiate, confidentiel, patience, ambitieux, tertio, patio, consortium, Helvétius, etc.
  b. -tia:
  initiative, initiation, insatiable, opuntia, etc.
  > EXCEPTIONS. t=t in the following words and their derivatives:
  > centiare, *sɑ̃tjaːr* ; châtiable, *ʃɑtjabl* ; éléphantiasis, *eleﬁɑ̃tjazis* ; galimatias, *galimɑ-tjɑ*; tiare, *tjaːr* .

c.-tie:
aristocratie, idiotie, suprématie.
EXCEPTIONS: t=t:
1. If preceded by a written consonant:
dynastie, $dinasti$; hostie, $osti$; garantie, $garãti$; ortie, $orti$; partie, $parti$; apprentie, $aprãti$; etc.
However in the two following words, although preceded by a written consonant, tie=si :
ineptie, $inɛpsi$; inertie, $inɛrsi$.
2. In verb forms:
elle est assujétie, $asyʒɛti;$ elle est rebâtie, $rəbati;$ elle s'est appesantie,$apəzãti;$ il l'a abrutie, $abryti;$ il l'a pressentie, $prɛsãti;$ etc.
However in the four following verbs t=s:
elle différentie, $difɛrãsi$; il balbutie, $balbysi$; il transsubstantie, $trãsybstãsi$; j'initie, $inisi$; etc.
3. In the following words, although preceded by a vowel:
chrestomathie, $krɛstomati$; Claretie, $klarti$.

d.-tien:
capétien, Le Titien.
ONLY EXCEPTIONS: t=t:
chrétien, $krɛtjɛ̃$; entretien, le tien, maintien, Sébastien.

e.-tiens, -tient:
impatient, quotient, etc.
EXCEPTIONS: t=t:
In all the forms of the verb tenir:
il tient, $iltjɛ̃$; je tiens, $ʒətjɛ̃$; etc.

f.-tier. In the following verbs only:
balbutier, différentier, initier, transsubstantier, throughout their conjugation.
NOTE: In all other words in -tier, t=t:
cafetier, $kaftje$; châtier, $ʃatje$; papetier, $paptje$.

g.-tiole:
gratiole, pétiole and their derivatives.
> EXCEPTIONS: t=t:
> In the following words, and
> their derivatives:
> bestiole, $bestjɔl$; étiole,
> $etjɔl$.

h.-tion-, -tion:
action, actionner, constitutionnellement,
fraction, fractionnel, etc.
> EXCEPTIONS: t=t:
> In the termination -tions, of
> verb forms only:
> nous éditions, $nuzeditj\tilde{ɔ}$ but
> les éditions, $edisj\tilde{ɔ}$; nous
> portions, $nuportj\tilde{ɔ}$ but les por-
> tions, $leporsj\tilde{a}$.

i. In the following words: t=s:
a fortiori, amphictyon, propitiateur and its derivatives; satiété.

II. At the end of a word the sound t is written:
-te, -tes, -the, -tte, -ttes:
bête, tu habites, Marthe, labyrinthe, chatte, tu
luttes, etc.

SILENT T
The letter t is usually silent at the end of a word:
avocat, Bossuet, debut, delicat, dent, doigt,
effet, et, forêt, fret, Hérault, influent, inquiet, jouet, maintenant, Rembrandt, salut,
tribut, vingt, etc.
and in verb forms:
elle allait, elle est, but est (east) est;
il boit, il rompt, il sent, il veut, etc.
> EXCEPTIONS: t is pronounced in
> the following common words:
> abject, abrupt, accessit, aco-
> nit, affidavit, Apt, Brest,
> brut, Bucarest, cet, Christ but
> Jésus-Christ; chut, compact,
> concept, contact, direct, dis-
> tinct, but succinct, instinct;
> district, dot, entre le zist et
> le zest; Ernest, est (east) but
> est (verb); fat, granit, huit,
> incorrect but aspect, respect,
> suspect; indirect, infect, in-
> tact, introït, Japhet, Josaphat,
> Lot, mat, net, ouest, prétérit,
> rapt, sept, soit, (meaning: so

be it, agreed) but qu'il soi̶t̶;
stric̲t̲, tac̲t̲, transep̲t̲, transi̲t̲,
verdic̲t̲.
Note 1. In the two following
words, the pronunciation of t is
optional:
aoû̶t̶ or aoû̲t̲; bu̶t̶ or bu̲t̲.
Note 2. In the following word the
pronunciation of ct is optional:
exa̶c̶t̶ or exac̲t̲.
Note 3. In liaison d is sounded t:
quand‿il viendra, second‿enfant,
grand‿h̶omme, il prend‿une
fourrure.

Chapter XLIV.
THE SOUND AND LETTER D, d

D-, -D-, -DD-, -DE-, -DH-; -D, -D(S), -DS, -DE, DE(S), -DES.

I. At the beginning or in the middle of a word the sound d is written:
  d-, -d-, -dd-, -de-, -dh-:
  aid̲e̲r̲, dam̲e̲, add̲i̲t̲i̲o̲n̲, avid̲e̲ment, adh̲érer, etc.
II. At the end of a word the sound d is written:
  1. -de, -des:
  j'aid̲e̲, avid̲e̲, tu vid̲e̲s̲, etc.
  2. -d, in the following endings:
  -ad, -ed, -ud:
  Alfre̲d̲, Bagda̲d̲, Caï̲d̲, Ci̲d̲, Davi̲d̲, Port-Saï̲d̲, su̲d̲, Valladoli̲d̲, etc.
  SILENT D
  1. The letter d, and the spelling ds are silent when they are the mark of the first, second and third persons singular of the present indicative of verbs of the third conjugation.
  il mou̶d̶, je per̶d̶s̶, tu confon̶d̶s̶, etc.
  2. The letter d is silent in the following endings:
  -ai̶d̶, -an̶d̶, -ar̶d̶, -au̶d̶, -au̶d̶, -ie̶d̶, -o̶d̶, -oeu̶d̶, -oi̶d̶, -on̶d̶, -or̶d̶, -ou̶d̶, -our̶d̶:
  lai̶d̶, marchan̶d̶, billar̶d̶, La Rochefoucaul̶d̶, chau̶d̶, pie̶d̶, Gouno̶d̶, noeu̶d̶, froi̶d̶, blon̶d̶, abor̶d̶. nor̶d̶. Sainte Menehou̶l̶d̶. sẽtmənəu or sẽtmənu; lour̶d̶.

ONLY EXCEPTION:
George San̲d̲
NOTE: With the following com-

pound words, liaison (with d) or linking (with r) is optional: nord-est, nord-ouest.
D is silent in the following words in -id: crid, muid, nid.
NOTE. In Madrid the pronunciation of d is optional. Madrid, or Madrid.

Chapter XLV.
THE SOUND AND LETTER K, k

C-, -C-, -CC-, -CCH-, CH-, -CH-, -CK-, -QUE-, K-, -K-, KH-, Q-, X-, -Q-, QU-, -QU-; -C, -C(S), -CH, -CH(S), -CK, -CK(S), -K, -Q, -Q(S), -QUE, -QUE(S), -QUES, -C(in liaison) -CT(in liaison), G(in liaison).

I. At the beginning or in the middle of a word the sound k is written:
  1. c-, -c-, before a, o, u, or any consonant:
    académie, codifié, curé, clavecin, acné, acrobate, cravate, etc.
    EXCEPTION:
    c=g in the following word and its derivatives:
    second, $səg\tilde{o}$.
  2. -cc-:
    acclamer, baccalauréat, raccommoder, etc.
    NOTE: cc before e or i=ks:
    accent, accident, etc.
  3. ch-, -ch-.
    a. Before any consonant:
    achromatique, chloroforme, chrétien, Christ, chrysanthème, ichtyologie, etc.
    b. In most scientific or unusual words and their derivatives. The most common are:
    archaïque, archange, archéologue, archiépiscopat, but archevêque with ʃ; Bacchus, catéchumène, but catéchisme with ʃ; Cham, chaos, choeur, chorus, écho, eucharistie, lichen, machiavel, but machiavélique with ʃ; Michel-Ange, but Michel with ʃ; orchidée, psychologie.
    Note 1. In the following word, ch is pronounced either ʃ or k: pachyderme.
    Note 2. In common words except those mentioned above, ch=ʃ: acheter, chacun, chose, etc.
  4. -cch-:

ecchymose, saccharine.
5. -ck-, -cqu-, k-, -k-, kh-:
nickel, jockey, Mecklembourgeois, becquée, képi, kilo, balkanique, khédive, etc.
6. q(+ua)-, -q(+u):In scientific or unusual words from Latin.The most usual are:
adéquat, aquarelle, aquarium, équateur, équation, in-quarto, obséquieux, quadrangulaire, quadruple, quartette, quatuor, quaternaire, quiet, quintuple, square.
7. qu-, -qu-.In all the common words not mention in 6: marquis, qualité, quantité, quatre, qui, quiconque, etc.
8. -que-:
manquement.
9. x-.In the two following words:
Xérès, *keres*; Ximénès, *kimenes*.
II. At the end of a word the sound k is written:
-c, -ch, -ck, -cq, -cque, -k, -q, -que, -ques:
avec, Forbach, Melchisédech, Roch, bock, Ourcq, La Mecque, Danemark, coq, casque, tu critiques, etc.

SILENT K:
The letter c, usually sounded k, is silent in the following words:
accroc, ajonc, banc, blanc, broc, caoutchouc, clerc, cric, but alambic, chic, etc; croc, escroc, estomac, flanc, franc, jonc, il vainc, lacs (net) but lac(s) (Eng. lake), hamac, sac, etc; marc (grounds of coffee)but Marc (proper name); porc (meat) but porc (living animal); Saint-Brieuc, tabac, tronc.

Note 1.In the following expressions only, the letter c is sounded in liaison, and is pronounced k:
franc-alleu, franc-archer, franc-étrier.
In other words in which final c is silent, liaison never takes place.
Note 2.In the following expression only, ct is sounded in liaison, and is pronounced k:
respect humain.
In other words in which final ct is silent, liaison never takes place.
Note 3.In the following expres-

sions only, g is sounded in
liaison and is pronounced k:
sang impur, suer sang et eau.

Chapter XLVI.
THE SOUND AND LETTER G, *g*

-C-, G-, -G-, GH-, -GH-, GU-, -GU-, -GUE-; -C(S), -G(S), -GUE, -GUE(S), -GUES.

I. At the beginning or in the middle of a word the sound g is written:
  1. -c-. In the following word and its derivatives:
    second,
  2. g-, -g-.
    a. Before a, o, u, l, m, or r:
      garçon, glace, gorille, gangrène, grande, gymnase, gutturale, flegme, bigote, Victor-Hugo, etc.
                    NOTE: gn=g+n: that is to say,
                    two consonant sounds, in scientific or unusual words. The
                    most common are:
                      agnat, agnus, diagnostic, gnome, inexpugnable, magnétisme, magnificat, magnolia, recognition, stagnant, Wagner.
                    In all other common words with gn, g melts with n to make a single sound, ɲ:
                      magnifique, répugnant, signer, etc.
      SILENT G
      The letter g is silent:
        1. In words compounded with long before a consonant:
          Longchamp, longtemps, etc.
        2. In the following words:
          amygdale, doigt, Magdeleine, sangsue, vingt.
    b. Before e in a few words of German or Scandinavian origin:
      Bergen, Gessler, Hegel, etc.
  3. gh-, -ghi-:
    ghetto, Enghien.
  4. gu-, -gu-. Before any vowel:
    guêpe, guide, vigueur, etc.
              Note 1. gu=two sounds: *g*+*u*:
              In the following common words and their derivatives:
                aiguille, aiguiser, ambiguité,

arguer, inextinguible,
linguiste.
Note 2.gu=two sounds: $g+w$:
In the following words and their
derivatives:
Guadalquivir, Guadeloupe,
jaguar, lingual, Nicaragua,
Paraguay.
5.-gue-:
vaguement.
II.At the end of a word the sound g is written:
-g, -gue, -gues:
Dantzig, zigzag, bague, Copenhague, tu distingues,
etc.

SILENT G
The letter g is silent after a nasal vowel or in
words ending in -berg and -bourg:
Bourg, Cherbourg, coing, Estaing, faubourg,
gong, Gutemberg, hareng, long, Luxembourg,
Meung, Nuremberg, poing, rang, sang, seing,
Strasbourg, Wurtemberg, etc.
Note 1.In the following words
the pronunciation of g is optional:
joug or joug; iceberg or iceberg
Note 2.c=g or k in the following
word:
zinc, $z\tilde{\varepsilon}{:}k$ or $z\tilde{\varepsilon}{:}g$.
Note 3.In legs s is silent and
the pronunciation of g is optional:
$l\varepsilon$ or $l\varepsilon g$.
Note 4.In the following expressions only, g is pronounced in
liaison and is sounded k:
suer sang et eau, sang impur.

Chapter XLVII.
THE SOUND AND LETTER F, f

F-, -F-, -FF-, -FFE-, PH-, -PH-; -F, -F(S), -FE, -FE(S),
-FES, -FF-, -FFE, -FFE(S), -FFES, -PHE, -PHE(S), -PHES.

I.At the beginning or in the middle of a word the sound
f is written:
f-, -f-, -ff-, -ffe-, ph-, -ph-:
faire, infidèle, offense, attiffement, étouffement,
philosophe, morphine, etc.

II. At the end of a word the sound f is written:
   -f, -fe, -fes, -ff, -ffe, -ffes, -phe, -phes:
   infinitif, girafe, tu agrafes, Falstaff, je griffe,
   étoffe, tu chauffes, philosophe, tu triomphes, etc.
   SILENT F
   The letter f is silent in the following words:
   boeufs but boeuf; cerf, cerf-volant, chef-
   d'oeuvre but chef, chef-lieu; clef, nerf but
   in the following expression f is pronounced:
   avoir du nerf; oeufs but oeuf.

Chapter XLVIII.
THE SOUND AND LETTER V, v

V-, -V-, -VE-; W-, -VE, -VE(S), -VES, -F(in liaison).

I. At the beginning or in the middle of a word the sound v is written:
   1. v-, -v-, -ve-:
      vendredi, avant, avenir, etc.
   2. w-, -w-. In words of German, Flemish or English origin, and their derivatives:
      Wagner, Wagram, Weimar, Wissembourg, Wurtembourgeois, Brunswick, Wallon, Waterloo, Watteau, wagon, wallace, warrant.
              EXCEPTIONS (w):
              tramway, $tramwɛ$, whist, $wist$.
II. At the end of a word the sound v is written:
   -ve, -ves:
   cave, tu laves, etc.
              NOTE: In liaison in the two following expressions only, f=v:
              neuf ans, $nœvã$, neuf heures, $nœvœːr$.

Chapter XLIX.
THE SOUND AND LETTER S, s

C-, -C-, ç-, -ç-, -C-, -CE-, S-, -S-, SC-, -SC-, -SS-,
-SSE-, -T(I)-, -X-; -CE, -CE(S), -CES, -S, -SCE, -SCE(S),
-SCES, -SSE, -SSE(S), -SSES, -Z, -TZ.

I. At the beginning or in the middle of a word the sound s is written:
   1. c-, -c-. Before e, i, oe:
      cette, ciel, coecum, acide, monceau, ici, etc.
   2. ç-, -ç-. Before a, o, u:

aperçu, ça, garçon, etc.
3. -ce-:
lancement.
4. s-:
sage, scrupule, sucrer, etc.
5. -s-:
a. Before or after a consonant:
absent, absolu, destrier, verser, Montespan
Nestor, de Maistre, etc.
EXCEPTIONS. s z, in the following words:
Alsace, Arsace, balsamine, subside.

SILENT S:
The letter s is silent in the following words:
Ai/ne, A/nière/, Ave/nes, Co/me, Deli/le, De/borde/, De/carte/, De/préaux, Duche/ne, Duque/ne, Fi/mes, I/le-Adam, Leconte de Li/le, Ne/le/, Pre/le/, Prévo/t, Sure/ne/, Vi/me/, de/quel/, -elle/; le/quel/, -elle/; Vo/ges.

b. Preceded by a nasal vowel and followed by any vowel or semi-vowel:
bonsoir, consul, tension, transi, etc.
EXCEPTIONS. s z in words derived from transi:
transit, intransigeant, etc.
However, in the following words s=s:
transept, transi, Transylvanie.
c. Between two ordinary vowels in many scientific or unusual words, and their derivatives. The most common of these words are:
antisémite, antiseptique, antiseptie, antisocial, aseptie, aseptique, asymétrie, cosinus, désuet, dysenterie, entresol, Lesage, Lesueur, monosyllabe, parasol, présalé, préséance, présupposer, primesautier, resalir, resaluer, resécher, résection, resonger, soubresaut, tournesol, vivisection, vraisemblable, etc.
6. sc-, -sc-, -sce-, -ss-, -sse-:
science, sceptique, disciple, acquiescement, dessert, assez, bassement, etc.
7. -t(+i)-:
See t(+i)-, pp. 187, 188, 189.
8. -x-: In the following words only:
Auxerre, Bruxelles, Saulxure, Xaintonge, written also Saintonge.
II. At the end of a word the sound s is written:

1. -ce, -ces, -sce, -sces, -ss, -sse, -sses, -x:
   Alice, face, tu divorces, acquiesce, tu t'immisces, express, basse, tu lasses, dix, etc.
2. -s. In the following common words classified according to termination:
   a. -aëns. In the following word only:
   Saint-Saëns.
   b. -as:
   alcarazas, as, Barabbas, Carabas, Cujas, Damas, d'Assas, Jonas, Mathias, Ménélas, Midas, pancréas, Stanislas, vasistas.
   c. -ès:
   Agnès, aloès, cacatoès, Cérès, Damoclès, ès, Méphistophélès, palmarès, pataquès, Périclès, Xérès.
   d. -is, -ïs:
   Adonis, bis (encore) but bi$/$ (color); cassis, Clovis, de profundis, fi$/$s (Eng. son and sons) but fil$/$ (wires); gratis, ibis, iris, jadis, lis but the pronunciation of s in fleur de li$/$ is optional; maïs, Médicis, Memphis, métis, myosotis, oasis, orchis, Senlis, tennis, Thémis, tamaris, Tunis, vis (screw) but je vi$/$; volubilis.
   e. -eims:
   Reims.
   f. -ens (sɑ̃:s) and (ɛ̃:s):
   cens, sɑ̃:s; contresens, kɔ̃trəsɑ̃:s; non-sens, nɔ̃sɑ̃:s; Rubens, rybɛ̃:s; sens, sɑ̃:s.
   g. -os:
   albatros, albinos, Burgos, Calvados, Carlos, intra-muros, mérinos, os (singular) but o$/$ (plural); rhinocéros, rinoseros or rinoseros, tétanos.

   NOTE: In proper names derived from the Greek, the letter s is pronounced and o may be either closed or open:
   Argos, Eros, etc.

   h. -aps:
   laps, relaps.
   i. -eps:
   biceps, forceps, reps.
   j. -ars:
   Mars.
   k. -us:
   Agnus, Angélus, autobus, chorus, Crésus, eucalyptus, hiatus, lapsus, lotus, Marius, motus, omnibus, prospectus, sinus, syllabus, terminus, typhus, Vénus, virus.

1. -ous:
tou<u>s</u> (pronoun) but touø (adjective).

> NOTE: In the following word, the letter <u>s</u> may be silent or may be sounded <u>s</u> or <u>z</u>:
> obus, ɔby, ɔbys, ɔby:z.

> NOTE: In the following word the pronunciation of <u>s</u> is optional:
> moeur<u>s</u>, mœrs or moeurø,
> mœ:r.

SILENT S
The letter <u>s</u> is silent:
a. When it is the mark of the plural:
cent histoireø, ceø alléeø, ceø cuisineø, ceø enfantø, ceø fenêtreø, deø femmeø, deø filleø, deø hommeø, deø jardinø, douze livreø, huit pierreø, leø mienø, leø murø, leø tableø, leø verreø, leø vitreø, meø cahierø, meø crayonø, seø amiø, teø soeurø, voø frèreø, etc.
b. When it is the termination of a verb:
je boiø, je diø, j'écriø, j'entendø, je faiø, je haiø, prendraiø, je travaillaiø, nous faisonø, nous parlionø, tu rompø, tu valuø, vous faiteø, etc.

> NOTE: The letter <u>s</u> of the plural forms and of verb terminations may be pronounced in liaison under certain circumstances, then it is sounded <u>z</u>.

c. And in all the common words which are not included in special lists for sounded <u>s</u>:
ailleurø, alorø, Angerø, Anglaiø, brebiø, chaoø, corpø, danø, fondø, fontø, garø, horø, Lourdeø, nouø, payø, poulø, procèø, puitø, Pyrénéeø, remordø, suspenø, tapiø, tempø, etc.

3. -z, -tz. In the following words:
Alvare<u>z</u>, bat<u>z</u>, Coblent<u>z</u>, Corte<u>z</u>, Fe<u>z</u>, Met<u>z</u>, quart<u>z</u>, ran<u>z</u>, ruol<u>z</u>, Sue<u>z</u>, Velasque<u>z</u>.

> NOTE: In Saint-Jean-de-Luz, the letter <u>z</u> may be pronounced <u>s</u> or <u>z</u>:
> lys or ly:z.

Chapter L.
THE SOUND AND LETTER Z, z

-S-, -SE-, Z-, -Z-; -S, -SE, -SE(S), -SES, -Z, -ZE, -ZE(S),

-ZES; S(in liaison), X(in liaison).

I. At the beginning or in the middle of a word the sound z is written:
1. z-, -z-:
zèle, azur, etc.
2. -s-:
  a. Between two vowels:
  aisance, basé, liaison, etc.
  EXCEPTIONS s=s:
  1. When the first vowel is a nasal:
     nous dansons, panser, penser, etc.
     However, in the following words formed with trans-, and in their derivatives, s=z:
     transaction, transalpin, transatlantique, transiger, transit, transitaire, transitif, transitoire.
     But in the four following words s=s:
     transept, transi, transir, Transylvanie.
  2. In many scientific or unusual words, and their derivatives. The most common of these words are:
     antisémite, antiseptique, antiseptie, antisocial, aseptie, aseptique, asymétrie, cosinus, désuet, dysenterie, entresol, Lesage, Lesueur, monosyllabe, parasol, présalé, préséance, présupposer, primesautier, resalir, resaluer, resécher, résection, resonger, soubresaut, tournesol, vivisection, vraisemblable, etc.
  b. Between a consonant and a vowel in the following words, and in their derivatives:
  Alsace, Arsace, balsamine, subside.
3. -se-:
embrasement.
4. x-, -x-: In the following words and their derivatives:
  a. Xavier, deuxième, dixième, sixième, etc.
  b. In liaison:
  deux enfants, dix-huit, six hommes, etc.
II. At the end of the word the sound z is written:

1. -se, -ses, -ze, -zes:
Anglaise, tu jalouses, douze, tu gazes, etc.
2. -z:
Berlioz, fez, gaz, Rodez, etc.

    Note 1. z=s in the following words:
        Alvarez, batz, Coblentz, Cortez, Fez, Metz, quartz, ranz, ruolz, Suez, Velasquez.
    Note 2. In Saint-Jean-de-Luz the letter z may be pronounced z or s:
        lys or ly:z .
    Note 3. The letters s and x=z in liaison:
        deux enfants, deux ou trois, dix élèves, dix héroines, doux ami, etc.

SILENT Z
The letter z is silent in words ending in -ez except those just mentioned:
assez, chez, nez, vous parlez, etc.
and in the following word also:
riz.

Chapter LI.
THE SPELLING AND SOUND CH, ʃ

CH-, -CH-, -CHE-, SCH-, SH-; -CHE, -CHE(S), -CHES.

I. At the beginning or in the middle of a word, the sound ʃ is written:
ch-, -ch-, -che-, sch-, sh-:
Michel but Michel-Ange with k; chacun, achat. acheter, schéma, schampooing, trachée but trachéal, trachéen, etc., with k; chic, choc, choir, chute, etc.

    Note 1. ch=k before any consonant: chloroforme, chrétien, Christ, chromatique, chrysanthème, Chrysostome.
    Note 2. ch=k in most scientific or unusual words and their derivatives. The most common are: archaïque, archange, archéologue, archiépiscopat but archevêque with ʃ ; Bacchus, catéchumène but catéchisme with ʃ;

Cham, chaos, choeur, chorus,
écho, eucharistie, lichen,
machiavel but machiavélique
with ʃ; Michel-Ange but Michel
with ʃ; orchidée, psychologie.
Note 3. In the following word ch
is pronounced ʃ or k:
pachyderme.

II. At the end of a word the sound ʃ is written:
-ch, -che, -ches, -sch, -sh:
sandwich, Autriche, que tu saches, haschisch,
kirsh, etc.

NOTE: ch=k. In the following words:
aurochs, Melchisédech, Moloch,
Munich, Saint-Roch, Zurich.

SILENT CH
The letters ch are silent in the following word:
almana̸c̸h̸.

Chapter LII.
THE SOUND ʒ

G-, -G-, GE-, -GE-, J-, -J-; -GE, -GE(S), -GES, -JE.

I. At the beginning or in the middle of a word the sound ʒ is written:
g-, -g-, ge-, -ge-, -(g)g-, j-, -j-:
 1. g-, -g-. Before e, i, y:
 gendre, girafe, agiter, gynécée, dégingandé, etc.
 2. ge-, -ge-. Before a, o, u or a consonant:
 geai, geôle, geôlier, mangeons, gageure, engagement, jugement, etc.
 3. j-, -j-:
 juge, majeure, etc.
 4. -(g)g- (gʒ):
 suggestion, sygʒestjɔ̃, etc.
II. At the end of a word the sound ʒ is written:
-ge, -ges, -je:
loge, je siège, tu protèges, ai-je, etc.

Chapter LIII.
THE SOUND AND LETTER M, m

M-, -M-, -ME-, -MM-; -M, -M(S), -ME, -ME(S), -MES, -MME, -MME(S), -MMES.

I. At the beginning or in the middle of a word the sound

m is written:
 m-, -m-, -me-, -mm-:
   mari, demoiselle, sixièmement, hommage, immense, etc.

   SILENT M
   The letter m is silent in the following words:
   auto~~m~~ne but auto<u>m</u>nal; da~~m~~ner and its derivatives.

   Note 1. Before b and p, m is merely the mark of the nasalization of the preceding vowel:
   accompagner, camp, aplomb, imbécile, etc.

   Note 2. mm is pronounced as one or a double consonant (p. 144) and the preceding vowel is not nasalized:
   ho-m~~m~~age, i-m~~m~~ense, etc.

   EXCEPTIONS: However, in the following words, and their derivatives, the first m nasalizes the preceding vowel:
   em-magasiner, ãmagazine ; em-mailloter, ãmajote ; em-mancher, ãmãʃe ; em-mener, ãmne ; em-murer, ãmyre.

   NOTE: In the following words, and their derivatives, i may or may not retain its nasal quality: immangeable, ɛ̃mãʒabl or imã-ʒabl ; immanquable, ɛ̃mãkabl or imãkabl ; immesurable, ɛ̃məzyrabl or iməsyrabl.

II. At the end of a word the sound m is written:
  1. -me, -mes, -mme, -mmes:
   j'acclame, dame, tu réclames, comme, dilemme, tu nommes, etc.
  2. -m:
   album, Amsterdam, intérim, Jerusalem, muséum, Potsdam, Stockholm, Wagram, etc.

   SILENT M
   The letter m is silent in the following words, and their derivatives. It is merely the mark of the nasalization of the preceding vowel, and consequently is not sounded:
   Adam, dam, daim, dom, essaim, étaim, faim, nom, parfum, Riom.

Chapter LIV.
THE SOUND AND LETTER N, n

N-, -N-, -NE-, -NN-; -N, -N(S), -NE, -NE(S), -NES, -NNE, -NNE(S), -NNES.

I. At the beginning or in the middle of a word the sound n is written: n-, -n-, -ne-, -nn-:
non, faner, crânement, donner, honnête, etc.

>Note 1. Before a consonant other than n, n is the mark of the nasalization of the preceding vowel, and consequently is not sounded:
>défunte, honte, mince, ondulation, tante, etc.
>
>Note 2. nn is sounded as one or a double consonant and the preceding vowel is not nasalized:
>do-nner, paysa-nne, etc.
>
>EXCEPTIONS: However in the following words and their derivatives, n, although placed before another n, is the mark of the nasalization of the preceding vowel, and the second n is sounded:
>en-nui, ã-nyi; en-noblir, ã-no-bli:r; etc.
>
>To these exceptions should be added the following words and their derivatives in which a single n, first nasalizes the preceding vowel, then sounds as an initial consonant, with the following vowel:
>enamourer, ãnamure ; enivrant, ãnivrã ; enorgueillir, ãnorgœji:r .
>
>Note 2. n placed after g is pronounced separately in scientific words, as well as in the following more common words and their derivatives:
>agnat, agnus, diagnostic, gnome, inexpugnable, magnificat, magnétisme, magnolia, recognition, stagnant, Wagner.

II. At the end of a word the sound n is written:

1. -ne, -nes, -nn, -nne, -nnes:
que je prenne, Seine, âne, tu mènes, djinn, bonne, que tu donnes, etc.
2. -n. After a consonant:
Béarn, Tarn, etc.

SILENT N
The letter n placed after a vowel, is usually the mark of nasalization of the preceding vowel and consequently is not sounded:
examen, an, rien, quelqu'un, bon, etc.

EXCEPTIONS. In the following common words n is pronounced: abdomen, albumen, amen, Beethoven, cyclamen, eden, gluten, hymen, lichen, Lohengrin, Mendelssohn, pollen, Reischoffen, specimen, clown,

Chapter LV.
THE SOUND AND SPELLING GN, gn or ɲ

GN-, -GN-, -GNE-; -GNE, -GNE(S), -GNES.

I. At the beginning or in the middle of a word the sound ɲ is written:
gn-, -gn-, -gne-:
gnangnan, gnognote, agneau, Agnès, magnifique, signification, ignorance, ignominie, incognito, répugnant, éloignement, etc.

EXCEPTIONS: gn=two sounds, g+n, in scientific or unusual words, of which the most common are:
agnat, agnus, diagnostic, gnome, inexpugnable, magnificat, magnétisme, magnolia, recognition, stagnant, Wagner.

II. At the end of a word the sound ɲ is written:
-gne, -gnes:
signe, il daigne. tu peignes, etc.

Chapter LVI.
THE SOUND AND LETTER L. l

L-, -L-, -LE-, -LL-, -LLE-; -L(S), -LE, -LE(S), -LENT, -LES, -LL, -ELLE, -ELLE(S), -ELLES, -LS.

I. At the beginning or in the middle of a word the sound

l is written:
 1. l-, -l-, -le-:
    là, talent, tabler, blond, parler, bêlement, etc.
    SILENT L
    The letter l is silent in the following words:
    Be/fort, cu/ blanc and all other derivatives of cu/; hou/que, Méni/montant.
 2. -ll-:
    a. Preceded by any vowel except i:
       aller, ballon, belladone, bulletin, mollesse, etc.
    b. Preceded by i. In words derived from scientific or unusual words and from the following more common words:
       distille, distiller; Lille, Lillois, mille, millionnaire; Millet; pupille, pupillaire; tranquille, tranquillement; ville, village; etc.
       Note 1. ill=j:
       In all other common words:
       billard, cédiller, fillette, etc.
       Note 2. (i)ll=ll:
       In scientific or unusual words, and their derivatives, the two l's are pronounced double l (p. 144):
       illégal, illicite, illusion, désillusion, illustration, etc.

II. At the end of a word the sound l is written:
 -l, -le, -les, -ll, -lle, -lles:
 Brésil, cil, fil, Nil, je file, seule, tu parles, (Guillaume) Tell, j'appelle, tu t'appelles, etc.
 NOTE: When preceded by i, l or ll combines with it, thus producing the sound of yod:
    bille, cédille, de Noailles, fille, je réveille, travail.
 However, in scientific or unusual words as well as in the following words, -ille=i+l:
    distille, Lille, mille, Millet, pupille, tranquille, ville.
 SILENT L
 The letter l is silent in the following words:
 au/x (plural of ail); bari/, cheni/, courti/, couti/, douzi/, fau/x, feni/, fi/s (son; sons); fourni/, fusi/, genti/ but gentille with yod, ʒɑ̃tij ; genti/shommes but gentilhomme with yod, ʒɑ̃tijom; gri/; Hérau/t and in all other

words with -au/t; La Rochefoucau~~ld~~ and in all
other words with -au~~ld~~; nombri~~l~~, outi~~l~~, persi~~l~~,
pou~~ls~~, Sainte-Menehou~~ld~~, saou~~l~~ or soû~~l~~, sou~~l~~,
sourci~~l~~ but ci<u>l</u>.

Chapter LVII.
THE SOUND AND LETTER R , *r*

R-, -R-, -RE-, RH-, -RH-, -RR-, -RRE-, -RRH-; -R, -R(S),
-RC(S), -RD, -RD(S), -RDS, -RE, -RE(S), -RENT, -RES,
-RF(S), -RG, -RG(S), -RPS, -RRE, -RRE(S), -RRENT, -RRES,
-RRHE(S), -RS, -RT, -RT(S).

I. At the beginning or in the middle of a word the sound
r is written:
r-, -*r*-, -*re*-, *rh*-, -*rh*-, -*rr*-, -*rre*-, -*rrh*-:
rare, arabe, perte, rhubarbe, rarement, enrhumé,
terrain, errement, catarrhal, etc.

II. At the end of a word the sound *r* is written:
1. -*rd*, -*rds*, -*re*, -*res*, -*rg*, -*rps*, -*rre*, -*rres*, -*rrhe*,
-*rs*, -*rt*.
il perd, d'abord, tu perds, j'admire, cigare,
pauvre, tu admires, bourg, Cherbourg, corps,
beurre, j'abhorre, tu te terres, catharrhe, ailleurs, alors, tu cours, Albert, il sort, expert,
etc.

   SILENT R
   The letters *rs* are silent in the following words:
   Angey~~s~~, Coulommier~~s~~, Poitier~~s~~, Louvier~~s~~, volontier~~s~~, Messieur~~s~~, mesjø ; but sieur~~s~~, sjœ:r
2. -*r*:
air, Arthur, César, dormir, martyr, mentor, amer,
mer, sieur but Monsieu~~r~~, məsjø ; soeur, etc.

   SILENT R
   The letter *r*, when preceded by *e* without written accent, is usually silent:
   aime~~r~~, bouche~~r~~, Alge~~r~~, Gerardme~~r~~, épicie~~r~~,
   boulange~~r~~, pommie~~r~~, etc.

   > EXCEPTIONS: However, the letter
   > *r* is pronounced in the following
   > common words:
   > ame<u>r</u>, cance<u>r</u>, enfe<u>r</u>, éthe<u>r</u>, fe<u>r</u>,
   > fie<u>r</u> (adjective) but fie~~r~~ (verb)
   > hie<u>r</u>, hive<u>r</u>, me<u>r</u>, revolve<u>r</u>, te<u>r</u>,
   > ve<u>r</u>.

3. -*rc*:
cler~~c~~, mar~~c~~ (coffee grounds) but Marc; por~~c~~ (meat)
but por<u>c</u> (living animal)

4. -rf. In the following words:
cerf but serf; cerf-volant, nerf.
   NOTE: In the following expression, f is pronounced:
   avoir du nerf.

Chapter LVIII.
A FEW COMMON WORDS OFTEN MISPRONOUNCED

	Incorrect Pronunciation	Correct Pronunciation
Alexandre	alεgzã:dr	alεksã:dr
appartement	apartmã	apartəmã
appeler	apεle, apεle	aple
auxiliaire	ogziljε:r	oksiljε:r
besoin	bɛzwɛ̃	bəzwɛ̃
capitaine	kaptεn	kapitεn
déjeuner	dəʒne	deʒœne
développe	develop	devlop
élever	elεve	elve
ennui	ãɥi	ãnɥi
ennuyeux	ãɥijø	ãnɥijø
enveloppe	ãvelop	ãvlop
Eugène	jyʒεn	øʒεn
Eugénie	jyʒeni	øʒeni
genre	ʒã:dr	ʒã:r
inutile	ɛ̃ytil, ɛ̃nytil	inytil
justement	ʒystmã	ʒystəmã
leçon	lεsɔ̃	ləsɔ̃
magasin	magazɛ̃	magazɛ̃
magnifique	magnifik	maɲifik
ordinaire	ordnε:r	ordinε:r
réchauffer	rəʃoʃe	rəʃoʃe
Victor-Hugo	viktor hygo	victorygo
vingt-et-unième	vɛ̃teãnjεm	vɛ̃teynjεm
voyage	voadʒ	vwajã:ʒ

INDEX OF SPELLINGS

With the exception of regular forms for the plural of nouns, pronouns, and adjectives, and for the third person plural of verbs, this index contains the different spellings of the sounds discussed in Part III.

a-, 158, 159, 163
-a-, 159, 160, 161, 162, 163
-a, 158, 160
â-, 159, 160
-â-, 159, 160, 162
-ac, 160
-acs, 158
-ae-, 168
-aë-, 159
-aen, 175
-aëns, 176, 197
ai-, 169
-ai-, 169, 170
-aid, 169
-aie-, 168, 170
-aie, 169
-aim, 178
ain-, 179
-ain-, 179
-ain, 178
-ainc, 178
-aincs, 178
-ains, 178
-aint, 178
-ais, 167, 169
-ait, 167, 169
-aît, 169
-aix, 169
am-, 176
-am-, 176
-am, 175
-amp, 175

an-, 176
-an-, 176
-an, 175
-anc, 175
-and, 175
-ang-, 177
-ang, 175
-ans, 175
-ant, 175
ao-, 167
-ao, 163, 167
-aô-, 164, 167
-aon, 167, 175
-aon-, 167
aou-, 172
-aoul, 172
août, 172
-ap, 160
-ars, 158
-as, 158, 161, 197
-at, 158, 161
-ât, 158, 161
-ats, 161
au-, 164, 165
-au-, 164, 165, 166
-au, 163
-aud, 163
-ault, 163
aulx, 163
-aux, 163
ay-, -ay-, 185
-ay, 169
-aye, 184

b-, 186
-b-, 186
-b, 186
-bb-, 186
-bbe, 186
-be-, 186
-be, 186
-bh-, 186
-bs, 187

c-, 191, 195
-c-, 191, 193, 195
-c, 192
ç-, 195
-ç-, 195
-(c)c-, 191
-cch-, 191
-ce-, 195
-ce, 197
ch-, 191, 200
-ch-, 191, 200
-ch, 192, 200
-che-, 201
-che, 201
-ck-, 191, 192
-ck, 192
-cq-, 192
-cq, 192
-cqu-, 191
-cque, 192
-ct-, 179, 192
-ct, 179

d-, 190
-d-, 190
-d, 190, 191
-dd-, 190
-de-, 190
-de, 190
-dh-, 190
-ds, 190

e-, 170
-e-, 162, 163, 168, 170
é-, 168
-é-, 168
-é, 168
-è-, 170
-ĕ-, 170

-ê-, 162, 169, 170
-ea-, 163
-ean, 175
-eau, 163
-ect-, 170
-ect, 170
-ed, 168
-ée-, 168
-ef, 168
-egs, 169
eh! -eh, 168
-ei-, 170
-eim-, 179, 197
-ein-, 179
-ein, 178, 179
-eing, 179
-eins, 179
-eint, 179
em-, 176
-em-, 176
-em, 177
-emp-, 177
-emps, 175
-empt, 175
en-, 177, 179
-en-, 177, 179, 180
-en, 175, 179
-end, 175
-ends, 175
-eng, 175
-ens, 175, 197
-ent, 117, 176
-er, 168
-ers, 168
-es, 117, 168, 169
-ès, 170, 197
est, 169
-est, 189
et, 168
-et, 169
-êt, 169
-ets, 169
eu, 174
eu-, 171, 174
-eu-, 170, 171
-eu, 170
-eû-, 170, 174
eue, 174
-eue, 170

eues, 174
-eun, 180
-eung, 180
eus, 174
-eus, 170
eut, 174
-eut, 170
eût, 174
-eux, 170
-ey-, 170, 185
-ey, 169
-eye, 184
-ez, 168

f-, 194
-f-, 194
-f, 194, 195
-fe, 195
-ff-, 194
-ff, 195
-ffe-, 194
-ffe, 195

g-, 193, 201
-g-, 193, 201
-g, 193, 194
ge-, 201
-ge-, 201
-ge, 201
-(g)g-, 201
gh-, 193
-gh-, 193
gn-, 193, 204
-gn-, 193, 204
-gne-, 204
-gne, 204
gu-, 183, 193, 194
-gu-, 183, 193, 194
(g)u(a), 182, 183
-gue-, 194
-gue, 194

haie, 169,
hais, 169
hait, 169
heu-, 171, 172
-heu-, 171, 172
hi-, 174, 185
-hi-, 174, 184

-hi, 173
-hô, 165
hou-, 172, 181
houe-, 172
houe, 172
houl-, 172
houx, 172
hu-, 174, 183
-hu-, 174, 183
-hu, 174
-hue, 174
-hues, 174
hum-, 181
hun, 180
hut, 174
hy-, 185

i-, 174
-i-, 174
-i, 173
-î-, 174
-ï-, 174, 184
-ï, 173
-ic, 173
-id, 173
-ie, 173, 174
-ïe, 173
-(i)en, 179
-(i)ens, 179
-(i)ent, 179
-ies, 173
-il, 173, 184
ill-, 184
-ille, 184
-lle, 184
-im-, 180
-im, 180
in-, 180
-in-, 179, 180
-în-, 180
-inct, 179
-ing, 179
-ingt, 179
-ins, 179
-int, 179
-înt, 179
-is-, 174, 196
-is, 173, 174, 197
-ïs, 173

-it, 173
-ît, 173
-ı̋t, 173
-ix, 173, 174
-iz, 173

j-, 201
-j-, 201
-je, 201

k-, 191
-k-, 191
-k, 191
kh-, 191

l-, 205
-l-, 205
-l, 205, 206
-le-, 205
-le, 205
-lh-, 185
-ll-, 184, 205
-ll, 205
-lle, 205

m-, 202
-m-, 202
-m, 202
-me-, 205
-me, 202
-mm-, 202
-mme, 202

n-, 203
-n-, 203
-n, 204
-ne-, 203
-ne, 204
-nn-, 204
-nne, 204

o-, 165
-o-, 164, 165, 166, 167
-o, 163
ô-, 165
-ô-, 164, 165
-ô, 163
-oc, 163
-od, 163

oe-, 169
-oe-, 181
-oê-, 181
-oeud, 170
oeufs, -oeufs, 170
oi-, 162, 181
-oi-, 159, 162, 182
-oi, 158, 159, 161, 162
oî-, 159, 162, 181
-oid, 158, 181
-oids, 158, 159, 181
-oie, 158, 159, 161, 181
-oigt, 161, 181
-(o)in, 181
-(o)ing, 181
-(o)ins, 181
-(o)int, 181
-ois, 158, 159, 161, 181
-oit, 159, 161, 181
-oît, 159
-oix, 159, 161, 181
om-, 178
-om-, 178
-omb, 178
-omp-, 178
-omp, 178
-ompt, 178
on-, 178
-on-, 117, 178
-on, 178
-onc, 178
-ond, 178
-onds, 178
-ong-, 178
-ong, 178
-ons, 178
-ont-, 178
-ont, 178
-oo, 163
-op, 163
-os-, 164
-os, 163, 197
-ost, 163
-ot, 164
-ôt, 163, 164
ou-, 172
-ou-, 172, 182
-ou-, 172
-ou, 172

-oubs, 172
-oud, 172
-ouds, 172
-oue-, 172
-oue, 172
-oûl, 172
-ould, 172
-ouls, 172
-oup, 172
-ous, 172
-out, 172
-oût, 172
-oux, 172
-ow-, 172
oy, 182, 185
oy-, 185
-oy-, 185

p-, 186
-p-, 186
-p, 186
-pe, 186
ph-, 194
-ph-, 194
-phe, 194
-ppe-, 186
-ppe, 186
-ps, 186

q-, 192
-q-, 192
-q, 192
qu-, 183, 192
-qu-, 183
-qua-, 182, 183, 192
-que-, 192
-que, 192

r-, 206
-r-, 206
-r, 206
-rc, 206
-rd, 206
-rds, 206
-re, 206
-rf, 206, 207
-rg, 206
rh-, 206
-rh-, 206

-rps, 206
-rr-, 206
-rre-, 206
-rre, 206
-rrhe, 206
-rs, 206
-rt, 206

s-, 196
-s-, 196, 199
-s, 198
sc-, 196
-sc-, 196
-sce-, 196
-sce, 197
sch-, 200
-sch-, 201
-sch, 201
-se-, 199
-se, 200
sh-, 200
-sh-, 200, 201
-ss-, 196
-sse-, 196
-sse, 197

t-, 187
-t-, 187, 196
-t, 189, 190
-te-, 187
-te, 189
th-, 187
-th-, 187
-th, 189
-the, 189
-tt-, 187
-tte-, 187
-tte, 187
-tz, 198, 200

u-, 174
-u-, 167, 174, 182
-u, 182
-û-, 174
-û, 174
-ü, 174
-ue, 174
-ûe, 174
-uë, 174

-um, 167, 180
un-, 178, 181
-un-, 178, 181
-un, 180
-unt, 180
-us, 174
-ut, 174
-ût, 174
-ux, 185
-uy, 174

v-, 195
-v-, 195
-ve-, 195
-ve, 195

w-, 195
-w-, 195

x-, 192, 196
-x-, 196, 199
-x, 197

y-, 185
-y-, 174, 185
-y, 173
-ys, 173
-ye, 173
-ym-, 180
-ym, 179
-yn-, 180

z-, 199
-z-, 199
-z, 198, 200
-ze, 200

INDEX OF WORDS USED AS EXAMPLES

In this index will be found the words given as examples to illustrate rules or explanations. The definitive edition will include in addition, all those used in the reading lessons as well as the phonetic transcription of every word.

a (il), 160
abbaye, 173
abbé, 136
abcès, 142
abdiquer, 86
abdomen, 175, 179, 204
abhorre (j'), 206
abhorrer, 186
abîme, 174
abject, 170, 189
Abner, 86
abolir, 186
abord, 136, 190, 206
Abraham, 161
abrupt, 189
abrutie (il l'a), 188
absent, 196
absolu, 174, 196
absolument, 142
abstraction, 87
académie, 191
accable (il l'), 159, 161
accent, 191
accent aigu, 130, 131
accessit, 173, 189
accident, 191
acclame (elle), 159, 161
acclame (j'), 202

acclamer, 191
accompagner, 178, 202
accroc, 163, 192
accueil, 171
achat, 200
acheter, 191, 200
Achille, 184
achromatique, 191
acide, 195
acné, 191
aconit, 173, 189
acquérir, 144
acquerrez (vous), 144
acquiesce, 197
acquis, 183
acrobate, 191
acte, 128, 162
action, 189
actionner, 189
activité, 86
Adam, 137, 175, 202
addition, 190
adéquat, 182, 192
adhérer, 190
adieu, 170
admirable, 86, 128
admirablement, 130
admire (j'), 206

admires (tu), 206
Adonis, 197
adorable, 128, 161
adorer, 85
adosse, 164, 166
adosser, 165
affectueux, 155, 183
affidavit, 173, 189
afflux, 174
affre, 159
affût, 174
a fortiori, 189
agace (il l'), 161
âge, 159
Agen, 175, 179
agenda, 177, 180
agent, 176
agile, 14
agiter, 201
agnat, 193, 203, 204
agneau, 204
Agnès, 170, 197, 204
agnus, 193, 197, 203, 204
agrafes (tu), 195
agrémenté, 86
agronome, 164, 166
ah! 132, 141
ai(j'), 167
aide (j'), 144, 190
aider, 143, 190
aies (que tu), 168
aient (qu'ils), 168
aïeul, 171, 184
aigu, 143, 169
aiguë, 143, 174
aiguille, 123, 183, 193
aiguiser, 183, 193
ai-je, 201
ail, 161
ailé, 143
ailleurs, 198, 206
aimable, 161
aimaient (elles), 117
aimâmes (nous), 159, 162
aimasses (que tu), 162
aiment (elles, ils), 117, 134
aimer, 132, 134, 144, 168, 206

aimerai (j'), 167
aimerais (j'), 169
aimerez (vous l'), 119
aimez (vous), 143, 168
Ain, 179
aine, 179
ainsi, 179
air, 136, 206
aisance, 199
aisé, 169
Aisne, 196
Aix, 147, 169
Aix-la-Chapelle, 147, 169
Aix-les-Bains, 147, 169
Ajax, 147, 162
ajonc, 178, 192
alambic, 173, 192
alangui, 183
albâtre, 159
albatros, 163, 197
Albert, 170, 206
albinos, 163, 197
album, 167, 181, 202
albumen, 167, 175, 179, 204
alcarazas, 197
Alexis, 173
Alfred, 190
Alger, 206
algue, 162
Alice, 197
allait (elle), 189
allant, 134
allât (qu'il), 158
allées, 198
allemand, 175
aller, 85, 130, 205
allés (nous sommes), 133
alliez (vous), 155
allons (nous) 178
allouions (que nous), 156, 182
allouons (nous), 155
almanach, 201
aloès, 170, 197
alors, 198, 206
alouette, 155
Alsace, 196, 199
Alvarez, 198, 200
amas, 158

amazone, 164, 166
ambassadeur, 176
ambiguïté, 183, 193
ambitieux, 187
ambition, 176
amen, 175, 179, 203
amener, 85, 176
amer, 168, 170, 206
américain, 168, 179
Amérique, 53
ami, 198
ammoniaque, 176
amnistie, 176
amphictyon, 189
Amsterdam, 202
amusant, 8
amygdale, 193
an, 204
analyse, 174
ananas, 158
ancêtre, 176
ancien, 138
âne, 204
anéantir, 85
anecdote, 176
anémone, 166
ange, 176
angelus, 197
Angers, 198, 206
anglais, 198
anglaise, 200
angoisse, 162
animal, 14
animaux, 128
Anne, 159, 162
Annecy, 173
année, 85, 176
ânonner, 160
anspect, 170
antisémite, 196, 199
antiseptie, 196, 199
antiseptique, 196, 199
antisocial, 196, 199
aoriste, 167
aorte, 167
août, 1, 172, 190
aoûteron, 172
aperçu, 196
aphone, 164, 166

aplomb, 186, 202
appareil, 184
appartement, 123, 133, 186
appartins (j'), 179
appas, 158
appelle (j'), 205
appelles (tu l'), 205
appelles (tu t'), 119
appendice, 177, 180
appesantie (elle est), 188
apportions (nous), 155
apprend (il), 175
apprentie, 188
après, 129
Apt, 189
aquarelle, 182, 192
aquarium, 182, 192
arabe, 162, 206
arbre, 87, 119, 140
archaïque, 191, 200
archange, 191, 200
archéologue, 191, 200
archevêque, 191, 200
archiépiscopat, 191, 200
architecture, 143
arcs-en-ciel, 132
Argos, 197
arguer, 183, 194
aristocratie, 188
arme, 162
arome, 162
arrose, 164
Arsace, 196, 199
art, 162
Arthur, 206
as, 197
as (tu), 161
ascenseur, 177
aseptie, 196, 199
aseptique, 196, 199
Asnières, 196
aspect, 170, 189
Assas (rue d'), 197
assens (j'), 175
asseoies (que tu), 182
asseye (que j'), 184
assez, 168, 196, 200
assiette, 155
Assomption, 155, 186

assujétie (elle est), 188
asthme, 187
astre, 162
astronome, 164, 166
asymétrie, 196, 199
atelier, 121
atome, 164, 166
atone, 164, 166
attifement, 194
attrape (j'), 162
attrapez-le, 126
attribut, 174
aucun, 137, 139
aucune, 174
augmentation, 165
augmentatif, 165
augmenter, 165
aujourd'hui, 183
aulx, 163, 205
aurai (j'), 165
aurochs, 201
aussitôt, 135
autant plus (d'), 148
Auteuil, 184
auto, 165
autobus, 165, 197
autochtone, 164, 166
automnal, 202
automne, 202
automobile, 165
autonome, 164, 166
autorité, 165
auto-suggestion, 165
autre, 128, 164
autres (les), 128, 132
autrement, 165
Autriche, 201
autrui, 156
Auxerre, 146, 196
avaient-elles? 129
avais (tu), 134
avant, 129, 195
avant-hier, 130
avec, 170, 192
avenir, 195
Avesnes, 196
aveugle, 171
avide, 199
avidement, 190

aviez (vous), 134
avis, 173
avocat, 161, 189
avons (nous), 134
axiome, 164, 166
azur, 199

Babylone, 166
bac, 162
baccalauréat, 191
Bacchus, 191, 200
bâchelier, 121
bacillaire, 185
bacille, 184
Bagdad, 190
bagne, 162
bague, 162, 194
baie, 169
bailli, 185
balafre, 159
balayer, 185
balbutie (il), 188
balbutier, 188
balkanique, 192
balle, 162
ballon, 205
balsamine, 196, 199
banc, 175, 192
baptême, 186
Barabbas or Barrabas, 197
Barcelone, 166
baril, 173, 205
baron, 160
bas, 158
bas étage, 136
base, 159
basé, 199
basse, 159, 162, 197
bassement, 196
Bastille, 184
bât, 158
batailleur, 160
bataille, 159
bâton, 160
bats, 161
batz, 198, 200
Bayard, 185
Bazaine, 179
bazar, 160

Béarn, 204
beau, 15, 163, 186
beaucoup, 135, 186
beaux ou laids, 130
bébé, 3
becquée, 192
Beethoven, 175, 179, 203
bel, 87
bêlement, 205
Belfort, 205
belladone, 205
belle, 85, 119, 140, 141
belles, 128
benéfice, 168
benjamin, 177, 180
benzine, 177, 180
Bergen, 193
Berlin, 178
Berlioz, 200
besace, 121
bestial, 187
bestiole, 189
bêta, 158, 160
bête, 170, 189
Bethléem, 177
bêtise, 169
beugle, 171
beurre, 172, 206
biceps, 197
bien, 2, 137, 138, 155, 175, 184
bien entendu, 138
bienfaisance, 118
bienfaisant, 118
bienfaisante, 118
bien plus, 148
bigote, 193
billard, 190, 205
bille, 184, 205
billet, 185
binocle, 180
bis (color), 173, 197
bis (encore), 173, 197
bizarre, 162
blanc, 192
blessure, 143
bleu, 171
bleuir, 171
blond, 190, 205

bock, 192
boeuf, 171, 195
boeufs, 170, 171, 195
bois (je), 198
boit (il), 189
boîte, 162
bombement, 186
bon, 138, 204
bonheur, 145
bonne, 204
bonnement, 176
bonté, 168, 178
bonsoir, 196
bord à bord, 140
bosse, 166
Bossuet, 189
boucher, 168, 206
boulanger, 206
bouquet, 133
bourg, 194, 206
bout à bout, 131
bout à l'autre (d'un), 130
boxe, 147
boxes (tu), 147
boyard, 182, 185
bras, 161
brasero, 168
brasier, 160
brave, 140, 162
brebis, 173, 198
Brésil, 173, 205
Brest, 189
broc, 163, 192
brosse, 166
brouette, 155, 182
bruit, 156
brunette, 181
Brunswick, 195
brut, 189
Bruxelles, 146, 196
bruyamment, 185
bruyère, 185
Bucarest, 189
bulletin, 205
Burgos, 163, 197
but, 190
but à but, 131
but en blanc, 131

ça, 160, 196
cacahuète, 183
cacatoès, 170
cadenas, 161
Cadix, 147, 174
cadre, 159
cadrer, 160
Caen, 137, 175
cafetier, 188
cahier, 132, 184, 198
Caïd, 190
Caïn, 85
calme, 162
Calvados, 163, 197
camp, 175, 186, 202
campos, 163
cancer, 168, 206
candélabre, 159
canevas, 161
caoutchouc, 192
cap, 186
capable, 8
capacité, 85
capétien, 188
car, 1
Carabas, 197
carbone, 166
Carlos, 163, 197
carosse, 160
carré, 160
carreau, 160
cartable, 122
cas, 53, 131, 158
casque, 192
casse, 159, 131, 158
cassis, 197
cataplasme, 142
catarrhal, 206
catarrhe, 206
catéchisme, 191, 200
catéchumène, 191, 200
catholicisme, 142
cauchemar, 165
cave, 53, 195
ce, 1, 123, 125, 126
ceci, 173
cédille, 205
cédiller, 206
ceinture, 179

ce le, 125
célèbre, 122
celtique, 86
celui, 121, 155
ce me, 124, 125
cendrier, 155
ce ne, 124, 125
cens, 175, 177, 197
cent, 128, 154
  cent un, 154
  cent deux, 154
  cent trois, 154
  cent dix, 154
  cent onze, 154
  cent douze, 154
  cent vingt, 154
  cent vingt et un, 154
  cent vingt-deux, 154
Centaure, 164, 166
centiare, 187
cep (de vigne), 186
cependant, 135
ce que, 124, 125, 126
Cérès, 170
cerf, 136, 195
cerf-volant, 195
certain, 138
cervelas, 158
ces, 128, 168, 198
César, 2(6
ce te, 124, 125
cette, 140, 142, 195
chacun, 2, 137, 191, 200
chaise, 117
chahut, 174
Cham, 175, 191
chambres à coucher, 132
champ, 186
champlevé, 186
champmêlé, 186
Champs-Elysées, 131
chancelier, 121
chandelier, 121
chantai (je), 167
chantas (tu), 161
chantât (qu'il), 161
chanteriez (vous), 121
chantes (tu), 119
chantez (vous), 168

chaos, 163, 191, 198, 201
chapeaux, 133
Charlotte Corday
charron, 160
chasse, 162
chasselas, 161
chat, 3, 131
Châteauroux, 162
châtiable, 187
châtier, 188
chatte, 189
chaud, 163, 190
chaud et froid, 133
chauffes (tu), 195
chef, 170
chef-d'oeuvre, 195
chef-lieu, 195
cheminée, 119
chenil, 173, 205
cheptel, 186
cher, 140, 168
Cherbourg, 194, 206
chercher, 143
chère, 140
chez, 129, 133, 200
chic, 192, 200
chloroforme, 191, 200
choc, 200
chocolat, 158, 161
choeur, 191, 201
choix, 159, 161, 182
choléra, 191, 201
chorus, 191, 197, 201
chose, 164, 191
chrestomathie, 188
chrétien, 188, 191, 200
Christ, 173, 189, 191, 200
Christophe Colomb, 178, 186
chromatique, 200
chrysanthème, 191, 200
Chrysostome, 164, 166, 200
chut, 189
chute, 200
Cid, 173
ciel, 195
cigare, 2(6
cil, 173, 205, 206
cinq, 150
   cinq cents, 154

cinq cent un, 154
cinq cent deux, 154
cinquante, 153
   cinquante et un, 153
   cinquante-deux, 153
   cinquante-trois, 153
   cinquante-quatre, 153
   cinquante-cinq, 153
   cinquante-six, 153
   cinquante-sept, 153
   cinquante-huit, 153
   cinquante-neuf, 153
circonspect, 170
Claretie, 188
classe, 159, 162
clavecin, 191
clé, 168
clef, 168, 195
clerc, 136, 192, 206
climat, 158, 161
clos, 163
Clovis, 197
clown, 172, 204
club, 172, 186
Coblentz, 198, 200
code, 167
codex, 147
codifié, 191
coecum, 195
coeur, 172
coing, 182, 194
colis, 173
coloris, 173
combien, 137
comme, 202
comment, 130, 132, 133
commerce, 170
commis, 173
commun, 139
compact, 189
compas, 158
complexe, 147
compromis, 173
compte, 178, 186
comte, 178
concept, 186, 189
concis, 173
confidentiel, 187
confluent, 86

confonds (tu), 178, 190
conquérir, 144
conquerrons (nous), 144
consent (il), 175
consortium, 187
consitution, 14
constitutionnellement, 189
consul, 196
contact, 189
contempteur, 186
contes et légendes, 130
contresens, 175, 177, 197
convaincs (tu), 179
convainquit (il), 183
conversation, 137
coopérative, 167
copeau, 144
Copenhague, 194
coq, 192
Corday (Charlotte), 169
corps, 198, 206
corps à corps, 140
correct, 170
Cortez, 198, 200
cosaque, 165
cosinus, 196, 199
Cosme, 196
côté, 165
côtelette, 165
coud (elle), 172
Coulommiers, 206
coup, 186
courir, 144
courrais (je), 144
courtil, 173, 205
courtois, 195, 161
coutelas, 158
coûtelier, 121
coûter, 172
coutil, 205
crabe, 159
craindre, 179
craint (il), 179
crânement, 203
cravate, 191
crayon, 198
crier, 26, 46
Crésus, 197
Creuse, 170

cric, 173, 192
crid, 173, 191
crispe-le, 122
critiques (tu), 192
croc, 163, 192
croc-en-jambe, 131
crois (je), 158
croît (il), 158
croître, 159
croix, 158
croquis, 173
croup, 186
croyant, 182
croyons (nous), 185
cruauté, 183
crucifix, 173
cruel, 85, 155
cruelle, 183
cueille, 17, 171
cuisine, 183, 198
Cujas, 197
cul, 205
cul-blanc, 205
curaçao, 163, 167
cure, 123
curé, 191
cyclamen, 175, 119, 203
cyclone, 164, 166

daigne, 204
daim, 202
dam, 175, 202
Damas, 197
dame, 161, 190, 202
damne, 159
damner, 160, 202
Damoclès, 170, 197
Danemark, 192
dans, 2, 3, 129, 136, 175, 198
dansâtes (vous), 159, 162
danse (il), 119
dansent (ils), 134
danser, 176
danserai (je), 169
danserions (nous), 121
dansons (nous), 199
Dantzig, 194
David, 173, 190

datte, 162
de, 119, 120, 121, 123, 125, 127
débarras, 161
debout, 120, 127
début, 189
décagone, 164, 166
de ce, 125
décembre, 176
déclame (elle), 159, 161
dedans, 120
défunte, 181, 203
dégingandé, 201
dehors, 145, 146
déjeune, 171
de le, 125
délicat, 161, 189
délicatesse, 85
Delisle, 196
demande, 125
demande (il ne), 121
dame, 125
démêler, 143
demoiselle, 202
démontre, 87
de ne, 125
dent, 189
de profundis, 177, 197
dépens, 175
depuis, 120, 126, 173
dérape, (il), 159
dernier, 128, 129
dérobe (je), 186
dérobes (tu), 186
des, 15, 128, 130, 168, 198
désaxe, 122
Desbordes, 196
Descartes, 196
descendre, 169
de se, 124, 125
désillusion, 205
désosse, 164, 166
désossement, 165
Despréaux, 196
desquels, -elles, 196
dessein, 179
dessert, 196
dessiner, 169
dessous, 172

dessus, 174
destrier, 196
désuet, 196, 199
détail, 161, 183, 184
détester, 143
Deutéronome, 171
deux, 2, 132, 150, 200
deux à deux, 131
deux cents, 128, 154
  deux cent un, 154
  deux cent deux, 154
  deux cent trois, 154
deuxième, 146, 171, 199
deux ou trois, 131
devant, 119, 129
développer, 86
développes (tu), 186
devers, 121
devin, 125
devis, 173
dévotion, 165
dévouement, 172
dextrier, 147
diable, 122, 159, 161
diagnostic, 193, 203, 204
Diane, 162
diapason, 160
Didon, 178
Dieppe, 186
différentie (elle), 188
différentier, 188
difficile, 14
dilemme, 177, 202
direct, 170, 189
dis (je), 173, 198
disciple, 196
discipline, 14, 174
discipliner
disent (ils), 117
dis-le, 126
dispos, 163
distille, 184, 205
distiller, 145, 205
distinct, 179, 189
distinction, 179
distingues (tu), 194
district, 189
dît (qu'il), 173
divers, 136

223

divin, 139
divorce, 167
divorces (tu), 197
dix, 136, 146, 153, 197, 200
dixième, 146, 199
dix-huit, 132, 146, 153, 154, 199
dix-neuf, 153
dix-sept, 153
Djinn, 204
dogme, 167
doigt, 171, 182, 189, 193
doigt et à l'oeil (au), 133
dois (je), 129, 161
dom, 202
domino, 163
dompte, 178, 186
Domrémy, 178
donc, 147, 177
donné, 168
donnée, 168
donner, 203
donnerai (je), 167
donnerez (vous), 119
donnes-en, 136
donnes (que tu), 204
dont, 129
dormir, 206
dos, 163
dos à dos, 130
dossier, 165
dot, 164, 167, 189
dotaux, 144
Doubs, 172, 187
douzaine, 179
douze, 153, 200
douzil, 205
doux, 200
drame, 161
drap, 160, 186
droite, 162
drôle, 164
drôlerie, 165
druide, 156
du, 2
dû, 174
Duchesne, 196
dûe, 174

duel, 155, 183
dûes, 174
Dumas, 158
Dupanloup, 186
Duquesne, 196
dynastie, 188
dysenterie, 196, 199

éblouissement, 155, 182
ecchymose, 192
ecclésiastique, 169
échalas, 155
écho, 201
éclipse, 122
école, 167
économe, 164, 166
écoute-t-il, 144
écria (s'), 155
écris (j'), 198
éden, 175, 179, 203
éditions (les), 189
éditions (nous), 189
effacer, 169
effet, 189
égaye (qu'il), 184
égoïsme, 142
eh! 168
éléphant, 85
éléphantiasis, 187
élever, 85
elles, 129, 131
Elizabeth, 170
éloignement, 204
embarras, 161
embarrasse (que j'), 204
embrasement, 199
embrasser, 176
émeute, 170
emmagasiner, 202
emmailloter, 202
emmancher, 202
emmener, 176, 202
emmurer, 202
empereur, 176
emploie (que j'), 159, 161
emprunt, 180
emprunte, 181
en, 129, 7, 137
enamourer, 177, 203

encaustique, 165
encens, 175
enclos, 163
encoignure, 182
encore, 123
encrier, 156
endécagone, 179
endécasyllabe, 179
endiablé, 160
endosse, 164, 166
endroit, 158
enfant, 85, 128, 175
enfer, 168, 177, 206
enflamme, 162
engagement, 201
Enghien, 193
engrêlure, 143
enivrant, 177, 203
enlevé, 119
ennemi, 177
ennoblir, 177, 203
ennui, 177, 203
ennuyer, 185
ennuyeux, 183
enorgueillir, 177, 203
énorme, 177
enrhumé, 206
enrôlé, 165
entends (j'), 198
enthousiasme, 142, 162
entre, 140
entresol, 196, 199
entretien, 188
enveloppe, 119, 186
envelopper, 86
envers, 136
épaissir, 143
epicier, 206
épouvantable, 161
équateur, 182, 192
équation, 182, 192
équipement, 186
Ernest, 189
Eros, 197
errement, 206
es (tu), 169
ès, 170, 197
Esaü, 174
escargot, 164

escroc, 163, 192
espace, 159, 161
espacer, 160
essaim, 202
essayes (que tu), 184
est (elle, il), 129, 169, 189
est (east), 189
Estaing, 194
estomac, 160, 192
et, 132, 168, 189
étaim, 202
étais (j'), 144
était (elle), 129
Etats-Unis, 131, 173
et ce, 126
été, 2
êtes (vous), 133
éther, 168, 206
étiole, 189
étoffe, 195
étoile, 162
étouffement, 194
étroite, 162
eu, 174
eucalyptus, 171, 197
eucharistie, 191, 201
Eudes, 170
eue, 174
eues, 174
Eugène, 171
Eugénie, 171
Eulalie, 171
eûmes (nous), 174
euphonie, 171
eurent (ils), 174
européen, 26, 46, 175, 179
eus (j'), 174
eus (tu), 134, 174
eut (il), 174
eût (qu'il), 174
eûtes (vous), 174
évidemment, 162
exact, 146, 190
examen, 86, 146, 168, 175, 179, 204
exclame (il s'), 159, 161
exhumer, 168
exempt, 175, 186

exempte, 172
exempter, 177
exemption, 177, 186
exhumer, 146
expatrier, 147
expert, 206
exploit, 182
explorer, 86
exprès, 170
express, 197
exquis, 173
extraordinaire, 86, 167

fa (music), 158, 160
face, 197
fac simile, 168
faïence, 85, 184
faim, 137, 179, 202
faire, 194
fais (je), 198.
faisaient (ils), 118
faisais (je, tu), 117
faisait (il), 117
faisan, 118
faisandé, 118
faisanderie, 118
faisant, 118
faiseur, 118
faiseuse, 118
faisiez (vous), 118
faisions (nous), 118
faisons (nous), 118, 198
fait est (le), 131
faites (vous), 198
faix, 169
Falstaff, 195
famille, 184
faner, 203
faon, 167, 175
fat, 162, 189
fatigue, 187
fatras, 158
faubourg, 194
faulx, 205
Faust, 164, 166
faut (il), 129, 163
fauteuil, 64, 171
faux, 163
Fécamp, 175, 186

féerie, 168
Félix, 147, 173
femme, 162, 176, 198
femmelette, 162, 177
fenêtre, 53, 119, 198
fenil, 173, 205
fer, 168, 206
feras (tu), 161
feriez (vous), 121
ferions (nous), 121
fermier, 132
féroce, 167
feuille, 171
Fez, 198, 200
fiançailles, 159
fiat lux, 147
ficelier, 121
fier (adj.), 145, 168, 206
fier (verb), 168, 206
fidèle, 141
fil, 173, 205
file (je), 205
fille, 53, 64, 133, 198, 205
fillette, 185, 205
fils, 173, 197, 205
fin, 2
fis (tu), 173
Fismes, 174, 196
fit (il), 53, 173
fixe, 147
fixes (tu), 147
flamme, 159, 162
flammèche, 176
flanc, 192
flatteur, 187
flegme, 193
fleur, 133, 140
fleur de lis, 197
flûte, 174
foi, 159, 161
folle, 3
fond en comble (de), 131
fonds, 198
font (ils), 178
Forbach, 192
forceps, 197
forêt, 189
fort, 130, 136

fortement, 123
fosse, 164, 166
fossé, 165
fossette, 165
fossoyer, 165
fossoyement, 165
fossoyeur, 165
fournil, 173, 205
fracas, 158
fraction, 189
fractionnel, 189
franc, 192
français, 53
française, 53
franc-alleu, 131, 135, 192
franc-archer, 131, 135, 192
franc-étrier, 131, 135, 192
front, 151
frères, 198
fret, 189
frit, 53
frite, 53
froid, 158, 181, 190
froide, 159
froisse, 162
furent, 129
fusil, 173, 205
fût, (qu'il), 174
fûtes (vous), 174

gageure, 201
gagne, 3, 159
gagner, 160
gai, gaie, gaies, gais, 3, 167, 169
gaiement, 168
gaieté, 168
galetas, 161
galimatias, 187
galop, 163, 186
gangrène, 193
Gap, 186
garantie, 188
garçon, 193, 196
garçonnet, 131
garde, 122
gars, 158, 198
gaz, 159, 200
gazes (tu), 200

gazon, 160
geai, 168, 201
gemme, 177
gendre, 201
général, 168
genêt, 53, 169
gentil, 173, 205
gentilhomme, 205
gentille, 205
gentilshommes, 205
geôle, 201
geôlier, 201
Gérardmer, 206
Gessler, 193
geste, 122
ghetto, 193
girafe, 162, 195, 201
glace, 193
glas, 158
globe, 167, 186
gluten, 175, 197, 204
gnangnan, 204
gnognote, 204
gnome, 164, 166, 193, 204, 204
gobbe (je), 186
gobbes (tu), 186
gond, 194
gorille, 193
gosse, 166
Gounod, 163, 190
goût, 172
gouvernement, 123
graillon, 160
gramme, 162
grand, 128
grande, 140, 142, 144, 193
granit, 173, 189
gras, 130, 158
grasse, 155, 159, 162
grasseyes (que tu), 184
gratiole, 189
gratis, 197
grenouille, 184
griffe (je), 195
gril, 173
gris, 173
gros, 136, 163
grosse, 164, 166

groseillier, 185
gruyère, 185
Guadalquivir, 194
Guadeloupe, 182, 194
guêpe, 193
guet-apens, 131
guettez, 143
guettrez, 143
gui, 183
guide, 193
Guillaume Tell, 205
Gutenberg, 194
gutturale, 193
gymnase, 193
gynécée, 201

habites (tu), 189
hache, 145
hagard, -e, 146
haie, 145, 184
haïes (elles sont), 173
haillon, 145, 160
haine, 145
haïr, 146
hais (je), 198
haïs (je, tu), 173
haït (il), 173
hâle, 145
hall, 145
halle, 145
hallebarde, 145
halte, 145
hamac, 145, 192
hameau, 126, 146
hanche, 145
hanneton, 145
hanter, 146
harangue, 145
haranguer, 146
harasser, 146
hardi, -e, 146
hareng, 145, 175, 194
haricot, 145
harpe, 145
hasard, 145
hasard (par), 146
haschisch, 201
hâte, 145
hausser, 126

haut, 126, 133, 146
haute, 146
haut (en), 145, 146
hautain, 138
haut en bas (de), 131
Havane (La), 145
Hâvre (Le), 145, 159
Haye (La), 145
Hegel, 193
Helvétius, 187
hem! 177
hein, 179
héraut, 145
Hérault, 163, 189, 205
hère, 145
héroïne, 145, 146
héroïsme, 146
héron, 132, 145
héros, 126, 133, 145, 163
hêtre, 145
heure, 133, 172
heureuse, 140, 170
heureux, 128, 143, 146, 171
heurter (se), 146
hexagone, 146, 164, 166
hi! 132
hiatus, 197
hibou, 145
hideuse, 146
hideux, 146
hier, 168, 185, 206
hiérarchie, 146
hippodrome, 164, 166
hirondelle, 128
histoire, 128, 198
hiver, 168, 174, 206
hollandais, 146
hollandaise, 146
Hollande, 146
homard, 133
hommage, 202
homme, 128, 145, 198
Hongrie (La), 146
honnête, 203
honte, 145, 203
hop! 186
hôpital, 165
horde, 146
hormis, 146, 173

horrible, 141
hors, 130, 146, 198
Hortense, 126
hostie, 187, 188
hôtel, 165
hôtelier, 121
hôtesse, 165
houache, 181
houe, 172
houement, 172
houette, 181
houlque, 172, 205
houp, 186
hourra, 172
houx, 126, 172
hue, 174
hues (tu), 174
huguenot, 174
huile, 183
huit, 132, 133, 141, 152, 189
  huit cents, 154
  huit cent un, 154
  huit cent deux, 154
  huit cent trois, 154
huitaine, 183
humain, 138
humanité, 181
humble, 181
humilité, 181
humour, 181
Hun, 180
hurler, 146
hutte, 146
hyène, 185
hygiène, 174
hymen, 175, 179, 204

ibis, 197
iceberg, 136, 194
ichtyologie, 191
ici, 195
idéal, 174
idiome, 164
idiotie, 188
ignominie, 204
ignorance, 74, 204
illégal, 205
illettré, 145

illicite, 205
illogique, 145
illusion, 205
illustration, 205
illustre, 145
ils, 129, 131
image, 128, 180
imbécile, 180, 202
immangeable, 180, 202
immanquable, 180, 202
immense, 128, 145, 202
immesurable, 180, 202
immisces (tu t'), 197
immeuble, 122, 123
immobile, 180
immortels, 128
impatient, 188
impossible, 180
inaccessible, 122
incapable, 180
incognito, 204
incorrect, 189
incroyable, 182
inculpe-la, 122
index, 147
indirect, 189
inepte, 40
ineptie, 188
inertie, 188
inexorable, 146
inexpugnable, 193, 203, 204
inexplicable, 147
inextinguible, 183, 194
infect, 17(, 189
infidèle, 194
infinitif, 195
influence, 189
inhumain, 174, 180
initial, 187
initiale, 187
initiaux, 187
initiation, 187
initiative, 187
initie (j'), 188
initier, 188
innocence, 180
in-quarto, 182, 192
inquiet, 189
insatiable, 187

instiller, 185
instinct, 179, 189
instinctivement, 179
intact, 189
intelligence, 145
intelligemment, 163, 177
intérim, 180, 202
intra-muros, 163, 197
intransigeant, 196
introït, 173, 189
inutile, 40, 180
iras (tu), 161
iris, 197
Isaac, 159
Isabelle, 87
Isaïe, 173, 184
islam, 175
Isle-Adam, 196
Ismaël, 170
isthme, 187

Jacob, 160, 186
Jacques, 159
jadis, 197
jaguar, 182
jalouses (tu), 200
jamais, 135
Japhet, 189
jappement, 186
jardin, 198
Jason, 160
je, 119, 123, 126
Jean, 137, 174
Jeanne, 163
je le, 124
je me, 124
je ne, 124, 125
Jérusalem, 177, 202
Jésus-Christ, 173, 189
je te, 123, 125, 125, 126
je te le, 126
tiens (je), 142
jeudi, 171
jeûn (à), 180
jeune, 170, 171
jeûne (fasting), 170
Joachim, 180
joaillier, 183
jockey, 192

joie, 159, 161
jolie, 145
Jonas, 197
jonc, 178, 192
Josaphat, 189
joue (je), 172
jouer, 134, 155
joues (tu), 172
jouet, 132, 169, 189
joug, 194
jouons (nous), 134
journalisme, 142
Judas, 158
judaïsme, 142
juge, 3, 201
jugeaient (ils), 85
jugement, 201
juin, 183

képi, 192
khédive, 192
kilo, 192
kirsch, 201

la (music), 158, 160
la, 14, 22, 205
labyrinthe, 189
lace (elle), 159, 161
lacs, 158, 192
laid, 168, 190
laide, 170
lait, 2, 53
lampe, 175
lancement, 196
Laon, 167, 175
Laonnois, 167
laps, 186, 197
lapsus, 197
La Rochefoucauld, 163, 190, 206
larynx, 147, 180
las, 158
lasse, 149, 162
lasses (tu), 197
Laure, 164, 166
Laurence, 165
laves (tu), 195
le, 2, 14, 32, 119, 120, 121, 123, 125, 126, 144

leçon, 137
Leconte de Lisle, 196
lecture, 143
léger, 168
légère, 140
legs, 169, 194
légua, 183
Lefebvre, 187
Lenormand, 120
lentement, 187
les, 14, 128, 168, 198
Lesage, 196, 199
lesquels, -elles, 196
Lesueur, 196, 199
leucocyte, 171
leude, 170
leurs, 128
liaison, 199
licenciement, 174
lichen, 175, 179, 191, 201
lier, 156
lilas, 158
Lille, 184, 185, 205
Lillois, 205
limite, 180
lingual, 182, 194
linguiste, 183, 194
linx, 147
lis, 197, 198
lit, 2, 3, 131
livre, 64, 133, 198
location, 160
loge, 201
logis, 173
Lohengrin, 204
loi, 159, 161
loin, 182
lointain, 138, 182
long, 135, 178, 194
Longchamp, 186, 193
longtemps, 175, 178, 193
longuement, 135
loquace, 182
losange, 165
Lot, 164, 189
loto, 144
lotus, 197
Louis, 2, 155, 173, 182
louent (ils), 172

loup, 2, 172, 186
lourd, 190
Lourdes, 198
Louviers, 206
loyal, 182
loyauté, 182
lui, 2
luttes (tu), 189
luxe, 147
Luxembourg, 194
luxes (tu), 147
Lycaon, 175
lymphatique, 180
lyncher, 180
lynx, 147
lyx, 140

macadam, 175
Machiavel, 191, 201
machiavélique, 191, 201
maçon, 160
madame, 16, 123
madone, 166
madré, 160
Madrid, 173, 191
Maeterlink, 168
Magdeleine, 193
magnétisme, 193, 203, 204
magnificat, 193, 203, 204
magnifique, 74, 193, 204
magnolia, 193, 203, 204
maigrir, 143
maintenant, 175, 189
maintien, 179, 188
maintiens (tu), 176
maintînmes (nous), 180
mairie, 53
mais, 134
maïs, 197
Maistre (de), 196
majordome, 164, 166
malappris, 173
malfaisance, 118
malfaisant, 118
malfaisante, 118
malheur, 172
malheureusement, 143
malheureux, 143, 146
maman, 3

mammifère, 83, 201
manges (tu), 121
manquement, 192
marbre, 162
Marc, 192, 206
marc (de café), 192, 206
marchand, 137, 190
Margot, 163
mari, 202
Marius, 197
Marne, 162
marquis, 173, 183, 192
marron, 160
Mars, 197
Marthe, 189
martyr, 206
masse, 161
masure, 160
mât, 158, 189
matelas, 161
Mathias, 197
matrone, 166
Maubeuge, 170
maure, 164, 166
mauvais, 165
mayonnaise, 185
maximum, 167, 181
me, 119, 123
Mecklembourgeois, 192
Mecque (La), 192
médaille, 159, 161
médecin, 142
Médicis, 197
médiocre, 167
meilleur, 172
meilleure, 172
Melchisédech, 192, 201
me le, 124, 125
mêle (je)
mêmement, 144
Memphis, 197
Mendelssohn, 204
Ménélas, 197
mener, 168
mènes (tu), 204
Ménilmontant, 205
mens (tu), 175
mentor, 206
menu, 121

menuet, 121
menuisier, 121
Méphistophélès, 170, 197
mépris, 173
mer, 168, 206
Mercure, 143
mérinos, 163, 197
merveille, 184
mes, 128, 168, 198
messieurs, 206
mets (je), 169
métis, 191
métronome, 164, 166
mettez (vous), 143, 144
mettre (se), 140, 170
mettrez (vous), 143
Metz, 198, 200
meuble, 171
meuglais (je), 171
meugle (il), 171
meule, 171
Meung (Jean de), 180, 194
meunier, 171
Meurice, 171
meus (je me), 170
Meuse, 170
Metz, 198, 200
Michel, 191, 200, 201
Michel-Ange, 191, 200, 201
Midas, 197
mien, 137
miens (les), 198
mieux en mieux (de), 131, 136
Milhau, 185
mille, 154, 184, 185, 205
  mille un, 154
  mille deux, 154
  mille trois, 154
Millet, 184, 185, 205
milliard (un), 154
million (un), 154
millionnaire, 205
Miltiade, 187
mince, 203
Minotaure, 166
miracle, 159, 161
mis, 134
mistral, 86

mixtion, 187
modeste, 140
moelle, 162, 176, 181
moelleux, 162
moeurs, 198
moi, 161
moignon, 182
moins, 182
moins en moins (de), 131
mois, 159, 161
moitié, 181
mollesse, 205
Moloch, 201
momie, 165
mon, 2, 128, 137
Monceau, 195
monde, 178
Monod, 163
monosyllabe, 196, 199
monotone, 166
monsieur, 118, 206
monstre, 53, 87, 119
monstrueux, 155, 183
Montauban, 187
mont-de-piété, 178
Montenegro, 168
monter, 134
Montespan, 196
Montmorency, 178
Montmartre, 178, 187
Montparnasse, 178, 187
Montpellier, 187
Montréal, 187
Montrésor, 187
Montreuil, 187
moque, 167
morphine, 194
mort-aux-rats, 131
mort ou vif, 140
mot à mot, 131
motus, 197
moud (il), 190
mouds (tu), 172
mourrons (nous), 144
mouton, 172
moyen, 138, 179
moyennant, 130
muid, 173, 191
Munich, 201

murs, 64, 198
muséum, 202
myosotis, 143, 165, 197
mythologie, 187

naïf, 174
naître, 140
nappe, 162
narghilé, 168
nation, 1
naviguâ, 183
nazaréen, 46
ne, 119, 120, 123, 144
néant, 46
ne le, 124, 125
ne me, 124, 125
Neptune, 186
nerf, 195, 207
nerf (avoir du), 195, 207
ne se, 124
Nesles, 196
net, 189
ne te, 124, 125
nettement, 187
netteté, 144
neuf, 153, 171, 195
   neuf cents, 154
   neuf cent un, 154
   neuf cent deux, 154
neutralité, 171
neutre, 170
neuve, 2
nez, 3, 131, 168, 200
nez à nez, 133
Nicaragua, 182, 194
nickel, 192
Nicolas, 158
nicotiane, 187
nid, 173, 191
nier, 156
Nil, 173, 205
nions (nous), 156
Noailles (de), 159, 161, 205
noble, 140
noblement, 123
noeud, 170, 190
noie (que je), 159, 161
noix, 159, 161

Nolhac (de), 185
nom, 137, 178, 202
nombre, 178
nombril, 205
nommes (tu), 202
non, 145, 203
nonobstant, 130
non-sens, 175, 177, 197
Nord, 190
nord-est, 140, 191
nord-ouest, 140, 191
normand, 120
nos, 128, 163
note, 119
notion, 165
nôtre (le, la), 119, 164
nouiez (que vous), 156
nouiez (vous), 182
nous, 129, 198
nuage, 155
nuance, 183
nuit, 183
Nuremberg, 194
nymphe, 180

oasis, 197
obséquieux, 183, 192
obstacle, 87, 161
obstruer, 155
obstruèrent (ils), 183
obus, 198
océan, 26, 46, 175
octogone, 164, 166
odieux, 165
odeur, 165
Oedipe, 169
oeil, 171
oesophage, 169
oeuf, 171, 195
oeufs, 171, 195
offense, 194
oh! 132, 141
oie, 159, 161
oignon, 182
oiseau, 128, 162, 181
ombre, 178
omnibus, 197
on, 137, 138
oncle, 122, 123, 178

ondulation, 203
ont, 129
onyx, 147
onze, 126, 132, 141, 153
opéra, 160
opération, 186
opium, 181
opuntia, 187
oracle, 159, 161
orchidée, 191, 201
orchis, 197
organisme, 142
orient, 175
ortie, 188
os, 163, 167, 197
oserai (j'), 165
ossement, 165
ôte (j'), 164
ôterai (j'), 165
ouest, 182, 189
oui, 126, 132, 135, 141, 182
Ourcq, 192
outil, 173, 205
outrage, 172
ouvrier, 156
oyant, 182, 185
ozone, 164, 166

pachyderme, 191, 201
page, 162
paiement, 170
païen, 184
paient (ils), 117
paix, 147, 169
pâlir, 160
palmarès, 170, 197
panser, 199
pancréas, 197
paon, 167, 175
paonne, 167
papa, 3
papetier, 188
paradis, 173
paradoxal, 85, 147
Paraguay, 182, 194
paraît (il), 169
paraître, 140
parasol, 196, 199

parce que, 126
Pardalhac, 185
parfum, 137, 167, 180, 202
parlai (je), 169
parlât (qu'il), 158, 161
parlâtes (vous), 159
parle (il), 119, 127
parle (ne), 125
parlement, 123
parlent (ils), 176
parler, 205
parleront (elles), 129
parles (tu), 117, 205
parlez (vous), 200
parlions (nous), 198
paroisse, 162
paroxysme, 142
part (il), 136
part en part, 140
part et d'autre, 140
partie, 188
partie, 186
partout, 135
pas, 130, 158
pas à pas, 131
passage, 160
passe, 159, 162
passion, 160
pataquès, 170, 197
patatras, 158
pâte, 2
patiemment, 177
patience, 187
patio, 187
patte, 2
Pau, 163
Paul, 164, 166
Paule, 164, 166
Pauline, 165
pauvre, 164, 206
pauvreté, 165
pax, 147
paye (que je), 184
pays, 178, 198
paysanne, 208
pêche, 142
pédestre, 87
peignée, 144
peignes (que tu), 204

peindre, 179
peine, 179
peins (je), 179
pelouse, 121
pendant, 129
pénitentiaire, 187
penser, 199
pensum, 167, 177, 180
Pensylvanie, 177, 180
Pentateuque, 171
pentecôte, 177
perd (il), 206
perd-il? 136
perdit, 143
perdrix, 147, 173
perds (je), 190
perds (tu), 206
perds-en, 136
perdu, 86, 143
Périclès, 170, 197
perler, 143
permis, 173
Pernod, 163
persil, 173, 205
personne, 132, 133
perte, 206
peser, 121
peste, 119
pester, 143
pétiole, 189
petit, 119, 127, 128
petit à petit, 131
petite, 127, 140, 142, 144
pétunsé, 181
peureux, 143, 171
peut (il), 170
peut-on? 129
peuvent-ils? 129
peux (tu), 136
Pharaon, 175
pharynx, 147
phénix, 147, 174
philosophe, 143, 165, 194, 195
phonétique, 168
pied, 155, 168, 190
pied-à-terre, 131
pied en cap (de), 131
pierre, 198

pis, 173
pis-aller, 131
place, 161
plains (je), 179
plaintivement, 179
plaisir, 143, 144, 169
plâtras, 158
plâtre, 159
plein, 138, 179
plomb, 178, 186
plus, 148
plus (au), 148
plus de, 148
plus en plus (de), 131, 149
plusieurs, 128, 136
plus ni moins (ni), 148
plus ou moins, 149
plus-que-parfait, 148
Pô, 163
poêle, 162, 176
poêllée, 162
poète, 181
poids, 159, 181
poing, 179, 194
point, 182
pois, 159, 161
Poitiers, 206
poix, 159, 161
pollen, 175, 179, 204
polluiez (que vous), 156
polluions (que nous), 183
Pollux, 147
polygone, 164, 166
pommeau, 144
pommier, 206
Ponce-Pilate, 159, 162
pont, 178
Pontchâteau, 187
Pontoise, 187
ponts et chaussées, 130
pope, 167
porc, 192, 206
port, 53, 136
porte, 53, 117, 122, 167
porter, 168
portions (les), 189
portions (nous), 189
Port-Saïd, 190
position, 165

pot à eau, 131
pot à tabac, 133
pot-au-feu, 130
pot au lait, 130
pot aux roses, 131
pots-au-feu, 132
Potsdam, 202
poulailler, 160
pouls, 172, 198, 206
poupée, 168
pour, 140
pourraient (ils), 129
préalablement, 123
précis, 173
préfixe, 147, 174
premier, 128, 129
prend (il), 135, 190
prenne (que je), 204
prendrais (je), 198
prendrait, 169
prends-le, 126
près, 170
présalé, 196, 199
préséance, 196, 199
président, 144
Presles, 196
presque, 122
pressentie (il l'a), 188
présupposé, 196, 199
prêt, 133
préterit, 173, 189
Prévost, 163, 196
prie (je), 173
prient (ils), 173
prière, 156
primesautier, 196, 199
prince, 180
prix, 147, 177
procès, 198
prochain, 138
proclame (elle), 159, 161
profond, 178
profundis (de), 178
promener (se), 131
promis, 113
prompt, 178, 186
prompte, 178
promptitude, 178
propitiateur, 189

propos, 163
propos (à), 163
prospectus, 197
protèges (tu), 201
psaume, 186
psyché, 186
psychologie, 186, 191, 201
puis, 149, 155, 173
puisque, 149
puissante, 142
puits, 183, 198
punch, 178, 181
pupille, 184, 185, 205
pupillaire, 205
Pyrénées, 198

quadrangulaire, 182, 192
quadruple, 182, 192
quai, 167, 169
qualité, 183, 192
quand, 130, 135, 175, 190
quant, 130
quantité, 183, 192
quarante, 153
  quarante et un, 153
  quarante-deux, 153
  quarante-trois, 153
  quarante-quatre, 153
  quarante-cinq, 153
  quarante-six, 153
  quarante-sept, 153
  quarante-huit, 153
  quarante-neuf, 153
quartette, 182, 192
quartz, 198, 200
quasi, 160
quaternaire, 182, 192
quatorze, 153, 167
quatre, 3, 140, 150, 162, 183, 192
  quatre cents, 154
  quatre cent un, 154
  quatre cent deux, 154
quatre-vingts, 154
  quatre-vingt-un, 132, 155
  quatre-vingt-deux, 155
  quatre-vingt- trois, 155
  quatre-vingt-quatre, 155
  quatre-vingt-cinq, 155
  quatre-vingt-six, 155
  quatre-vingt-sept, 155
  quatre-vingt-huit, 132,155
  quatre-vingt-neuf, 155
  quatre-vingt-dix, 155
  quatre-vingt-onze, 155
  quatre-vingt-douze, 155
  quatre-vingt-treize, 155
  quatre-vingt-quatorze, 155
  quatre-vingt-quinze, 155
  quatre-vingt-seize, 155
  quatre-vingt-dix-sept, 155
  quatre-vingt-dix-huit, 132
  quatre-vingt-dix-neuf, 155
quatuor, 182, 192
que, 49, 125, 126
que ce, 124, 125
que de, 124, 125
que je, 124, 125
que le, 124, 125
quelle, 141
quelqu'un, 137, 204
que me, 124, 125
que ne, 124
querelle, 121
question, 187
que se, 125
que te, 124, 125
queue, 170
qui, 183, 192
quiconque, 192
quiet, 183, 192
quintuple, 183, 192
quinze, 153
qui plus est, 149
quoi, 161
quotient, 188

raccommoder, 120, 191
raccroc, 163
radis, 173
rafle, 159
ramification, 176
rang, 175, 194
ranz, 198, 200
rapidement, 135
rapt, 186, 189
rare, 206
rarement, 206

ras, 158
ravissant, 145
rebâtie (elle est), 188
réclame (il), 159, 161
réclames (tu), 202
recognition, 193, 203, 204
recommencer, 120
recommander, 120
redemande (je te le), 126
redemanderai (je te le), 126
redemandes (tu), 125
redis (je te), 126
redis-le, 126
redonne (je te le), 126
referas (tu), 125
Reims, 179, 197
reine, 170
Reischoffen, 175, 179, 204
relaps, 197
remarque, 162
Rembrandt, 189
remettez-vous, 120
remettre, 120
remis à neuf, 134
remords, 198
rendez-le, 126
reparlera (il), 123
repas, 158
répétait (il), 144
répond (il), 178
répondant, 134
repos, 163
reps, 197
répugnant, 193, 204
resalir, 196, 199
resaluer, 196, 199
resécher, 196, 199
résection, 196, 199
resonger, 196, 199
respect, 170, 189
respect humain, 131, 135, 192
respectueux, 170
resplendir, 86
restaurant, 165
reste, 170
réveille (je), 205
reverrai (je), 125
revolver, 168, 206

rhinocéros, 163, 197
rhubarbe, 206
rhum, 167
rien, 3, 137, 138, 155
ries (que tu), 173
Riom, 178, 202
rions (nous), 156
riz, 172, 200
riz au lait, 133
Roanne, 184
robe, 2, 119
Roch, 192
Rodez, 200
roi, 158, 181
roide, 159
romanesque, 170
romantisme, 142
Rome, 166
romps (je), 186, 198
romps (tu), 178
rompt (il), 186, 189
ronfle (il), 122
rose, 2, 3, 164
rosette, 165
rôt, 163
rôti, 165
rôtir, 165
Roubaix, 147, 169
Rouen, 155, 175, 179
ruban, 131
Rubens, 176, 197
rue, 53
ruelle, 183
Ruisdaël, 159
ruolz, 198, 200
Russe, 53
rustre, 53
Ruy, 155

sable, 122, 159, 161
sac, 192
saccharine, 192
saches (que tu), 201
sage, 196
saine, 140
saint, 179
Saint-Brieuc, 192
Saint-Denis, 173
Saint-Jean-de-Luz, 198, 200

Sainte-Menehould, 172, 190
200
Saint-Roch, 201
Saint-Saëns, 175, 197
sais (je), 167, 169
sais (tu), 167, 169
sait (il), 167, 169
salade, 162
salles à manger, 132
salut, 189
Sand (George), 190
sandwich, 201
sang, 135, 194
sang impur, 131, 135, 193, 194
sangsue, 177, 193
sanitaire, 176
sans, 129, 136
Saône, 164, 167
saoul, 172, 206
sarcasme, 142
sarreau, 160
satan, 160
satiété, 189
Saulxure, 147, 196
saute, 164
scabreux, 160
scepticisme, 142
sceptique, 196
schampooing, 182, 200
schéma, 200
schisme, 142
sciemment, 174
science, 177, 196
scintille, 184
scrupule, 196
sculpter, 186
se, 1, 123
Sébastien, 187, 188
second, 128, 135, 137, 190, 191, 192
secundo, 178, 181
sedan, 121
Seine, 204
seing, 179, 194
seize, 153
se le, 124
selon, 130
semonce, 53

Senlis, 197
sens, 149, 175, 197
sens (bon), 149
sens commun, 149
sens devant derrière, 149
sens dessus dessous, 149
sens (tu), 175
sent (il, 189
sentes (que tu), 117
sept, 152, 186, 189
    sept cents, 154
    sept cent un, 154
    sept cent deux, 154
septante, 186
septembre, 118
septentrion, 186
septième, 186
septièmement, 186
seraient (ils), 129
serions (nous), 134
sermon, 53
sert-elle? 136
serez-vous? 120
ses, 128, 168, 198
seul, 171
seule, 205
Seyne, 170, 179
sic, 173
siège, 155
siège (je), 201
sien, 175, 179
sieur, 206
signe, 204
signer, 193
signification, 74, 204
silhouette, 155
simple, 180
Simon, 166
Sinaï, 173
singulier, 128, 129
sinistre, 180
sinus, 197
sirop, 163, 186
six, 150
    six cents, 154
    six cent un, 154
    six cent deux, 154
sixièmement, 202
Sodome, 164, 166

soeur, 198, 206
soie, 159, 161
soient (qu'ils), 161
sois (que tu), 182
soit, 189
soit...soit, 130
soit (qu'il), 129, 182, 190
soixante, 147, 153, 155
  soixante et un, 153
  soixante-deux, 153
  soixante-trois, 153
  soixante-quatre, 153
  soixante-cinq, 153
  soixante-six, 154
  soixante-sept, 154
  soixante-huit, 132, 154
  soixante-neuf, 154
  soixante-dix, 154
  soixante et onze, 154
  soixante-douze, 154
  soixante-treize, 154
  soixante-quatorze, 154
  soixante-quinze, 154
  soixante-seize, 154
  soixante-dix-sept, 154
  soixante-dix-huit, 154
  soixante-dix-neuf, 154
solennel, 162, 176
solennité, 162
soleil, 2, 53, 183, 184
sommes (nous), 134
somptueux, 86
son, 3, 128, 137
sont (ce), 129
sort (il), 206
sosie, 165
sottement, 137
sou, 170
soubresaut, 196, 199
soûl, 172, 206
sourcil, 173, 206
sourd, 136
souris, 173
sous, 129
souverain, 138
square, 182, 192
spartiate, 187
spasme, 142
spécimen, 175, 179, 204

spectacle, 161
spectral, 86
Staël, 159
stagnant, 193
Stendahl, 177
strict, 190
subside, 196, 199
succès, 170
succinct, 179, 189
succincte, 179
sucrer, 196
sud, 190
suer sang et eau, 131, 135,
    193, 194
Suez, 198, 200
suggestion, 201
suis (je), 134
supplie (je), 14
supplier, 156
suprématie, 188
sur ce, 126
Suresnes, 196
surface, 161
surplomb, 186
suspect, 170, 189
suspecter, 170
suspens, 175, 198
stagnant, 203, 204
Stanislas, 197
Stockholm, 202
Strasbourg, 194
Styx, 147
syllabus, 197
syntaxe, 162

ta, 3
tabac, 160, 192
tabernacle, 159, 161
table, 53, 64, 117, 119,
    122, 123, 186, 198
tabler, 205
tact, 190
taffetas, 161
taille (il), 161
taille (il), 161
talent, 205
tamaris, 197
tandis que, 149
tant, 135
tant...que, 130

tant et plus, 148
tante, 203
taon, 175
tapes (tu), 186
tapis, 173, 198
Tarn, 204
tas, 53, 158
te, 123, 125, 126
te le, 124, 125
teint, 179
teinte, 179
téléphone, 166
Tell(Guillaume), 205
tellement, 85, 117, 135
temps, 175, 186, 198
temps en temps (de), 131
tendrement, 130
tenez, 120
tennis, 197
tension, 196
ter, 168, 206
terminus, 197
terrain, 85, 206
terrasse, 162
terre, 87, 119, 170
terres (que tu te), 206
terriblement, 123
tertio, 187
tes, 128, 168, 198
tétanos, 163, 197
thé, 187
Thémis, 197
théosophe, 165
théosophie, 143
thérapeutique, 171
Thomas, 158
thorax, 147
thym, 179
tiare, 187
tien (le), 188
tiens (je), 188
tient (il), 176, 179, 188
Tiers-Etat, 131
timbre, 180, 187
tînt (qu'il), 179
Titien (Le), 188
tohu-bohu, 174
toit, 159
tolle, 168

tome, 164
ton, 128, 137
topaze, 159
torse, 122
tort et à travers (à), 140
toujours, 123, 136
tournesol, 196, 199
tous, 149, 198
tout, 128, 129, 130, 132, 172
tout à coup, 131
tout à fait, 131
tout à l'égout, 131
tout à l'heure, 131
tout au plus, 148
toute, 140
tracas, 158
tracasse (je), 162
trachéal, 200
trachée, 200
trachéen, 200
trahi, 173
trahison, 174
tramway, 195
tranquille, 184, 185, 205
tranquillement, 205
transaction, 199
transalpin, 199
transatlantique, 190
transept, 186, 190, 196, 199
transi, 196, 199
transiger, 199
transir, 199
transit, 173, 190, 196, 199
transitaire, 199
transitif, 199
transitoire, 199
transsubstantie (il), 188
transsabstantier, 188
Transylvanie, 196, 199
travail, 161, 184, 205
travaillais (je), 198
travailles (tu), 161, 184
travailler, 185
treize, 153
trente, 153
   trente et un, 153
   trente-deux, 153

trente-trois, 153
trente-quatre, 153
trente-cinq, 153
trente-six, 153
trente-sept, 153
trente-huit, 153, 155
trente-neuf, 153
trépas, 158
très, 130, 170
triangle, 156
tribut, 189
triomphes (tu), 195
troène, 181
trois, 132, 150, 158
  trois cents, 154
  trois cent un, 154
  trois cent deux, 154
troisième, 160
tronc, 178, 192
trop, 135, 163, 186
trouer, 155, 182
tub, 172
tues (tu le), 174
tuiez (que vous), 156, 183
Tunis, 197
type, 186
typhus, 197

uhlan, 131, 141
ululement, 131, 141
ululer, 131
un, 38, 40, 49, 50, 69, 128, 132, 137, 139, 141, 149, 180
un à un, 139
un auprès de l'autre (l'), 140
un avec l'autre (l'), 139
uncial, 181
une, 41, 50
un et l'autre (l'), 140
union, 181.
un ou l'autre (l'), 139
uns (les), 128
usage, 128

va (il), 3, 160
vache, 162
vaguement, 194

vain, 138
vainc, (il), 179, 192
vais (je), 167, 169
valeureux, 143
Valladolid, 190
valse, 162
valus, (tu), 198
vasistas, 197
vas-y, 136
vécut (il), 173
vedette, 121
veiller, 185
Vélasquez, 193, 200
vélodrome, 164, 166
venant, 134
vendredi, 195
vends (tu), 175
venez, 120
venez (vous), 119
Vénus, 197
ver, 168, 206
Vercingétorix, 174
verdict, 190
Verdun, 180
vernis, 173
verre, 198
vers, 130, 136
Versailles, 159
verser, 196
version, 155
vert, 136
verte, 119
vertex, 147
vertu, 86
vertueux, 183
vestiaire, 187
veule, 171
veulerie, 171
veut (il), 189
veux (je), 136, 170
Vevey, 169
vice-versa, 168
Victor-Hugo, 140, 193
vides (tu), 190
viens (je), 176, 179
vient (il), 176
vif, 142
vigueur, 193
vilain, 138

village, 205
villageoise, 162
ville, 184, 185, 205
vin, 179
vingt, 128, 153, 179, 189, 193
  ving et un, 153
  vingt-deux, 153, 155
  vingt-trois, 153, 155
  vingt-quatre, 153, 155
  vingt-cinq, 153, 155
  vingt-six, 153, 155
  vingt-sept, 153, 155
  vingt-huit, 132, 153, 154, 155
  vingt-neuf, 153, 155
vînt (qu'il), 179
vint (elle), 179
virus, 197
vis, 197
vis (je), 173, 197
vis à vis, 131, 173
Vismes, 174, 196
vitre, 198
vivez, 145
vivisection, 196, 199
voeu, 170
voie (noun), 159, 161
voie (qu'il), 161
voie (que je), 181
voies (que tu), 161
voit-il, 129
voix, 161
volontiers, 168, 206
volubilis, 197
vomir, 165
vortex, 147
vos, 128, 163, 198
Vosges, 164, 196
votre, 140
vôtre (le, la), 164
vôtres (les), 119
voudrions (nous), 129
voyage, 155

voyager, 185
vous, 129
vraisemblable, 196, 199

wagon, 195
Wagner, 193, 195, 203, 204
Wagram, 195, 202
wallace, 195
wallon, 195
warrant, 195
Waterloo, 163, 195
Watteau, 195
Weimar, 195
whist, 195
Wissembourg, 195
Wurtembourgeois, 195
Wurtemberg, 194

Xaintonge, 146, 196
Xantippe, 146
Xavier, 146
Xénophon, 146
Xérès, 146, 170, 192, 197
Xerxès, 146
Ximénès, 146, 192
xylophone, 146

yacht, 131, 141, 185
yatagan, 131
yes, 131
yeuse, 131, 141
yeux, 131, 141,
yole, 131, 141, 185
ypréaux, 131, 141

zèle, 170, 199
Zeus, 171
zigzag, 194
zinc, 194
zist et le zest (entre le), 181
zone, 164, 166
zoologie, 167
Zurich, 201

INDEX OF SUBJECTS TREATED

Accent (The French) 8.
Accent (Vocalic) 9.
Anticipation (Law of) 52.
Aspirated h, 141.
Assimilation, regressive-, 142; progressive-, 142.
"Attack" or beginning (of a vowel) 17.
Beginning or "attack" of a vowel (see "Attack").
Bi-labials (see Consonants).
Breath-groups, 88.
Cavity (Nasal) 7.
Chords (Vocal) 5.
Classification of the vowels (see vowels).
Clauses introducing a direct quotation, 101
Closed vowels (see Vowels).
Consonants, 49. Classification: voiced, 49; voiceless, 49; plosives, 49; fricatives, 50; sibilants, 50; hushing sounds, 50; laterals, 51; liquids, 51; rolled, 51; uvular, 51; bi-labials, 52; dentals, 52; palatals, 52, instantaneous or momentary, 50; continuants, 51; description: p, b, 54-55; t, d, 56-57; k, 58-59; g, 60-61; f, v, 62-63; s, 64-65; z, 66-67; ch, ʃ, 68-69; j, ʒ, 70-71; m, n, 72-73; gn, ɲ, 74-75; l, 76-77; rolled r, uvular r, 78-79; Parisian r (or grasseyé) 80-81. Double consonant, 144.
Continuants (see Consonants).
Corners of mouth, 6.
Declarative sentences, 8, 92.
Dentals (see Consonants).
Détente (release) 53.
Double consonant (see Consonants).
Duration--of vowels, 20;--of

nasal vowels, 37.
Emphasis (see stress for emphasis).
Exclamatory sentence, 114.
Exercises for practice, 18.
Explosion, 50.
Falling part, 10, 94.
Figures, 18.
French accent (The) 8.
French syllable (The) 8.
French vowel (The) 14.
Fricatives (see Consonants).
Grasseyé (r) (see Consonants).
Groove, 16.
Groupe rythmique, 8.
H aspirate (see Aspirate).
H (pronunciation of) 145.
Hard palate, 7.
Harmony (Vowel) 143.
Hushing sounds (see consonants).
Immovable organs, 7.
Implosion, 50.
Instantaneous (consonants) (see Consonants).
Intensity, 9, 90.
Interrogative sentence, 111.
Intonation, 8, 87.
Jaw, 17.
Labio-dentals (see Consonants)
Larynx, 5.
Laterals (see Consonants).
Liaison, definition, 127; obligatory, 128; prohibited, 131, optional, 133, change of sound in liaison, 135; of the nasal vowels, 136.
Linking, 140.
Lips, 6, 16.
Liquids (see Consonants).
Mistakes to be avoided, 19.
Momentary (see Consonants).
Monosyllables (Mute e) 24.
Mouth (Corners of), (see Corners of mouth).

Movable organs, 5.
Musical pitch, 9, 90.
Mute e, 117.
Nasal cavity, (see Cavity).
Nasals (see Consonants).
Nasal vowels (see Vowels)
Normal stress, 9, 90.
Numerals (Pronunciation of the) 149.
Occlusion, 50.
Open vowels (see Vowels).
Organs (Movable, immovable or rigid) (see Movable and Immovable Organs).
Palatals, 52.
Palate (Hard, soft) (see Hard palate, Soft palate).
Parenthetical clauses, 100.
Parisian r (see Consonants).
Pause (tenue), 51.
Pharynx, 6.
Phonetic alphabet (Use of) 1.
Phonetics, 1.
Phonetic triangle (The) (see Introduction).
Phonograph records (see Introduction).
Plosives (see Consonants).
Preparation, 15, 51.
Prévoyance (Loi de) (see Law of Anticipation).
Progressive assimilation (see Assimilation).
Pronunciation (good) 3.
Pronunciation of h (see H).
Pronunciation of written ou+vowel, u+vowel, i+vowel, 155.
Pronunciation of x (see X).
Regressive assimilation (see Assimilation).
Relaxation, 15.
Release (détente) 51, 53.
Rigid organs (see Immovable organs).
Rising part, 10, 92.

Rolled r (see Consonants).
Semi-vowels (semi-consonants) description, 43;
semi-vowel ou, w, 44-45;
semi-vowel ü, $ɥ$, 44-45;
yod, j, 46-47.
Sibilants (see Consonants).
Soft palate, 6.
Speech-organs, 4.
Stress for emphasis, 91.
Stress-group, 8, 87.
Stress (normal) (see Normal stress).
Syllable (The French) 8.
Syllabification, 85.
Teeth, 7, 17.
Teeth-ridge, 7.
Tenue (see pause).
Tongue, 6, 16.
Uvula, 7, 52.
Uvular r (see Consonants).
Vocabulary, 18.
Vocal chords, 5, 6.
Voiced consonants (see consonants).
Voiceless consonants (see consonants).
Vowels, classification, anterior, posterior 19;
closed, 19; open, 20; mute, 19; nasal, 39. Description:
anterior a, a, 22-23; posterior a, $ɑ$ 22-23; ou, u, 24-25; closed o, 24-25;
closed e, 26-27; closed eu, $ø$, 26-27; i, 28-29; u, y, 28-29; open o, $ɔ$, 30-31;
open e, $ɛ$, 30-31; open eu, $œ$, 32-33; mute e, 32-33;
nasal vowels, an, $ã$, 38-39; on, $õ$, 38-39; in, $ɛ̃$, 40-41; un, $œ̃$, 40-41.
Vowel-harmony, 143.
X (Pronunciation of) 146.
Yod (see Semi-Vowels).